Absolute Beginner's Guide to

Personal Firewalls

201 West 103rd Street,
Indianapolis, Indiana 46290

Absolute Beginner's Guide to Personal Firewalls

International Standard Book Number: 0-7897-2625-4

Library of Congress Catalog Card Number: 20-01090292

Printed in the United States of America

First Printing: October 2001

04   03   02   01   4   3   2   1

Trademarks

Warning and Disclaimer

Associate Publisher

Greg Wiegand

Acquisitions Editor

Sharry Lee Gregory

Development Editor

Howard Jones

Managing Editor

Thomas F. Hayes

Project Editor

Tricia S. Liebig

Copy Editor

Kezia Endsley

Indexer

Chris Barrick

Proofreader

Andrea Dugan

Technical Editor

Johannes Ullrich

Interior Designer

Kevin Spear

Cover Designer

Alan Clements

Page Layout

Susan Geiselman
Michelle Mitchell

Contents at a Glance

Table of Contents

About the Author

Jerry Lee Ford, Jr. is an author, instructor, and a security analyst with over 13 years of experience in the information technology field. He holds a Masters in Business Administration from Virginia Commonwealth University in Richmond, Virginia and has over five years of teaching experience in information technology. Jerry is a Microsoft-certified Systems Engineer and has authored six other books, including *Practical Microsoft Windows Peer Networking*. He lives in Richmond, Virginia with his wife, Mary, and their sons, Alexander and William.

Dedication

To Mary, Alexander, and William.

Acknowledgments

This book is the result of the combined efforts of a number of individuals. I wish to thank Howard Jones for his work as the book's development editor, Johannes Ullrich for providing his services as technical editor, and Sharry Gregory, the book's acquisition editor. I also wish to thank everyone else at Que for working so hard to help make this book a reality. Finally, I want to thank my wife, Mary, for carrying more of the workload at home so that I could find the time to write this book.

Tell Us What You Think!

As the reader of this book, *you* are our most important critic and commentator. We value your opinion and want to know what we're doing right, what we could do better, what areas you'd like to see us publish in, and any other words of wisdom you're willing to pass our way.

As an Associate Publisher for Que, I welcome your comments. You can fax, e-mail, or write me directly to let me know what you did or didn't like about this book—as well as what we can do to make our books stronger.

Please note that I cannot help you with technical problems related to the topic of this book, and that due to the high volume of mail I receive, I might not be able to reply to every message.

When you write, please be sure to include this book's title and author as well as your name and phone or fax number. I will carefully review your comments and share them with the author and editors who worked on the book.

Fax: 317-581-4666

E-mail: feedback@quepublishing.com

Mail: Greg Wiegand
              Que
              201 West 103rd Street
              Indianapolis, IN 46290 USA

INTRODUCTION

Do You Need This Book?

It was not that many years ago that the personal computer was first introduced. The benefits of personal computers were obvious but limited because each computer was an island unto itself. Over the years a great deal of effort has gone into figuring out how to interconnect computer systems. From the first local area networks, we have now grown into the age of the Internet, where millions of computers around the world share a vast and open network of resources and information.

Connectivity is no longer the main issue. The new focus seems to be on how fast the connection is. This has led to 56kbps modems, and more recently, to cable and DSL connections. Because cable and DSL connections are always on, there is no waiting. Access is instantaneous. However, all this wonderful interconnectivity does have a drawback: security.

It turns out that the same tools that provide users with access to all the information and resources on the Internet can also be turned against them. Enter the hacker, a new breed of individual that thrives on breaking into computer systems.

Most people keep a lot of valuable information on their personal computers, such as personal financial records and electronic diaries, that they do not want to share with others. However, many people fail to realize that when they connect their personal computer to the Internet, they are also connecting the Internet to their personal computer, where anyone with a little know-how can try and break in and have a look around.

To guard against this exposure, you need to erect a barrier that prevents unwanted visitors from breaking into the home computers without inhibiting your ability to surf the Internet. This is where personal firewall comes into play. In this book, you learn about the security risks that occur when you connect to the Internet and how you can use a personal firewall to guard against external threats. You learn how personal firewalls work, how to install them, and how they protect your computer. Whether you have a dial-up or a high-speed cable or DSL Internet connection, you'll find that the *Absolute Beginner's Guide to Personal Firewalls* can help you surf faster and safer.

What You Need to Begin

To use this book effectively, all you need is a personal computer, a connection to the Internet, and a personal firewall. Your Internet connection can be dial-up, cable modem, or DSL. If you are not sure what personal firewall you want to use, go ahead and read this book first: it will help you to make that decision. This book covers a number of personal firewall products, both software- and hardware-based. You'll learn about the advantages and disadvantage of hardware and software firewalls and how to determine which one is right for you. You will also find information on where to go to download some really good, free firewalls.

How This Book Is Organized

This book is organized into 11 chapters and three appendixes. Chapters 1–4 lay the groundwork required for the rest of the book. The remaining chapters present specific topics.

Chapter 1, "Why Do You Need a Personal Firewall?," introduces you to high-speed Internet access and the need to protect your home computer with a personal firewall. You are also introduced to hackers and the hacker community.

Chapter 2, "High-Speed Internet Connections Equal Increased Vulnerability," provides additional information about cable and DSL connections and explains how to set up and configure your cable or DSL connection for maximum performance. This chapter also explains how high-speed connections are less safe and why you need to protect them with personal firewalls.

Chapter 3, "Firewalls Explained," covers the differences between hardware and software personal firewalls and provides additional insight on how personal firewalls operate. This chapter also provides an overview of TCP/IP and basic network communications.

Chapter 4, "Locking Down Windows Networking," discloses security holes built into Microsoft networking and discusses ways to lock some of them down. In addition, the chapter talks about the benefits up upgrading to a more secure version of Windows.

Chapter 5, "Hardware Firewalls," introduces cable/DSL routers and explains how they can be used as personal firewalls. This chapter shows you how to install and configure these devices. Topics include features such as IP address blocking and reviewing firewall logs.

Chapter 6, "McAfee Personal Firewall," shows you how to install, configure, and work with this personal firewall. You learn how to configure trusted applications and network security settings. Every major feature of this firewall is covered, including how to manage alerts and log files.

Chapter 7, "BlackICE Defender," provides complete coverage of this personal firewall. You learn how to install and configure it, as well as how to establish security settings. Every major product feature is covered, including how to analyze security events and information collected about attackers.

Chapter 8, "ZoneAlarm," provides thorough coverage of this personal firewall. The chapter shows how to install and configure the personal firewall and explains every major application feature. You learn how to apply ZoneAlarm security settings and configure trusted applications. You also learn how to analyze ZoneAlarm's log file and enable its automatic update feature.

Chapter 9, "How Secure Is Your Computer?," shows you how to run a free Internet security scan against your home computer so that you can test the effectiveness of your personal firewall. The chapter then goes over the results of a typical scan to help you analyze its results.

Chapter 10, "Habits of Security-Conscious Surfers," provides a collection of additional tasks that you can perform to further tighten your security when connected to the Internet. In addition, you'll find advice on good surfing habits and on keeping your computer and its applications up to date.

Chapter 11, "Home Networks and Internet Connection Sharing," shows you how to set up your own home network and secure it using a combination of hardware and software personal firewalls. The chapter presents several options for securing your home network and explains the differences between each option.

Appendix A, "Other Firewall Products," provides a list of additional personal firewall products and provides a brief high-level overview of each one.

Appendix B, "Other Web Sites That Will Test Your Security," supplements the material presented in Chapter 9 by supplying you with a number of additional Web sites that provide free Internet security scans that you can run to test your computer's defenses.

The Glossary provides a list of terms and definitions that you can reference as you are reading this book.

How to Use This Book

This book is designed to be read from cover to cover. However, depending on your experience and interests, you might find that you only need to read certain parts. Chapters 1–4 provide required background reading for the rest of the book. Chapters 5–8 cover specific personal firewall products. You will want to read at least one of these chapters. If you are interested in maximizing your security, you might prefer to read Chapter 5, "Hardware Firewalls," and then one of the three chapters covering software firewalls.

Learning how to run an Internet scan to test the strength of your firewall's security as shown in Chapter 9 should be essential reading. Chapter 10 provides additional advice on securing your computer that you might find useful. Chapter 11 is essential if you have a home network, otherwise you might want to skip it. Finally, the appendixes are intended to be used as supplements to the material in the chapters.

Conventions Used in This Book

Commands, directions, and explanations in this book are presented in the clearest format possible. The following items are some of the features that make this book easier for you to use:

- *Commands that you must enter*—Commands that you'll need to type are easily identified by special **bold monospace** format. For example, to view IP configuration information (IP address, subnet mask, and default gateway), I display the command like this: `ipconfig`. This tells you that you'll need to enter this command exactly as it is shown.

- *Other commands*—Commands that I do not expect you to type are listed as plain `monospace` text.

- *Glossary terms*—For all the terms that appear in the glossary, you'll find the first appearance of that term in the text in *italic* along with its definition.

- *Notes*—Information related to the task at hand, or "inside" information is off-set to make it easy to find this valuable information.

- *Tips*—Pieces of information not necessarily essential to the current topic but that offer advice or help you to save time.

- *Caution*—A warning explaining the need to be careful when performing a particular procedure or task.

PART I

INTRODUCING PERSONAL FIREWALLS

WHY DO YOU NEED A PERSONAL FIREWALL?

Because you are reading this chapter's introduction chances are very good that you already know a little about the Internet and why it is both an incredible and dangerous place to visit. The Internet is gold mine of information and opportunity. Unfortunately it has also become a hunting ground for less-than-scrupulous individuals who have both the tools and the know-how to penetrate your computer and steal your personal and financial information or who simply enjoy playing practical jokes or deliberately harming other people's computer systems.

The introduction of wide spread high-speed Internet access makes your computer an easier and more attractive target for these people. The mission of this book is to introduce you to personal firewalls and to help you protect your data and your privacy when you are surfing around the World Wide Web.

- Learn about the hacker community and the dangers of surfing unprotected on the Internet
- Examine the dangers of high-speed cable and DSL access
- Discover how easy it is to protect yourself by installing your own personal firewall
- Review the differences between software and hardware firewalls and decide which solution is best for you
- Find out which features you should look for when you go firewall shopping

The New Age of High-Speed Internet Access

Anytime that you surf the World Wide Web, you are electronically linking your computer to a vast network over which, unless you have installed a personal firewall, you have little control and from which you have little protection. Until recently, unless you worked for a company that provided high-speed Internet access, surfing the Internet meant dialing into Internet service providers (ISPs) via 56Kbps (56 kilobytes per second) connections over your local telephone line. These connections are relatively slow and never actually provide a 56Kbps connection. You are normally lucky to connect somewhere in the 44Kbps–49Kbps range.

Traditional 56Kbps Internet Access

Until recently, the Internet experience has meant using slow and sometimes frustrating dial-up connections that have a tendency to get disconnected, thus forcing you to redial and establish the connection over and over again. The situation is even more frustrating when you are unable to connect to the Internet because your computer receives a busy signal every time it tries to dial into your Internet service provider (ISP).

After you log on to your ISP, your computer is automatically assigned a temporary address, known as an IP address. This IP address uniquely identifies you across the entire Internet. IP address assignment is normally a dynamic process, which means that you are assigned a different IP address each time you log on.

All communication that your computer has with other computers on the Internet is based on the sending and receiving of data to and from your IP address. Your IP address therefore exposes your computer to the Internet and, once discovered by an intruder, provides a point of access to your computer. Fortunately, temporary dial-up connections combined with constantly changing IP addresses tend to make your computer a more difficult target for would-be intruders.

An IP address serves much the same purpose as your home address. It provides a means of identifying your computer on the Internet and allows other computers to communicate with your computer by sending messages to its assigned IP address. To learn more about TCP/IP addresses, check out *Special Edition Using TCP/IP*, by John Ray and published by Que; ISBN: 0-7897-1897-9.

To summarize, the characteristics of a traditional Internet connection are:

- Slow 56Kbps connections
- Temporary dial-up established connections
- A constantly changing IP address
- A tendency to get disconnected over time

The New Era in High-Speed Internet Access

Enter high-speed Internet access as the answer to the problems posed by 56Kbps dial-up connections. High-speed Internet connections can be classified as continuous network connections and come in two forms:

- **Cable**—A shared network connection with the Internet using the same coaxial cable that provides your local cable television connection.
- **DSL**—A dedicated network connection with the Internet using telephone wires provided by your local telephone company. (Does not, however, tie up your telephone lines.)

Both technologies provide up to 20 times faster connections than 56Kbps. They are always on, so you never have to waste time dialing up or risk getting busy signals and you do not get disconnected after being on for a lengthy period of time. Finally, because the connection is always on, the IP address assigned to your computer almost never changes.

High-speed connections are great. But, like anything, high-speed connections have drawbacks. Ironically, the very features that make high-speed connections attractive are also the things that make them vulnerable. In many ways, connecting to the Internet via a high-speed connection is like leaving your front door open and unlocked. This is because high-speed Internet connections have the following features:

- **A constant IP**—Makes it easy for an intruder who has discovered your computer on the Internet to find you again and again.
- **High-speed access**—Means that the intruder can work much faster when trying to break into your computer.

■ **An always-active connection**—Means that your computer is vulnerable anytime that it is on.

Because a high-speed Internet connection is simply another network connection, it is activated anytime the computer is started and remains active until it is shut down. Because of the way high-speed Internet access providers configure their DHCP servers, your IP address rarely ever changes. In fact, if you log on at least once every few weeks or so, your computer's IP address assignment might never change because your computer will continue to renew its IP address assignment over and over again. However, if you do not use your Internet connection for an extended period of time, you might find that your IP address has changed.

ISPs have a pool of IP addresses that they dynamically assign or lease to subscribing computers. The length of the lease varies depending on how the ISP has set things up. When you first log on, your computer is assigned an IP address from this pool. As long as your computer logs in often, your computer will continue to renew this lease. However, if you do not connect for an extended period of time the IP lease will expire and your ISP will reclaim it and place it back in the pool of available IP addresses. As a result, the next time that you connect, you will receive a new IP address. This process is completely transparent to the end user.

DHCP stands for Dynamic Host Configuration Protocol. ISP's use DHCP servers to manage the process of assigning IP addresses.

Because an IP address acts as a sort of home address for you when you connect to the Internet and because it might never change it makes you an easier target for those individuals on the Internet who like to break into computers (called crackers and/or hackers). After all, after they have identified your computer as a possible target, it is easy to come back to it again and again and attempt to break in because its IP address remains constant.

The high speed of the connection is also a double edged sword because although it provides you with blazing speed on the Internet, this same speed can be used against you by allowing your would-be assailant to work with the same lightening speed when trying to access your computer.

Finally, always-on connections make your computer or network a significantly more attractive target because it means that once it's targeted, your computer is easy to find and access any time that it is on.

If you are like the vast majority of people today, you use one of many Microsoft operating systems. Unfortunately, as you learn in Chapter 9, "How Secure Is Your

Computer?" although Microsoft operating systems might be simple and intuitive to use, they are not necessarily secure. This fact, when combined with the dangers of high-speed Internet access, can make the Internet a very dangerous place to visit.

Protecting Yourself with a Personal Firewall

So now you have an idea of how your always-on Internet connection makes you more vulnerable than an ordinary 56Kbps connection. What you now need to know is how you can defend yourself against the threats posed by this type of connection.

I hope that I have not led you to believe that 56Kbps Internet connections are somehow impervious to hacker attack because this is not the case. They are simply a little more difficult for hackers to attack thanks to their limited online time and constantly changing IP addresses.

As this book shows you, there are a few simple precautions that you can take that will make your computer or network a much safer place. If you are running a Microsoft operating system, you will want to change a few network configuration settings that leave unnecessary holes in your defenses. You learn how to make these configuration changes in Chapter 4 "Locking Down Windows Networking." You should also visit the Microsoft Web site regularly and apply any available security fixes and patches. In addition, you should make sure that your antivirus program is running and that it is up to date. If you do not have an antivirus program, you should get one when you purchase your personal firewall.

A computer virus is a software program that has been designed to infiltrate a computer system or network. Many viruses are relatively harmless and simply display a humorous message. Other viruses are designed to delete files or even reformat entire hard drives.

A couple years ago no one ever even heard of the term personal firewall. Firewalls were expensive hardware and software programs that were required only by large companies to protect their multi-million dollar data centers. However, things have changed. The personal firewall has become a necessary product for anyone with a high-speed Internet connection. Its purpose is to prevent hackers from being able to penetrate or even to see your computer when you are surfing on the Internet. A good firewall not only prevents current and future attacks but also alerts you of the presence and activity of a Trojan horse program that might have snuck its way onto your computer before you installed your personal firewall.

A *Trojan horse* is a program that, once installed, communicates back to the hacker's computer and performs whatever instructions it is told to do, including attacking other computers. This is what happened in February 2000 when two distributed denial-of-service attacks shut down the Yahoo and Ebay Web sites. You learn more about Trojan horses later in this chapter.

A distributed denial-of-service attack occurs when a hacker plants a Trojan horse program in thousands of computers and then instructs these computers to continuously connect to a company's network or Web site. This floods the site with network traffic. The objective of the distributed denial-of-service attack is to flood the target with more traffic than it can handle, thus preventing it from being able to service any real customer requests.

There are a number of companies making personal firewall products. Some of these products are hardware-based and others are implemented as software programs. This book reviews four of the most popular firewall products:

- Linksys EtherFast cable/DSL router—www.linksys.com
- McAfee Personal Firewall—www.macfee.com
- BlackICE Defender—www.networkice.com
- ZoneAlarm Personal Firewall—www.zonelabs.com

In addition to these personal firewalls, you'll find information on a number of other personal firewalls in Appendix A.

Makers of firewalls sometimes sell antivirus programs as well. Look for combo software packages that include both an antivirus program and a firewall application. You usually save some money when you buy them bundled together this way.

The Typical Internet Connection

Today's high-speed Internet connection is either cable modem or DSL. Cable modem, of course, is a solution in which your TV cable service provider also provides you with Internet access via a cable modem. Your telephone carrier, on the other hand, provides a DSL connection. High-speed access modems generally come equipped to work with either medium connection and require no configuration on your part other than attaching the modem to the cable or DSL connection and then plugging it into your computer.

Figure 1.1 depicts a typical high-speed Internet connection. Either an Ethernet or Universal Serial Bus (USB) connection to a cable/DSL modem connects the computer. The modem is then connected to the Internet service provider.

FIGURE 1.1

Cable and DSL high-speed Internet connections provide blazing connection speeds but leave your system vulnerable to attack from virtually anyone on the Internet.

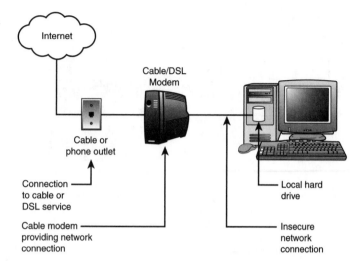

This connection is similar to any other network connection in that your computer can send and receive messages to and from other computers on the network. Only instead of a safe corporate network with trusted co-workers and a dedicated staff of security and networking professionals, it's just you and the entire Internet. This is why a personal firewall is so important.

Figure 1.2 depicts the role of a software firewall. In this case, a program such as McAfee's Personal Firewall is installed on your computer. After asking you a few simple questions, it configures itself and goes right to work acting as a filter for all network traffic to and from your computer and making sure that nothing passes through unless you have specified that it is okay to do so.

Software firewalls allow you to determine which traffic is permitted and which is blocked via policies that are created when you first install the firewall. Generally, a wizard asks you a series of simple questions that you answer. The wizard then creates the policies according to the information you supplied.

 Note

The reason that the firewall filters outbound IP traffic is to guard against any Trojan horses. If a Trojan horse does make its way on to your computer or was already there before the firewall was installed, it will be caught the first time that it tries to connect to the Internet.

Personal firewalls are packaged in two forms:

- **Standalone**—A software firewall installed on the computer.
- **Appliance**—An external piece of hardware that sits between your cable computer and your computer and provides firewall protection.

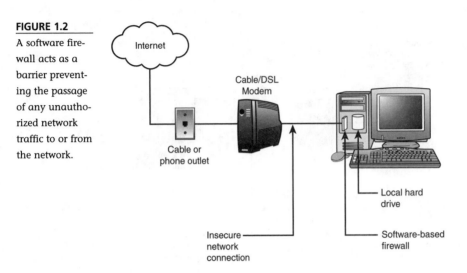

Unlike a software firewall, a hardware firewall does not require configuration. In
addition, a hardware firewall usually includes additional networking functionality
not provided by software firewalls including:

- **Hub**—A network device used to connect multiple computers on the same
  local area network.

- **Switching**—A technique for creating a dynamic dedicated communication
  session between two computers on a network.

- **Routing**—A feature that instructs the device to route Internet-based traffic to
  the Internet while keeping local area network traffic local.

The additional networking functionality provided by a hardware firewall is relevant only
if you have or plan to create a local area network. Otherwise, these are unnecessary features that, in addition to the cost of the hardware, help explain why hardware firewalls
cost more than software firewalls. More information about working with local area networks is provided in Chapter 11, "Home Networks and Internet Connection Sharing."

The manner in which a firewall filters IP packets depends on the type of firewall that
you have. There are several types of firewalls, as listed here:

- **Application gateway**—Also known as a proxy server. It filters based on IP
  addresses and the action an application is attempting to perform.

- **Circuit-level**—Checks packets for pre-approved Internet services and IP
  addresses. After a connection is established, it allows traffic to proceed without additional checking.

- **Stateful inspection**— Examines the contents of packets and allows or blocks them based upon a comparison against the characteristics of approved packet types.
- **Packet filter**—Filters packets based on pre-approved IP addresses. This option involves a lot of configuration and upkeep.

> **Note**
>
> Personal firewalls are just that, personal. They are intended for home use and lack the complexity and flexibility required to manage communications on a massive scale. To learn more about the industrial strength firewalls used by corporations, check out *Practical Firewalls*, by Terry Ogletree and published by Que; ISBN: 0-7897-2416-2.

Hardware firewalls present an alternative solution whereby the firewall is moved outside of the computer that it protects to an external device, as depicted in Figure 1.3. This option in effect moves the battle from inside your computer to outside of it. It also frees up precious resources on your computer for purposes other than running your personal firewall. Personal hardware firewalls tend to be a little less flexible than software firewalls. The main drawback to the hardware firewall is cost, which is between three to five times the cost of a typical software firewall.

FIGURE 1.3

A hardware firewall performs the same job as its software counterpart without requiring any resources from the computer or network that it protects.

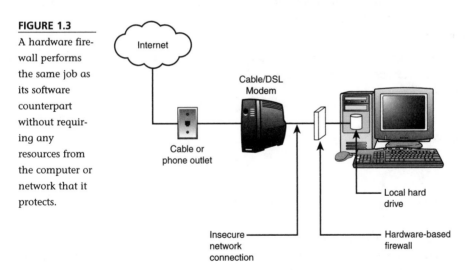

Who Are Hackers Anyway?

Up to this point, this chapter has explained why, any time you access the Internet, you are opening yourself up to some risk. You also learned that the element of risk increases when you upgrade from a 56Kbps connection to high-speed connection. A personal firewall provides a protective barrier between your computer and the would-be intruders on the Internet. But you might be wondering why in the world anyone would want to bother trying to break into your computer or home network. To understand this, you must take a look at a special group of people on the Internet, sometimes called hackers, and understand who they are, or who they think they are, and what they might find interesting about your computer and its contents.

To most people, the term hacker has come to describe an individual who breaks into computers or networks with the intent of doing harm. This is a broad and overly simplistic definition.

In reality, there are many levels of "hackers," each of which has a varying skill set and different set of objectives. It is the intent of this section to introduce you to the hacker community and to help you better understand why they do what they do.

The Hacker Community

Hackers are more than just isolated individuals roaming the Internet looking to cause trouble. In fact, you might be surprised to know that there is an active hacker community flourishing on the Internet. This community has a heritage that goes back to the 1960s and can trace its roots back to the first hackers who used to hack into the phone company to steal long-distance service. These people eventually gave themselves the title of phone freaks. As you will see, colorful names abound in the hacker community.

Perhaps the best way to learn about and understand the hacker community is to examine its various self-named members. These classifications include:

- Hacker
- Cracker
- Whacker
- Samurai
- Larva
- Demigod

Note You can learn more about this unique collection of individuals by checking out the `alt.2600` newsgroup. However, keep a low profile and try not to make anybody mad while you're there (…just in case).

Hacker

A *hacker* is an individual who possesses a technical mastery of computing skills and who thrives on finding and solving technical challenges. This person usually has a very strong UNIX and networking background. A hacker's networking background includes years of experience on the Internet and the ability to break into and infiltrate other networks. Hackers can program using an assortment of programming languages. In fact, this person can probably learn a new language in a matter of days. The title of hacker is not something that you can claim. Instead, your peers must give it to you. These people thrive on the admiration of their peers. In order to earn this level of respect, an individual must share his or her knowledge. It is this sharing of knowledge that forms the basis of the hacker community.

> UNIX is one of the oldest and most powerful operating systems in the world. It's also one of the most advanced. UNIX provides most of the computing infrastructure that runs the Internet today and a comprehensive understanding of UNIX's inner workings is a prerequisite for a true hacker.

One basic premise of this community is that no one should ever have to solve the same problem twice. Time is too precious to waste reinventing the wheel. Therefore, hackers share their knowledge and discoveries and as a result their status within the hacker community grows as does the community itself.

Hackers believe that information is meant to be free and that it is their duty to make sure that it is. Hackers are not out to do any harm. Their mission, they think, is to seek a form of personal enlightenment, to constantly learn and explore and to share. Of course, this is a terribly self-gratifying view but that is how hackers see each other. They see their conduct as honorable and noble.

But the bottom line is that hackers use their computing skills to break into computers and networks. Even though they might not do harm, it is still an unethical and illegal act. Hacking into someone else's computer is very much the same thing as breaking into their home. Whether it makes them more enlightened or not is insufficient justification for the crimes that they commit.

Cracker

Another group in the hacker community is the group that gives hackers a bad name. The individuals in this group are known as crackers. *Crackers* are people who break into computers and networks with the intent of creating mischief. Crackers tend to get a great deal of media attention and are always called hackers by the TV news and press. This, of course, causes hackers much frustration. Hackers have little respect for crackers and want very much to distinguish themselves from them. To a hacker, a cracker is a lower form of life deserving no attention. Of course, crackers always call themselves hackers.

Usually, a cracker doesn't have anywhere near the skill set of a true hacker, although they do posses a certain level of expertise. Mostly they substitute brute force attacks and a handful of tricks in place of the ingenuity and mastery wielded by hackers.

Whacker

Whacker is another title that you might have heard. A whacker is essentially a person who shares the philosophy of the hacker, but not his or her skill set. Whackers are less sophisticated in their techniques and ability to penetrate systems. Unlike a hacker, a whacker is someone who has never achieved the goal of making the perfect hack. Although less technically sophisticated, whackers still posses a formidable skill set and although they might not produce new discoveries, they are able to follow in the footsteps of hackers and can often reproduce their feats in an effort to learn from them.

Samurai

A *samurai* is a hacker who decides to hire out his or her finely honed skills in order to perform legal activities for corporations and other organizations. Samurai are often paid by companies to try to break into their networks. The samurai is modeled after the ancient Japanese Samurai and lives by a rigid code of honor that prohibits the misuse of his or her craft for illegal means.

Larva

Larvas are beginner hackers. They are new to the craft and lack the years of experience required to be a real hacker. They idolize true hackers and in time hope to reach true hacker status.

So what do hackers, crackers, whackers, Samurai, or larva want with you or your computer? After all there are plenty of corporate and government computers and networks in the world that must offer far more attractive targets. Well, although hackers, whackers, and Samurai might not be targeting them, home computers can often be viewed as low lying fruit for crackers who want easy access to financial information and a fertile training ground for larva to play and experiment.

But the biggest threat of all might come from a group of people not associated with the hacker community. This group consists of teenagers and disgruntled adults with too much time on their hands. These people usually have little if any real hacking skills. And were it not for the information sharing code of the hacker community, these people would never pose a threat to anybody. However, even with very little know-how, these people can still download and execute scripts and programs developed by real hackers. In the wrong hands, these programs seek out and detect vulnerable computers and networks and wreak all kinds of destruction.

Other Hacker Terms

In addition to the more common titles previously presented, there are a few other hacker terms that you should be aware of. For example, a *wannabee* is an individual who is in the beginning larva stage of his or her hacking career. Wannabees are seen as very eager pupils and can be dangerous because of their inexperience even when their intentions are good. A *dark-side hacker* is an individual who for one reason or another has lost their faith in the hacker philosophy and now uses their skills maliciously. A *demigod* is a hacker with decades of experience and a worldwide reputation.

Just remember that somebody is always watching you; that on the Internet nothing is private anymore and it's not always the bad guys that you need to be worried about. In early 2000, the FBI installed a device called the Carnivore at every major ISP that allowed them to trap and view every IP packet that crossed over the wire. It has since been renamed to a less intimidating name of CDS1000. The FBI installed this surveillance hardware and software, they say, so that they can collect court-ordered information regarding specifically targeted individuals. It's kind of scary but it is true. Just be careful with whatever you put into your e-mail because you never know who will read it.

Where Do They Get Their Toys?

The tools of the hacker trade are free and easily accessible to anyone with an Internet connection. Because hackers believe that information must be shared and that it is their duty to make it so, they have developed an incredible collection of hacking tools over the years. Many of these tools rival and even surpass the quality of programming found in commercial applications. These tools have been created by highly skilled individuals. Their source code is made available to the public and, unlike software developed by giant corporations, their code undergoes the scrutiny of expert programmers around the world.

The purpose of this book is to provide you with all the information you need to know about selecting and implementing your own personal firewall and not to glorify the role of hackers or to help further their craft. Therefore, you will not find any hacking tricks or references to specific hacking tools in this book. They are all too readily available and easily found by any search engine. In fact, there are even a few books that have been published and are readily available in bookstores that provide this very information.

Although there are distinct differences between hackers, whackers, crackers, and the other members of the hacker community, the point of this book is that you do not want any of these people gaining access to your computer or home network regardless of their intentions, motives, or levels of technical skill. The purpose of this book then is to help you prevent the breach of your computer systems, data, and privacy.

Some hacker tools that you should know about are port scanners and password crackers. Port scanners search the Internet looking for online computers that have open TCP/IP ports. TCP/IP ports are software-created communications ports that are assigned to network applications. Network applications communicate with other network applications by sending and receiving data to the appropriate TCP/IP port. Hackers have many tools and tricks that they use to try to gain access to your computer through these open ports. One of your most basic anti-hack defenses is to close any unnecessary ports. You learn more about these ports and how to close them in Chapter 9. You also look at how personal firewalls can hide your ports so that they cannot be seen from the Internet in Chapter 3, "Firewalls Explained."

Note

TCP/IP is the language of the Internet and most corporate networks. TCP/IP is composed of a set of standards and protocols that your computer uses when it communicates over the Internet using TCP/IP-based applications such as Web browsers and e-mail programs.

Microsoft operating systems provide added security by allowing you to implement user account and password requirements. However, there is absolutely nothing built into most Microsoft operating systems that allow them to defend against a hacker's brute force password attack. A brute force password attack is an attack on your computer by a software program that attempts to gain further access to computer resources by locating user accounts and guessing their passwords using a list of commonly used passwords. Microsoft Windows NT, 2000 and XP can be configured to disable accounts when to many unsuccessful attempts are made against them. This provides a degree of protection against brute force password attacks. However, most people are not running these operating systems on their home computers and are therefore virtually defenseless against this type of attack. In fact, without a good firewall you will never know that you are under attack.

Note

Hackers can launch brute-force password attacks after gaining access to Windows NT 4 and Windows 2000 computers. Other Windows operating systems, such as Windows 98 and Windows Me, do not incorporate the same security model as Windows NT 4 and 2000 and therefore, do not implement a password-based access scheme. This of course makes the hacker's job a lot easier when hacking into these operating systems.

It might seem obvious that you need to take great care when creating passwords and to make sure that they are strong. A strong password has at least eight characters, uses a combination of numbers, upper- and lowercase letters, and uses at least one special character (such as !@#$%^&()*).

What Do They Want from You?

So the question remains: What could anyone possibly find on your computer or home network that would be of value to him or her? The answer might surprise you. For example, they might want to:

- Steal your Microsoft Money and Quicken files, where you store personal financial information.
- Get their hands on your personal saving and checking account numbers.
- Search for your personal pin numbers.
- Steal electronic copies of your taxes that have been prepared using desktop tax reporting applications.
- Steal your credit card numbers or any other financial information that is of value.
- Steal important business information on your computer that might be of value to a competitor.
- Launch distributed denial of service attacks against other Internet computers and Web sites.

All these types of information can easily be captured and sent to the hacker using a *worm* program, as depicted in Figure 1.4. A worm can be initially implanted on your computer by hiding inside an e-mail attachment which, when double-clicked, silently installs the worm on your hard drive. The worm then goes to work searching your hard disk for valuable information that it can relay back to its creator.

FIGURE 1.4
Worms allow hackers to work behind the scenes using your computer's resources to gather and steal your personal information.

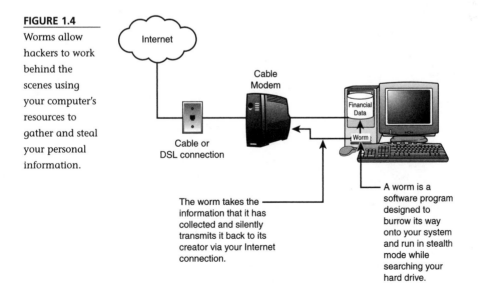

Money and personal secrets might not be the only things of value your computer can provide to hackers. Some people simply delight in causing trouble or playing practical jokes. It is not fun to find out that somebody has hacked on to your computer and deleted important files or filled up your hard drive with useless garbage, but to some crackers this is a form of amusement.

A cracker can also take control of your computer without your knowledge and use it and thousands of other computers to launch attacks on commercials Web sites and other corporate communications systems. Crackers achieve this task by breaking into individual computer systems and planting Trojan horses that, after installed, communicate back to the cracker's computer and perform whatever instructions they are told to do. To prevent this sort of silent hostile takeover, you need to install a personal firewall and configure it to block all unapproved outgoing traffic from your computer. As you will see in Chapter 3 you can configure your firewall with a list of approved Internet applications such as Internet Explorer and Outlook Express. Your personal firewall will then deny access to the Internet to any application that is not on this list, including any Trojan horse applications.

The term *Trojan horse* comes from the trick that the Greek attackers used to penetrate the defenses of the city of Troy. It describes a program that sneaks onto your computer by hiding within a seemingly legitimate piece of software. The horse later begins to run amuck. Back Orifice made the Trojan horse software attack famous. Back Orifice is a Trojan horse program whose name mimics the Microsoft Back Office suite of network applications. Once planted, the Back Orifice program provides the hacker with complete control over the infected computer.

HIGH-SPEED INTERNET CONNECTIONS EQUAL INCREASED VULNERABILITY

*T*his chapter equips you with the information that you need when deciding what type of high-speed access to purchase. You also learn everything you need to know to purchase, install, and go online with your cable or DSL modem. You learn how to tweak your connection and improve its performance as well as find out how to test and verify its speed.

- Compare the strengths and weakness of cable and DSL Internet access
- Install required hardware and software
- Install your modem and set up your high-speed Internet access
- Test the speed of your connection

Selecting a High-Speed Connection: Cable Versus DSL

When it comes to the selection of a high-speed Internet connection, you usually do not have many choices. Both cable and DSL are being aggressively deployed across most of North America. However, this does not mean that both of these technologies are available everywhere. In fact, in many places only one of these two options is available. However, if you live in an area where both options are available, you need to know enough about the strengths and weaknesses of these two technologies to be able to make an informed decision when choosing between them.

Cable for example, does not have any distance restrictions, whereas you typically must reside within three miles of one of the telephone company's central offices to receive DSL service. Unlike cable, the further away your DSL connection is from a central office the slower it will be. Of course, the only way that you can find out whether you have any DSL service restrictions is to contact a local ISP that provides DSL service.

Although both cable and DSL provide high-speed Internet access, cable represents a shared connection with your neighbors whereas DSL employs dedicated communication lines between your house and the telephone company. This means that your cable connection might slow down noticeably as more people in your neighborhood come online. The next two sections explore the strengths and weaknesses of cable and DSL in greater detail.

High-Speed Cable Internet Access

High-speed cable Internet access is delivered over the same TV cable that is probably already in your house. So unless you want to set up your computer in a room that does not already have a cable outlet, you shouldn't need to run any new cable.

Cable access is capable of offering connection speeds as high as 1MB, but speeds of 300–500Kbps are more common. Although downloads can occur at these speeds, uploads are usually slower. This is because cable access is usually asymmetric. This means that you can receive data much faster than you can send it. In fact, one cable provider, @Home, limits the maximum upload speed to 128Kbps. Still this is a lot better than your old dial-up connection, which was capable of no better than 33.6Kpbs. Fortunately, except for Internet gaming, most user access requirements are asymmetric in nature. For example, a mouse click at a Web site involves a very small amount of data, whereas downloading pictures and multimedia content requires considerably larger amounts of bandwidth or transmission capacity to handle all the extra data.

The Issue of Shared Access

Cable access represents a shared connection. Your cable provider in effect sets up a local area network in your neighborhood to which you and your neighbors connect. Because you must share the network, not all the bandwidth is available to you all the time. In fact, as more of your neighbors come online, you can expect a bit of a slowdown. At peak hours of the day, your connection speed might not be much more than double or triple your old dial-up connection's speed. Still, that's a big improvement over conventional 56Kbps modems.

Cable modem access is an insecure connection because anyone on your local area network has the ability to inspect the data that flows to and from your Internet connection. This means that one of your neighbors can potentially observe all your activity on the Internet, including finding out what kinds of Web sites you have been visiting. Unfortunately, this is one problem that you can do nothing about. It is simply a characteristic of this type of connection. However, your neighbors will require some fairly sophisticated knowledge and experience to do this. It should also be noted that most modern cable systems use encrypted communications. This means that the data sent to and from your computer is automatically encoded so that only your computer and the computer that is communicating with you can decrypt or decode it. So, although the Web sites that you visit when surfing the Internet are potentially visible, the actual data that you send or receive is safely encoded.

RoadRunner and @HOME

When it comes to finding a cable ISP, you really have no choice. Either your current cable provider offers the service or it does not. Cable companies have exclusive territories, so you do not have the option of choosing one vendor over another.

The two largest cable-access ISPs in North America are @HOME and Road Runner. Together they represent 80% of all cable installations. Two other smaller ISPs, Softnet Systems and High Speed Access Corp, service most of the remaining areas. These ISPs partner with local cable companies to provide Internet cable access and sell their services under a joint name. For example, in my area, MediaOne Road Runner provides Internet cable access.

It's the job of the local cable company to help install your cable connection and make sure that it is operating correctly. The ISP then provides the rest of the ISP service. Today, a single cable connection typically runs between $30–$50 per month and includes the following features:

- Unlimited access
- Cable modem rental fee
- Technical support
- Free software, including browsers and diagnostic utilities

High-Speed DSL Internet Access

DSL stands for Digital Subscriber Line. DSL provides a high-speed Internet connection over the existing telephone wiring found in your home. DSL is capable of providing connections from 144Kbps to 1.5Mbps. DSL is limited by an approximate distance of three miles from a telephone company's central office. The farther your house is from the central office, the slower your connection will be.

A telephone company's central office represents a junction point for phone and data connections. There are thousands of these offices spread out all over North America. With luck, your home will be within three miles of one of these central offices.

Locating a DSL Service Provider

There are several ways to determine whether you can get DSL service in your home. You can call your local phone company and ask if it provides this service and then try to find an ISP that has an agreement with your company to provide the service. Alternatively, you can go straight to a local ISP that advertises DSL service and ask it to set everything up with the telephone company. Finally, there are a number of Web sites that list areas where DSL service is available, including:

- www.thelist.com
- getconnected.com
- www.dslreports.com

Even if DSL is available in your area, you have one more hurdle to get over. The local phone company might need to visit your house and perform a test of your internal wiring to make sure that it will support the data traffic. A poorly wired home or a home with older telephone wiring might not be able to support a DSL connection. If this is the case, you'll need to replace or add new wiring or find out if your cable provider offers Internet cable access.

Depending on your local phone company, you might be able to get a do-it-yourself kit
that allows you to perform a self-install.

DSL Variations

There are a large number of DSL options. The three most common are outlined here:

- **ADSL (Asynchronous Digital Subscriber Line)**—Targeted at home users
  and small businesses. Provides less bandwidth for uploads than for downloads. This means that you'll be able to receive data faster than you can
  send it.

- **SDSL (Synchronous Digital Subscriber Line)**—Targeted at businesses
  with heavier Internet access requirements. Provides equal bandwidth for
  uploads and downloads. This type of access is more expensive and is targeted
  as business users.

- **IDSL (Integrated Digital Subscriber Line)**—Provides a slower level of
  service. This type of access is targeted at customers who are more than three
  miles from the central office.

Like cable connections, ADSL is an asymmetric connection, which means that it supports faster downloads than uploads. ASDL data signals are piggy backed on top of
the same connection that carries voice signals. The signals are later split at the central office with voice traffic routed over the public switched telephone network and
data traffic routed to the Internet.

A DSL connection is a dedicated connection between your house and the phone
company's central office. This means that your connection is more secure than a
cable connection because your neighbors do not share it. It also means that your
connection might be less subject to congestion because you do not share the connection with your neighbors. However, back at the central office, you do share the telephone company's connection to the Internet with all other DSL users serviced by
that office, so you might still experience slowdowns during peak usage periods.

Cable and DSL Modems

Cable and DSL Internet connections each require their own special type of modem.
These modems are expensive, usually over $200. DSL customers and a large number
of cable subscribers have no choice but to lease their cable modem as a part of their
high-speed Internet access package. Usually this adds an extra $10 to the monthly
bill. Often, the ISP that provides the service has systems in place that are designed to

work with modems created by specific manufacturers. Therefore, you cannot easily swap one modem for another.

A cable modem standard, known as DOCSIS, was developed in 1998 and is gradually being adopted by the cable industry. An organization called CableLabs is responsible for determining whether cable modems comply with this standard. Those that do are labeled "CableLabs Certified." If your cable company supports CableLabs-certified modems then chances are they will also allow you to purchase your own modem and save the $10 per month lease fee. You can usually find CableLabs-certified modems at your local computer store.

Features

Both cable and DSL modems support the same basic set of features. Their primary difference is that cable modems have a connection for a coax cable, whereas DSL modems use a standard telephone connection.

Figure 2.1 shows the Toshiba PCX1100 cable modem.

FIGURE 2.1

A front view of the Toshiba PCX1100 cable modem.

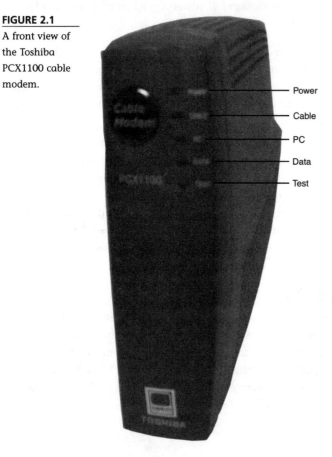

- Power
- Cable
- PC
- Data
- Test

This particular device is representative of a typical high-speed connection modem. It provides a number of LED indicators that specify the status of the modem and its network status. These LEDs include:

- **Power**—Lit when powered on.
- **Cable**—Lit when a good connection is established.
- **PC**—Lit when the computer is powered on and its network connection is active.
- **Data**—Flashing when transmitting data.
- **Test**—Flashing when a modem self-test is executed and solid if the test fails.

Figure 2.2 shows a rear view of the Toshiba PCX1100 cable modem.

FIGURE 2.2

A rear view of the Toshiba PCX1100 cable modem.

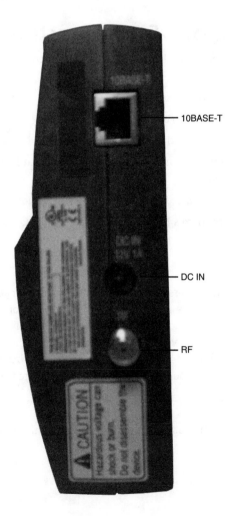

— 10BASE-T

— DC IN

— RF

The following connection ports are provided.

- **10BASE-T**—Connects the computer and modem using the network cable supplied with the modem.

- **DC IN**—Connects the modem's power adapter.

- **RF**—Connects to the coaxial cable connection supplied by your local cable company.

Support for Universal Serial Bus (USB) technology is being added to many newer cable and DSL modems. USB provides the option of replacing a traditional network connection with a simple plug-and-play external USB connection.

Setting Up Your Cable or DSL Connection

There are several steps involved in getting your cable or DSL connection up and running. These include:

- Performing pre-installation tasks

- Installing a network interface card (NIC)

- Installing the NIC's software driver

- Connecting your modem to your computer, its high-speed Internet access connection, and power supply

- Running the installation wizard that came with your modem

- Giving your ISP your modem's MAC address and the MAC address of your computer's NIC

MAC addresses are unique numbers assigned to network devices that identify the devices on a network. A MAC address is a 48-bit number. Both your cable modem and your NIC have their own MAC addresses. Your ISP permits only authorized Internet connections. They control these connections by preventing any unauthorized MAC addresses (such as modem and NIC addresses) from connecting to the network. Therefore, when you provide your MAC addresses to your ISP, they use this information to block out network traffic from your home that does not originate from these addresses.

Each of these steps is described throughout the remainder of this chapter.

Pre-Installation Tasks

There are a few tasks that you should complete before you begin installing your cable or DSL modem. These tasks are designed to make your connection work better and be more reliable when you are surfing the World Wide Web.

Updating Your Operating System

One of the smartest things that you can do before going online is make sure that you are using the most current software updates and fixes on your operating system. Microsoft posts these updates on its operating systems' home pages, which as of the writing of this book are located at `www.microsoft.com/windows/default.asp`.

Windows 98, Me, 2000, and XP can also assist you in keeping your operating system current with their Windows Update utility. When started, this utility automatically connects to your operating system's update site. The site analyzes your computer's current level of software and generates a list of recommended downloads. From there, you can automatically download and install any update.

Updates to look out for include:

- Updates and fixes that affect Windows networking
- Updates and fixes that address security issues
- Updates and fixes that address base operating system functionality and stability

In addition, you should make sure that your antivirus software is working properly and that it is current. If you do not have an antivirus program, you should really think about getting one.

Speeding Up Your Internet Access

As was noted in Chapter 1, "Why Do You Need a Personal Firewall?," TCP/IP sends and receives information in packets. TCP/IP ensures that every packet is delivered by requiring an acknowledgement from the receiving computer. However, to be as efficient as possible, TCP/IP does not require an acknowledgement for every individual packet. Instead, it allows the receiving computer to collect as many data packets as its TCP/IP receive window can hold before sending one acknowledgement for all the packets in the current receive window. The TCP/IP receive window is a container that stores TCP/IP packets when they're first received.

By increasing the size of the TCP/IP receive window, you increase the amount of data that your computer can receive without having to send an acknowledgement. This can result in a big performance increase when surfing the Internet. However, you need to be careful not to make the TCP/IP receive window too big because if a packet should get lost on its way to your computer it will not be acknowledged. In fact, none of the data packets currently residing in the TCP/IP receive window will be acknowledged. Eventually, the sending computer will resend all the unacknowledged packets.

Windows 95, Windows 98, and Windows Me automatically set their TCP/IP receive window to 8KB. Windows NT and Windows 2000 operating systems set their TCP/IP receive window to 16KB. These sizes are optimized for slower 28.8Kbps to 56Kbps modem connections. Unfortunately, Microsoft has yet to develop a way to automatically adjust the TCP/IP receive window for high-speed connections.

The proper setting for the TCP/IP receive window depends on the amount of latency present in your Internet connection. *Latency* is a measurement of the time required for a packet to travel to and from your computer on the Internet. Higher latency is often caused by congestion at your ISP or by slow server response at the Web sites that you visit.

You can test your level of latency using the Microsoft **TRACERT** command. Tracert identifies the number of hops (for example, the number of computers on the Internet that your data had to travel through) your computer encounters on its way to the destination computer and lists the amount of time required by each hop. You can test the latency related to your ISP by typing the following command:

Tracert www.*yourisp*.com

The following example shows the partial results of such a test and indicates that the maximum latency experienced was 30ms (millionths of a second) for any hop. You should run this test against your ISP and any other sites where you spend a lot of time. When determining your latency, use the highest value of any hop.

C:\>tracert www.mediaone.rr.com

```
Tracing route to www.mediaone.rr.com [24.30.203.14]
over a maximum of 30 hops:

  1   <10 ms    10 ms     10 ms   va-24-168-254-1.va.mediaone.net
[24.168.254.1]
  2    10 ms    10 ms     10 ms   va-24-30-224-53.va.mediaone.net
[24.30.224.53]
  3   <10 ms   <10 ms    <10 ms   va-24-30-224-49.va.mediaone.net
[24.30.224.49]
  4    10 ms    10 ms     11 ms   va-24-30-224-9.va.mediaone.net
[24.30.224.9]
  5    10 ms    10 ms     10 ms   24.93.64.41
```

```
6    10 ms    20 ms    10 ms   24.93.64.129
7    30 ms    20 ms    30 ms   24.93.64.45
8    20 ms    30 ms    20 ms   pos0-1.hrndva1-brt1.rr.com [24.128.6.2]
9    20 ms    20 ms    30 ms   24.218.188.169
```

Low latency is generally considered to be 100ms or less. High latency is above 200ms. A normal rate is somewhere in between.

If you are experiencing normal latency, you should adjust your computer's TCP/IP receive window to 32KB. If you have high latency, you should set your TCP/IP receive window to 64KB.

You can change the size of your TCP/IP receive window by editing your Windows Registry. The Registry is a Windows database that stores operating system, user, and application settings. Running the Regedit program shown in Figure 2.3 does this. Regedit is a Registry edit utility supplied with Microsoft's operating systems.

FIGURE 2.3

The Regedit program allows you to view and change Registry database settings.

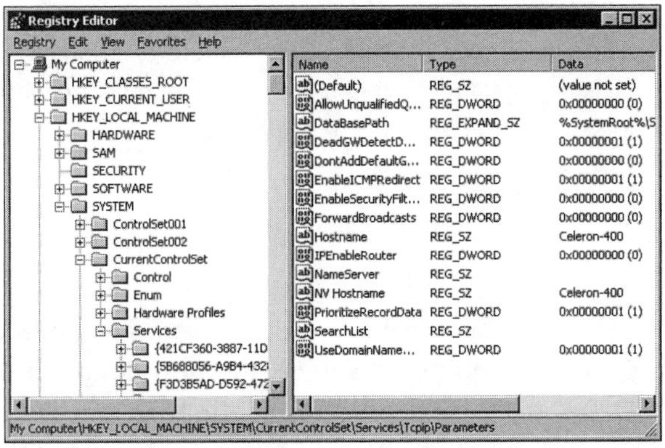

Regedit is a tool designed for use by advanced users and system administrators. It provides a Windows Explorer look and feel. Working with the Registry is a complex process and is beyond the scope of this book. However, you might want to check out the *Microsoft Windows 2000 Registry Handbook* (ISBN: 0-7897-1674-7) and the *Windows 98 Registry Handbook* (ISBN: 0-7897-1947-9) for detailed information about how to change Registry settings.

The following list provides the appropriate Registry key to edit based on the operating system and the amount of latency.

■ To configure your Windows 95, 98, or Me computer for low latency:

```
Set HKEY_LOCAL_MACHINE\System\CurrentControlSet\Services\XvD\MSTCP\

DefaultRcvWindow = 32767
```

■ To configure your Windows 95, 98, or Me computer for high latency:

```
Set HKEY_LOCAL_MACHINE\System\CurrentControlSet\Services\XvD\MSTCP\

    DefaultRcvWindow = 65535
```

■ To configure your Windows NT or 2000 computer for low latency:

```
Set HKEY_LOCAL_MACHINE\SYSTEM\CurrentControlSet\Services\Tcpip
➥\ Parameters\

    TcpWindowsSize = dword:00007fff
```

■ To configure your Windows NT or 2000 computer for high latency:

```
Set HKEY_LOCAL_MACHINE\SYSTEM\CurrentControlSet\Services\Tcpip\
➥ Parameters\

    TcpWindowsSize = dword:0000ffff
```

The Registry is a database that Windows operating systems use to store critical system and application settings. Editing your Registry is serious business and if you should make a mistake you can render your computer inoperable. Make sure that you make a backup copy of the registry before making any changes to it. Therefore, if you are not absolutely comfortable making this change, I recommend that you ask someone who has experience in working with the Registry to make the change for you.

NIC Installation

For your computer to connect to a cable or DSL modem, you have to install a network interface card (NIC) in your computer. This section provides general instructions for installing your NIC. Before you begin, make sure that you have at least one expansion slot open on your computer. Expansion slots allow you to extend the capabilities of your computer by adding new hardware that plugs directly onto the computer's motherboard. The motherboard is the main circuit board that ties all the components of your computer together.

Opening a computer and installing new hardware can be intimidating. If you are not completely comfortable with this task, I suggest that you have somebody else do it for you. You might be able to get the store that sold you your NIC to install it for free. For a small fee, your cable technician will install it too.

PCI expansion slots are preferable to ISA expansion slots. They represent the newer technology and have greater throughput, meaning that they are capable of handling more data faster. Check your computer's documentation to determine which type of expansion slots you have available and be sure to purchase a NIC that matches one of your open slot types.

Computer manufacturers have very rigid warrantees that prohibit the installation of peripheral devices such as NICs by people other than trained and certified technicians. Although this does not stop most people from doing it themselves, you should consider the possible repercussions should something go wrong. Usually this means that your warrantee is voided and your computer manufacturer can refuse to provide you with technical support.

The following steps outline the general procedure for physically installing the NIC. Installing a NIC:

1. Open and remove your computer's case.

2. Remove a metal slot cover in order to provide access to an open expansion slot.

3. Firmly insert and secure the NIC into the expansion slot.

4. Replace the computer's cover.

5. Start the computer. Windows plug and play should automatically recognize the card and begin the software portion of the install.

Installing the Software Driver

After you have performed the physical installation of your NIC, you then need to install the software that enables the operating system to communicate with it. This software is known as a software driver. Windows plug and play should automatically detect and begin the process of installing the NIC's software driver when you turn your computer back on. In the event that Windows fails to automatically detect the NIC, you can manually invoke this process from the Add/Remove Hardware icon in the Windows Control Panel.

Every peripheral device that is added to your computer requires the installation of an additional piece of software known as a software driver. Because there are so many versions of Windows operating systems today, it is difficult to describe the process of installing a software driver that applies to every operating system. The following procedure outlines in general terms how to complete the software portion of install process.

1. If plug and play automatically detects your NIC, follow the instructions presented by the installation wizard. Otherwise, click Start, Settings, Control Panel and then double-click Add/Remove Hardware. The Add New Hardware wizard starts.

2. Click Next and follow the instructions presented to begin the installation.

3. Windows will display a dialog box stating that is performing a search for the new hardware. The wizard will then display a list of any new hardware that it has discovered. Make sure that your NIC is on the list. If it is not, select the option that allows you to select a new piece of hardware from a list. If you select this option, you are presented with a list of hardware manufacturers. Select the NIC's manufacturer from the list and then select its model. If you are unable to locate either of these pieces of information, you can select the Have Disk option, which prompts you for a disk or CD that came with your NIC.

4. Supply the disks or CDs that the installation process requests.

5. When you're presented with a confirmation dialog box, make sure that everything looks correct and click Next.

6. Windows completes the installation. Click Finish when prompted. Depending on which Windows operating system you are running, you might be prompted to reboot your computer in order for the changes that you have made to take effect.

Network Configuration

Windows automatically configures itself to work on a TCP/IP based network, like the Internet, when a NIC is installed. This includes the installation of a number of software components. The specific components installed vary based on the version of Windows that you are running. Windows 98, Windows Me, and Windows 2000 Professional automatically install your NIC's software driver, the TCP/IP protocol, and the Client for Microsoft Networks. The purpose of each of these components is outlined here.

■ **Client for Microsoft Networks**—Provides support for connecting to Microsoft local area networks and is not required to support your Internet connection.

■ **NIC software driver**—Provides the operating system with instructions for controlling your NIC.

■ **TCP/IP**—A software implementation of a set of communication rules and standards that permits your computer to communicate with the Internet.

Other software components will be installed but vary based on the version of your Windows operating system. You learn more about the specifics of each of these components in Chapter 4, "Locking Down Windows Networking."

Installing Your High-Speed Modem

Modem installation is a multistep process. First you must physically install your modem. This involves the following steps:

- Unpacking the modem and attaching it to its Internet connection (for example, a cable or telephone wire)
- Attaching the modem's power supply
- Running the modem's installation wizard
- Contacting your ISP

Each of these steps is outlined in the remaining sections of this chapter.

Hooking Up Your Modem

Your first step is to ensure that you have either a phone outlet or a cable outlet in the location where you plan to make your Internet connection. If you do not, you have to arrange for one to be installed. The next step is to attach your modem to your computer and its Internet connection. This process is depicted in Figures 2.4 and 2.5 and is very straightforward.

FIGURE 2.4

A depiction of the process of hooking up your cable modem.

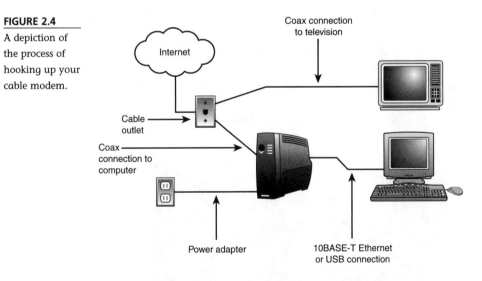

To make things go as smoothly as possible, try to avoid placing your modem close to other electrical devices. Every electrical device produces a small amount of electromagnetic interference. Modems are sensitive pieces of equipment and might not work properly when placed too close to other electrical devices.

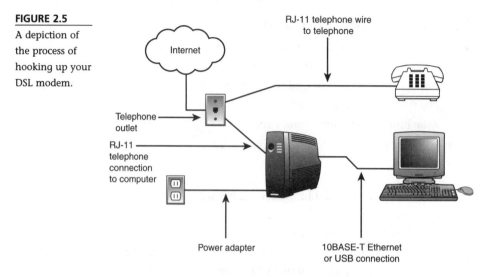

Running the Modem's Installation Wizard

Most cable and DSL modems come with an installation wizard that steps you
through the process of installing your modem. Otherwise, you should receive a
detailed set of instructions. Because of the number of cable and DSL modems available today it is impossible to provide you with specific instructions for installing
each one. By way of providing a typical example, this section reviews the installation process for the Toshiba PXC1100 cable modem. Although the steps involved in
installing your modem might vary, the overall process should be very similar.

1. Close any open applications and insert the CD that came with your modem.
   The modem's installation wizard should automatically start, as demonstrated
   in Figure 2.6.

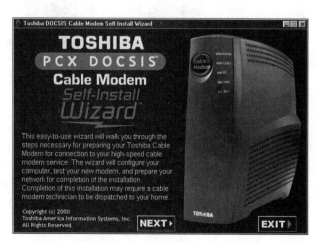

2. The wizard presents an overview of the installation process. Begin the installation process.

3. A list of cable providers is displayed. Select your cable provider, as demonstrated in Figure 2.7.

FIGURE 2.7

The wizard provides configuration for a number of major ISPs, including an option to support IPSs not listed there.

4. The wizard performs a system check to verify that your computer has the appropriate hardware to support the connection. Verify the results before continuing.

5. Next, you will see several dialog boxes that present detailed instructions for physically installing the modem. Verify that you have already performed these steps or complete them now.

6. Next, you will see several dialog boxes stating that the wizard is configuring your computer's TCP/IP settings and testing communications between your modem and your computer. After this configuration is complete, you should see results similar to those shown in Figure 2.8.

FIGURE 2.8

The wizard completes the modem installation and provides a confirmation of the connection between the computer and the modem.

7. Next, the wizard displays the internal MAC address of the cable modem. Make sure that it matches the MAC address listed on the outside of your modem.

8. Finally, the wizard finishes configuring your computer. You might be asked to reboot your computer.

Contacting Your ISP

The final step in activating your high-speed Internet access connection involves providing your Internet service provider with the MAC addresses of your modem and NIC. If the installation wizard doesn't tell you your modem's MAC address, you can usually find it on a label affixed to the modem. If not, it should be supplied as part of the documentation that accompanied the modem.

If your NIC's MAC address is not provided by the installation wizard, you can get it on Windows NT and 2000 systems by opening a command prompt and typing **IPCONFIG**. Look for a line of output similar to the following:

```
Physical Address. . . . . . : 00-00-00-00-00-00
```

The term physical address identifies the MAC address.

You'll find a Windows 95, 98, or Me computer's MAC by clicking Start, Run, and then typing **WINIPCFG**. This opens the IP Configuration dialog box that, among other things, displays your NIC's MAC address.

When you call your ISP, you will be asked for your MAC addresses. Your ISP will then use your MAC addresses to register your Internet account. Typically, this process is instantaneous. After you're done, you will be ready to go online.

After you have your high-speed access connection working, you might want to test your connection speed. There are a number of sites on the Web that offer free connection testing. Basically, these tests provide you with a file to download and then measure how long it takes for your computer to download it. To visit one of these sites, go to www.toast.com and look for its free performance test. However, the accuracy of the information that you get from this site might vary depending on how busy the Internet is, as well as how busy your ISP and the test site is. Running the test late at night or early in the morning might give you a better idea of your true connection speed.

Windows also supplies a utility that you can use to continuously monitor your connection speed. For Windows 95 and 98 users, look for a utility named the Network Monitor Agent located on the Windows CD. Windows NT and 2000 users can use the Performance Monitor utility to monitor their connections. Choose Start, Programs, Administrative Tools and select the Network Interface object.

FIREWALLS EXPLAINED

In this chapter, you learn about the differences between hardware and software firewalls and gain the knowledge required to determine which type of firewall is right for you.

You also get an overview of TCP/IP and learn how firewalls try to manage and protect TCP/IP connections to keep your computer or home network safe from outside intruders. This chapter also discusses the types of threats that you expose your computer to when you go online and how firewalls guard against these dangers. The chapter ends by breaking firewalls down into several categories to provide a complete explanation of their functions and features.

- Examine the difference between hardware and software firewalls
- Learn about the TCP/IP protocol and how it facilitates communication over the Internet
- Learn about the dangers posed by port scanners, Trojan horses, and denial-of-service attacks
- Discover how personal firewalls defend against both internal and external threats

Understanding Personal Firewalls

Personal firewalls are hardware devices or software programs that are designed to detect and defend against external and internal threats to your computer or home network. As you learned in Chapter 1, "Why Do You Need a Personal Firewall?," every computer connected to the Internet is exposed to the possibility of attack and that possibility of attack grows when you switch from a dial-up Internet connection to a cable modem or DSL broadband connection.

Personal firewalls are designed to afford you a level of protection that until recently was only available to large corporations.

What to Look for in a Personal Firewall

Not all firewalls are the same. They each have their own strengths and weaknesses that you need to be aware of before purchasing one. Regardless of whether you choose to go with a hardware- or software-based personal firewall, there are certain features that you should look for and expect to find in a good personal firewall. You'll often find some of these features listed on the back of the box that contains the personal firewall software. If you do not see the information listed there, check out the vendor Web sites for more information. Features to look for include:

- A set up and configuration wizard—Most personal firewalls come with an installation wizard that configures firewall policies based on the answers to a few simple questions.
- Pre-defined security policies—These are built-in policies that are implemented based upon your specified criteria.
- Filtering of both inbound and outbound IP traffic—The firewall should guard against external attacks as well as internal attacks from Trojan horse programs.
- Automatic blocking of Internet file sharing—The firewall should automatically unbind Microsoft's file and print sharing from any Internet connections.

■ Controlled-use Internet applications—You should be able to specify precisely which applications you want to permit to communicate with the Internet and which ones you do not.

■ Port stealth—The firewall should hide TCP/IP ports from Internet port scanners.

■ Detection of port scans—In the event that a hacker discovers an exposed port, the firewall should be able to detect and report on the hacker's scan.

■ Recognition and defense against denial-of-service attacks—The firewall should be able to recognize when an attack has been launched and be able to terminate it by blocking the attacker's access.

■ Alerting and logging—Your firewall should alert you when it detects a security breach or attack and keep a detailed log for you to review.

■ Support for home networking—Some personal firewalls work with home networks while others may prevent them from functioning.

Hardware Firewalls

Hardware firewalls are external devices that provide a buffer between your computer and your Internet connection. Most hardware firewalls are designed to connect to cable and DSL connections. Hardware personal firewalls are self-contained devices that interface with your computer via a Web browser. Beyond the Web browser, no additional software is required.

Like software firewalls, the features of hardware firewalls vary from vendor to vendor. The available feature set also varies based on price with some vendors offering a number of personal hardware firewalls at different prices. On the low end, you can purchase a hardware firewall that supports a single user PC connection for a little under a $100. For a little more, you can get a hardware firewall that doubles as a network hub/switch that can support a small local area network in your home. This option also allows you to share a single Internet connection with other members of your household. To see some up close examples of hardware firewalls, visit your local computer store. You'll also find plenty of information about them at Web sites such as www.compusa.com and www.egghead.com.

Note

A network hub/switch is an external device that facilitates the connection of computers into a local area network.

For example, Chapter 5, "Hardware Firewalls," demonstrates the use of a Linksys BEFSR41 EtherFast cable/DSL router, shown in Figure 3.1. Although called a cable/DSL router, this device provides a typical hardware-based personal firewall solution.

You can learn more about the Linksys EtherFast cable/DSL router at `www.linksys.com`.

In addition to the Linksys line of personal hardware firewalls, there are a number of really good personal hardware firewalls on the market. You can find them in most computer stores or online at Web sites such as `www.egghead.com` or `www.compusa.com`. For example, you might also want to look at the DI-704 Homegateway cable/DSL Internet sharing and firewall router made by Dlink. The Dlink Web site is `www.dlink.com`.

FIGURE 3.1

The LinkSys BEFSR41 EtherFast cable/DSL router is also an example of a personal firewall.

To make things easier to read, the term Linksys personal firewall is used to represent the Linksys BEFFRS41 EtherFast cable/DSL router from this point on.

Hardware firewalls connect to your cable or DSL modem using an Ethernet network connection. Your ISP usually provides the equipment for this connection and for an extra fee they will hook everything up for you. First, the NIC is installed into an open expansion slot in the computer. Windows plug and play should automatically discover and step you through the NIC's installation process. Then it is connected to the hardware firewall using a RJ-45 twisted pair cable. Then the hardware firewall is connected to your modem using another RJ-45 cable. These cables should be supplied with your modem and hardware firewall. The complete configuration is shown in Figure 3.2. Unless you are familiar with computer hardware, you will probably want to see if your ISP will hook all this up for you.

FIGURE 3.2

A typical personal hardware firewall set up.

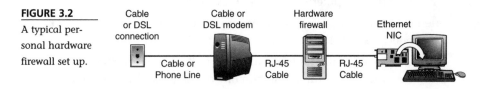

If you have a hardware firewall that provides more than one port, you can connect other computers to it and build a small home network. However, your ISP will want you to pay them an additional fee for each additional computer. Fortunately, as you will learn in Chapter 11, "Home Networks and Internet Connection Sharing," these devices have built-in features that provide a way to share this connection without incurring the additional fee.

Once you install it, you can communicate with your hardware firewall by using its self-assigned IP address and your Netscape or Internet Explorer Web browser. You'll probably need to run version 4 or higher of these browsers. For example, the Linksys personal firewall assigns itself an IP address of 192.168.1.1. To begin configuring it, you only need to start your browser and type `http://192.168.1.1` in the URL field and press Enter. You are asked to supply a password, which you can then change to prevent anyone else from being able to reconfigure your firewall. All administration from this point on is done via the browser connection. Chapter 5 provides you with a detailed review of how this process works.

Note

To learn more about the Linksys personal firewall, including how to configure it using its Web interface, refer to Chapter 5.

There are a number of personal hardware firewalls on the market. Most share a common set of characteristics. These characteristics include:

- Cable/DSL router—Built-in software that routes your outgoing network traffic (such as e-mail, file uploads, and so on) to the Internet and receives and forwards network Internet traffic sent to your computer. Any Internet traffic not addressed specifically to your computer is automatically disregarded.

- DHCP server—Dynamic Host Control Protocol or DHCP is a software feature used by people with small networks. It allows the hardware firewall to double as a DHCP server. DHCP servers dynamically assign IP addresses to computers connected to a home network, saving you the trouble of having to learn how to do it manually. More information is available about this software feature in Chapter 1.

- DHCP client—Allows your firewall to accept a dynamic IP address from your ISP so that the computer(s) that it services can establish a connection.

- Internet firewall—Software that protects your computer or small network from malicious attacks when connected to the Internet.

- Multiport hub—Additional hardware ports built into the hardware firewall that allow you to hook up more than one computer and share the Internet connection. This way, you can build a small home network.

- Switch—The capability to establish a temporary dedicated connection between two local computers on a home network, which helps make networking games run faster because their network traffic is more efficiently managed.

- Internet configuration—The capability to securely configure your firewall over an Internet connection.

- Browser configuration—The capability to configure your firewall using your Web browser.

Software Firewalls

Software firewalls are software programs loaded onto your computer that reside on its hard drive and are loaded into memory when the computer starts up. Unlike hardware firewalls, software firewalls are designed to work with your current hardware configuration and are just as effective for dial-up connections as they are for cable or DSL connections. Once installed, each software firewall is configured via its own custom interface.

Unlike hardware firewalls, software firewalls are designed to protect a single device and do not provide the capability to create local area networks. However, if you do not have a local area network, you might find that software firewalls offer a simplicity that makes them easier to work with and manage than their hardware-based counterparts.

Software firewalls are less expensive than hardware firewalls. Some perfectly good software firewalls are even free to the individual home user. For example, the ZoneAlarm personal firewall is free although there is also a professional version of ZoneAlarm that provides additional features that is not free. You get the opportunity to learn more about ZoneAlarm in Chapter 8, "ZoneAlarm."

MICROSOFT'S NEW INTERNET CONNECTION FIREWALL

As of the writing of this book, Microsoft is only a few months away from releasing the home version of its newest computer operating system, called Windows XP Home Edition. Among its many new features is a built-in firewall, which Microsoft calls the Internet Connection Firewall.

The Microsoft Home Networking Wizard will automatically install and configure both the computer's Internet Connection and its personal firewall. Microsoft says that this new firewall will block unsolicited Internet connections by rejecting any that did not originate from the home computer. In addition, if you have a small home network, you can use the personal firewall to protect it. However, although it is nice to see that Microsoft recognizes that its operating systems do lack protection when surfing the Internet, this firewall offering will be of no help except to those who convert to the Windows XP Home edition, which could prove to be a costly measure. Like all the Microsoft operating systems before it, Windows XP features an escalated set of hardware requirements that many home computer owners will not be able to accommodate without purchasing new computers. For example, you'll need a minimum of 128MB of memory to use Windows XP.

Software firewalls are designed to work with specific operating systems. However, most major personal software firewalls work with Windows 95, 98, Me, NT 4, 2000, and XP. Software firewalls provide easy-to-work-with wizards that step you through the setup and configuration processes. Each software firewall provides its own set of predefined security policies that allow you to specify a different level of security. For example, BlackICE Defender provides four canned security policies:

- Trusting—Allows all inbound traffic, essentially disabling the firewall.
- Cautious—Blocks all unsolicited Internet traffic that attempts to access networking or operating system resources.
- Nervous—Blocks all unsolicited Internet traffic with the exception of certain types of interactive traffic, such as streaming multimedia.
- Paranoid—Blocks all unsolicited Internet traffic.

You should expect about the same level of protection from a software firewall as from a hardware firewall. The major distinction between the two is that hardware firewalls defend your computer by attempting to block any attack from ever reaching it, whereas a software firewall, by virtue of being installed on the computer itself, must defend the computer from attacks that are already at the computer's front door. Software firewalls consume computer resources—including disk space and memory—and therefore (even when successful) will have a small impact on their computer host.

Typical Software Firewall Requirements

Hardware requirements can differ significantly between the various software firewall programs. Hardware firewalls, on the other hand, do not place any software requirements on the computers that they protect. Their only requirement is an Ethernet connection, which is the connection you established when you installed you NIC and cabled it to your cable or DSL modem, as described in Chapter 2, "High-Speed Internet Connection Equal Increased Vulnerablility."

Table 3.1 lists the hardware requirements of the firewall products that are going to be reviewed in this book.

Table 3.1   Software-Based Personal Firewall Hardware Requirements

Firewall	Operating System	CPU	Memory	Hard Disk
Linksys EtherFast cable/ DSL router	N/A	N/A	N/A	N/A
McAfee personal firewall	W95 or higher	486	32MB	4MB
BlackICE Defender	W95 or higher	Pentium	16MB	10MB
ZoneAlarm personal firewall	W95 or higher	-	-	-

Networking Overview

As was mentioned in Chapter 2, a cable or DSL Internet connection is a connection to a giant and highly complex network. To communicate on this network, your computer must use the appropriate network protocol. A *network protocol* is a set of rules, standards, and procedures for communicating and exchanging data over a network. There is only one set of protocols used on the Internet and they are collectively known as TCP/IP.

You can view your high-speed connection to the Internet as a layered set of protocols and applications, as shown in Figure 3.3 where each layer of protocols depend upon the services of the layer below.

Your connection from your home PC to your local cable or telephone ISP is an Ethernet connection. Ethernet is itself a protocol. However, it is a lower-level protocol and is used to transport the higher-level TCP/IP protocol. This allows your ISP to bridge the connection between itself and your computer. TCP/IP performs a number of jobs for you but at its most basic level, it facilitates the communications between applications running on two computers, such as Internet Explorer or Outlook Express.

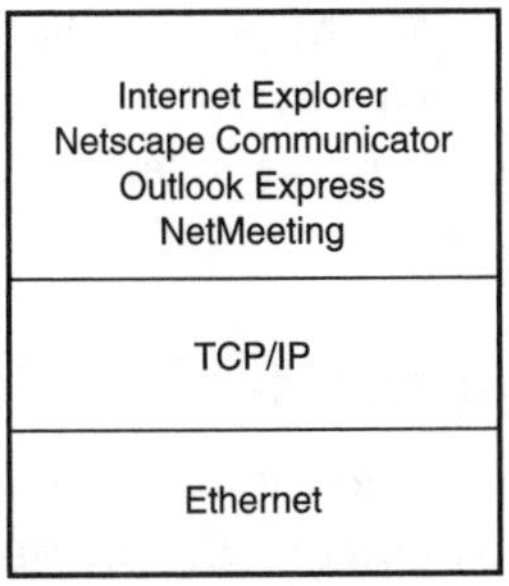

FIGURE 3.3

A representation of the typical broadband Internet connection.

Internet Explorer Netscape Communicator Outlook Express NetMeeting
TCP/IP
Ethernet

Understanding How Data Is Sent Between Network Computers

Communication over the Internet ultimately occurs between two computers, a source and a destination computer, or more specifically between the NIC on one computer and the NIC on another computer. During the communication session that occurs between two computers, they will often switch between these two roles. As data traffic is sent from one computer to the other, it must flow over the Internet. Because the Internet is a vast collection of computers, the data actually passes through a number of other computers on its way to the destination computer. TCP/IP is the protocol that makes all this possible.

In order for the computers that make up the Internet to know where to deliver all this data, it must be appropriately addressed. It's important to understand that when you send something such as e-mail to someone else on the Internet that the e–mail itself is not sent as a single document. TCP/IP actually breaks it up into more manageable units called *packets*. The individual packets are then sent across the Internet to the destination computer, as depicted in Figure 3.4.

FIGURE 3.4

A look at how files are broken into multiple packets and transported over the Internet.

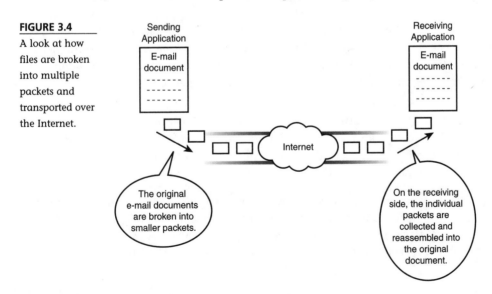

Not every packet will follow the same path. In fact the packets that make up your e-mail can travel over many different paths on their way to the destination computer. This is where they will ultimately be received and reassembled by TCP/IP. Finally, they are passed on to the recipient's e-mail client for viewing.

Understanding How Computers Communicate

Every computer that connects to the Internet is assigned a unique IP address. This address identifies the location of the source computer on the Internet as well as the address of the destination computer. Identifying the source and destination address of each packet is essential to completing the delivery of every packet.

When a data packet arrives, the destination computer inspects the packet. If the packet is addressed to the computer it is accepted and processed, otherwise it is disregarded.

The assignment of IP addresses is transparent to most users because most ISPs use a protocol known as *DHCP* or the *Dynamic Host Configuration Protocol*. DHCP automatically assigns an IP address to your computer every time you power on your cable- or DSL-connected computer. If you are using a dial-up connection, your IP address is assigned every time you establish a dial-up connection.

How ISPs Use MAC Addresses

Likewise, the MAC address need not cause you any concern either, unless you plan to share your Internet connection with other computers on a small home network. Cable and DSL ISPs track the number of computers using an Internet connection by looking at the MAC addresses of the data packets that pass over the connection. This is why you must call and provide the MAC addresses of your cable modem and NIC card when you first activate your cable or DSL service. By default, cable and DSL ISPs block computers with unregistered MAC addresses from sharing the Internet connection. Because both your cable modem and computer have a MAC address, you must register them before you can use your Internet connection.

Cable and DSL ISPs charge an extra fee for each additional computer that shares the connection. This fee is usually around an extra $5–$7 per month. You have to call your ISP to arrange for the extra connections and provide the ISP with the MAC addresses of the NICs in the additional computers. You can use the IPCONFIG /All command to gather the MAC addresses as was covered in Chapter 2.

Note There is another way you can share a single Internet connection with multiple computers without having to pay the extra fee charged by your ISP. Basically, you route all Internet traffic through a single computer, which communicates with the Internet on behalf of the other computers on the home network using Microsoft Internet

Connection Sharing. This is provided as a component of Windows 98 Second Edition, Me, 2000, and XP.

Another option is to use a personal hardware firewall such as the Linksys BEFSR41, which provides a similar service. You learn more about setting up shared Internet connection access in Chapter 11.

More About TCP/IP

TCP/IP is actually a suite of many protocols that works together to provide communications over large and small networks. TCP and IP are two of the protocols in the overall TCP/IP suite. TCP/IP is the default protocol for Windows 98, Me, 2000, and XP, and is automatically installed when plug and play discovers a computer's network card or modem.

TCP/IP networks, like the Internet, find computers using a combination of the destination computer's IP address and its MAC address as has already been explained. Just like the MAC address, every IP must be unique.

An IP address is a 32-bit address made up of a combination of 0s and 1s. However, because people have trouble remembering 32-bit numbers, IP addresses are translated into a dotted decimal notation made up of four decimal numbers, each of which is separated by a period. For example, an IP address of 10000011 01101111 00000111 00011011 equals 131.111.7.27. IP addresses can be either statically or dynamically assigned to a computer. A static address is specially assigned to a computer and never changes. Static IP addresses are very rare for Internet connections. Typically, ISPs use dynamic IP address assignment.

To make things as easy as possible on you, Windows 98, Me, NT 4, 2000, and XP automatically configure themselves for dynamic IP address assignment. For example, Figure 3.5 shows the TCP/IP properties dialog box for a Windows 2000 Professional computer that as been configured for DHCP.

FIGURE 3.5

TCP/IP configuration is performed on the TCP/IP Properties dialog box.

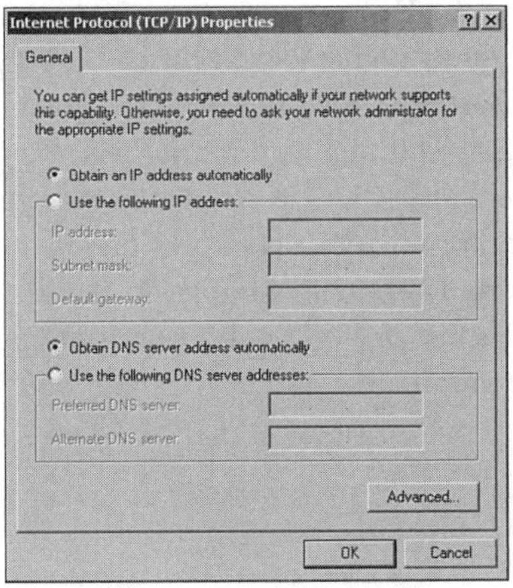

TCP/IP Ports

There is one additional component involved in communications that you need to understand, the TCP/IP port. Every packet that is sent out over the network also contains a target port that identifies the specific resource on the destination computer for which the packet is intended. For example, when you want to view a Web site, you type an address such as www.microsoft.com in the URL field of your Web browser. As initial communication is established between your computer and the Web server, the user-friendly Web site address is automatically substituted with the IP address of the destination computer. By the time a connection is established between your computer and the Web server, both computers know each other's IP addresses and automatically use them to address data packets for the rest of the session.

For example, servers that provide HTML content on the Internet are known as HTTP servers. To communicate with them and receive HTML content, you must use port 80. Without you even being aware of it, your Web browser automatically appends the port number to the end of the IP address. So if the address of the Microsoft HTTP server is 207.46.230.218, your data packets are ultimately addressed as 207.46.230.218:80.

By examining each packet for its port number, the destination computer knows to pass the resulting data to the application that has been assigned to that port number. In the case of a request to an http server for a Web page the packet will specify port 80.

There are over 60,000 possible port assignments on any computer running TCP/IP. In order to communicate over one of these ports, an application or service must be assigned to the port and actively listening. The first 1024 ports, numbered 1 through 1024, are considered to be well-known ports and each port in this range has already been assigned to a specific type of application or service. Ports above 1024 are known as ephemeral ports and can be used as necessary by any application, assuming that the port is not already in use by another application.

For example, port 80 is assigned to the HTTP service. Ports 20 and 21 are assigned to the File Transfer Protocol or FTP. Figure 3.6 depicts a view of TCP/IP port assignments. The first port in the list is port 80, which has been assigned to the Microsoft Personal Web Server, which is a Microsoft application that lets you turn your computer into a mini-HTTP Web server. Ports 137–139 are NetBIOS ports that are turned on whenever you enable the client for Microsoft Networks and its file and printer sharing. You learn more about ports 137–139 in Chapter 4, "Locking Down Windows Networking." Port 4444 is just one of the thousands of ephemeral ports that can be assigned to any application.

FIGURE 3.6

A demonstration of Microsoft TCP/IP port assignments.

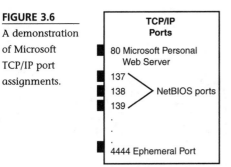

If you are interested in seeing a more complete listing of TCP/IP ports, check out `www.iana.org/assignments/port-numbers`.

Ports are a major source of exposure for any computer on the Internet. As you learn later in this chapter, intruders attempt to gain access to your computer by probing for open and unprotected ports.

Understanding How Firewalls Operate

Firewalls operate by examining the contents of packets in order to make a judgment about whether to allow the packet to pass through. For example, Figure 3.6 depicts two applications attempting to transmit data over the Internet. The data is broken into packets that are then sent out over the Internet. However, a firewall stands between two computers. The firewall in this example has been configured to permit all Internet Explorer traffic. Internet Explorer is designed to communicate with Internet Web servers using port 80. As Figure 3.7 demonstrates, packet targets at port 80 are being permitted through the firewall. However, Figure 3.7 also shows that a Trojan horse application has somehow managed to make its way onto the computer and is attempting to transmit data to another computer on the Internet using port 4444, which the firewall has been configured to block. In addition, the firewall is shown displaying a notification alert to its owner and recording a message in the personal firewall's log.

The rules for determining what is and is not allowed through the firewall are determined by the policies established on the firewall. Different firewalls have different capabilities and different policies. By appropriately setting the correct policy setting, you can enable strong firewall security. However, by improperly configuring firewall policies, you can render your firewall pretty much useless.

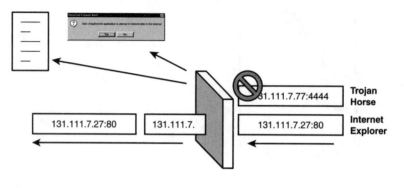

FIGURE 3.7

Your personal firewall can be configured to block traffic and report on any application that tries to make an Internet connection that is not allowed by policies.

Firewall Functions

Earlier in this chapter you saw a list of functions to look for in personal firewalls. This section and the sections that follow present a more detailed look at some specific firewall functions and explain how firewalls implement them. The basis for each of these functions is the firewall's ability to inspect packets and implement security policies that tell it what packets to let through and which to block.

Intrusion Detection

Some firewalls are designed to prevent unauthorized applications from communicating through the firewall. These firewalls can effectively block many attacks. However, firewalls that incorporate intrusion detection software afford an even greater level of security.

The problem with just examining packets for application and port information is that it still leaves a computer open to the possibility of an attack launched using approved applications. For example, many holes have been discovered in products such as Microsoft's NetMeeting and Personal Web Server (although Microsoft continues to plug each hole as is it discovered). This technique does not guard against buffer overflow attacks either. A buffer overflow attack occurs when an intruder attempts to use an approved application to flood a port. This can potentially crash the targeted computer or keep it so busy that it cannot perform any useful work.

Firewalls like BlackICE Defender that incorporate intrusion-detection software into its firewall can offer a defense against these kinds of attacks. For example, BlackICE is capable of analyzing hundreds of types of attacks. Intrusion-detection software is designed to examine the entire contents of packets and determine their intent. If a personal firewall with intrusion-detection software determines that its host computer is under attack, it can simply block the offending packets from passing through.

Detecting Attempts to Scan Your Computer

Intruders can use one of any number of freely available tools to search the Internet looking for victims. For example, there are plenty of ping-sweeper applications that can be used to search the Internet for active TCP/IP connections. *PING* is a TCP/IP command that can be used to poll the status of another TCP/IP computer and determine whether it is active. For example, to try to ping any computer on the Internet, type **PING** followed by its name or IP address. For example, you can ping a server, as shown here.

```
C:\>ping www.que.com

Pinging que.com [128.121.231.124] with 32 bytes of data:

Reply from 128.121.231.124: bytes=32 time=100ms TTL=234
Reply from 128.121.231.124: bytes=32 time=100ms TTL=234
Reply from 128.121.231.124: bytes=32 time=100ms TTL=234
Reply from 128.121.231.124: bytes=32 time=100ms TTL=234

Ping statistics for 128.121.231.124:
    Packets: Sent = 4, Received = 4, Lost = 0 (0% loss),
Approximate round trip times in milli-seconds:
    Minimum = 100ms, Maximum =  100ms, Average =  100ms
```

You can also type its IP address and receive the same results:

```
C:\>ping 128.121.231.124

Pinging 128.121.231.124 with 32 bytes of data:

Reply from 128.121.231.124: bytes=32 time=101ms TTL=234
Reply from 128.121.231.124: bytes=32 time=100ms TTL=234
Reply from 128.121.231.124: bytes=32 time=101ms TTL=234
Reply from 128.121.231.124: bytes=32 time=100ms TTL=234

Ping statistics for 128.121.231.124:
    Packets: Sent = 4, Received = 4, Lost = 0 (0% loss),
Approximate round trip times in milli-seconds:
    Minimum = 100ms, Maximum =  101ms, Average =  100ms
```

A ping-sweeper program can be used to ping thousands of IP addresses looking for active computers. After a hacker develops a list of active computers, another free program known as a port scanner can be run against the list that attempts to communicate with a range of ports on each active computer. More aggressive attacks can then be launched against computers that have open ports that are willing to accept connections. If for example, a hacker discovers that ports 137–139 are open, the hacker can easily collect a number of potentially helpful pieces of information such as your username and the name of your computer. If port 80 was discovered to be open and accepting connections (because you were running Microsoft's Personal Web Server), the intruder could try launching any number of attacks to exploit well-known weaknesses in this service.

A good firewall can detect when its ports are being scanned and can log the event and notify you if instructed. For example, ZoneAlarm can be configured to display a pop-up alert every time your computer is scanned. This way, if you hard drive suddenly begins spinning or things inexplicably slow down you can block the attack by temporarily disabling the connection. BlackICE Defender takes things a step further by tracking down and reporting the IP address of the offending computer where the scan originated.

However, not every scan is an attack. For example, someone may have accidentally typed the wrong IP address when trying to connect to an HTTP server or open a NetMeeting session with a friend. It's also possible that your ISP may be running some sort of test. Another false alarm that is known to occur comes from Internet-based WebTV services that sometimes contact the wrong IP addresses by accident.

It is important to keep an eye on the security logs created by your personal firewall and to be aware when your computer is scanned. Be sure to keep an eye out if the number of scans hitting your computer suddenly increases.

Guarding Against Trojan Horses

As you have already learned, a Trojan horse is a program that makes its way onto your computer and then attempts to communicate with its creator in stealth mode. It does so by attempting to open a TCP/IP port and then connecting to an external computer. The purpose of the program can be to seek out, find, and try to copy your Microsoft Quicken or other personal files. Or, its purpose can be to take control of your computer and use it in a distributed denial-of-service attack. Regardless, if such a program does make it onto your computer, its communication with the Internet needs to be blocked and you need to be informed.

Personal firewalls detect Trojan horses by trusting nothing, even network traffic generated from your own computer. This means that all packets, both incoming and outgoing, are constantly examined.

For example, the McAfee Personal Firewall lets you specify a list of applications that you want to let communicate through the firewall. Any application that is not on the list but that tries to communicate is blocked and an alert is generated. When alerted, you are notified of the name of the executable that made the communication attempt. If you recognize it as an application that you want to permit through the firewall, you can respond to the alert telling the firewall to add it to the approved application list. If you suspect that it is a Trojan horse, you can delete it and any threat that it might impose.

However, it's not always easy to tell whether an executable program is actually a part of an application that is important to you and by deleting it you could accidentally disable the application. Therefore you might want to move the program to a floppy disk or ZIP drive so that if it turns out to be something that you need, you can copy it back to its original location.

Examining All Network Traffic

Personal firewalls need to be able to distinguish new connection requests from other network traffic. The very first packet sent between two computers when establishing a connection is different from all the packets that follow. The first packet is used to initiate a connection. All packets that follow the first packet include an acknowledgement flag that indicates that it is a packet being returned in response to a request for service. Your firewall can then use this information to let the packets through.

This means that a firewall can be set up to block all unsolicited incoming connection requests while allowing communication with servers that your computer initiated. When used in this manner, the personal firewall makes the ports on your computer disappear from the Internet because when ping sweepers or port scanners attempt to initiate a session with your computer, your firewall will ignore the unsolicited connection requests. A port that does not reply to a connection request is for all essential purposes invisible.

Firewall Classifications

There are a number of firewall technologies. Some are more appropriate for personal use than others. However, a quick review of each can provide insight on the firewall technology as a whole. Various types of firewalls include:

- Application-gateway
- Packet-filtering
- Circuit-level
- Stateful Inspection

Each type of firewall inspects and manages packet flow using a different technology. Some personal firewalls, such as BlackICE, combine the features of more than one firewall technology. Each of these types of firewalls is examined in the sections that follow.

Application-Gateway Firewalls

The application-gateway firewall is the model for most personal firewalls. These types of firewalls are sometimes referred to as *proxy firewalls*. These firewalls can filter based on IP addresses and the specific function that an application is trying to execute. For example, application firewalls can prevent specified applications such as Microsoft NetMeeting, PCAnywhere, or FTP from getting through. By monitoring application function, the firewall can even permit some application operations while blocking others. One example of this is a FTP site that permits you to upload files to specified directories without permitting you to view or modify files in the directories. For example, McAfee, BlackICE, and ZoneAlarm all employ features of the application gateway model.

Packet-Filtering Firewalls

Packet-filtering firewalls are designed to monitor packets based on their IP address and to only allow communication with specific IP addresses. As you might imagine this can be a labor-intensive process that requires a lot of upkeep. This type of firewall is sometimes used by companies to permit remote dial-in access by their employees or trusted customers. But for the home user who is likely to surf the Internet and needs connection to any number of Web sites, it is not a practical option.

Circuit-Level Firewalls

Circuit-level firewalls permit traffic flow with pre-approved IP addresses, networks, and Internet service providers. Once a network session is established between the users on each side of the firewall, all remaining packets are permitted to flow through the router unchecked.

Stateful Inspection

Instead of limiting packet inspection to the port and application specifications, stateful inspection firewalls examine the entire packet and analyze its contents. Stateful inspection firewalls attempt to determine the type of data being transmitted. If this data is viewed as non-threatening, these firewalls allow it to pass through. For example, BlackICE incorporates a variant of this technology in its firewall.

PART II

TIGHTENING YOUR SECURITY

LOCKING DOWN WINDOWS NETWORKING

*T*his chapter provides an overview of how Microsoft networking works and how Microsoft has implemented TCP/IP and its other Internet technologies. You see how these components interact and affect your security when you're surfing the Internet. This chapter provides insight into the security holes created by Microsoft networking and shows you steps that you can take to make things a bit safer.

You also get an overview of the differences between surfing the World Wide Web with Windows 95, 98, and Me and surfing with Windows 2000 or XP. This material provides you with information regarding the importance of the Windows file systems and explains how choosing the right file system can help make your system more secure.

- Review the relationship of Microsoft's networking and Internet technologies
- Learn how to simplify your network configuration
- Learn how to make your Windows computer more secure
- Review strategies for making your computer less attractive to intruders
- Examine the advantages of upgrading your operating system to a newer version

An Overview of Microsoft Networking

When you are on the Internet you have access to a world full of resources. However, unless you have taken steps to secure your computer, you might be surprised just how much access the world has to your computer. The purpose of this chapter is to show that there are a number of things that you can do to help protect yourself before you begin surfing on the World Wide Web with your new, always-on, high-speed Internet connection. The actions that you can take to protect yourself include:

- Removing unnecessary Microsoft networking components
- Cleaning up your network bindings
- Using a more secure operating system
- Choosing stronger passwords
- Installing a personal firewall
- Installing an antivirus scanner

Introducing Microsoft Networking

The networking software built into Microsoft operating systems is designed to support your computer when you're participating on local area networks. A *local area network* is a collection of interconnected computers located within a small area such as a house or building. Microsoft networks are designed to allow the sharing of resources such as the files and folders located on the disk drives of networked computers.

 Note Within the context of this book, references to local area networks are meant to address personal home networks comprised of 2–3 computers.

The degree of security on a Microsoft network depends on the operating systems that are running on it. When a Windows home network consists of entirely Windows NT,

2000, or XP computers, it is much more secure than if it consists of Windows 95, 98, and Me computers. This is because the Windows NT line of operating systems features a secure file system known as *New Technology File System* (NTFS) that allows you to apply significantly stronger security over its disk and printer resources. However, the vast majority of home users are still running Windows 95, 98 or Me as their operating systems and these operating systems do not support the NTFS file system.

By definition, cable and DSL Internet connections are actually local area network connections. So whether or not you have a home network, your computer is still attached to a local area network. Microsoft operating systems automatically install a set of default network components whenever a network connection, such as one to the Internet or a home local area network, is established. These network components include:

- Client for Microsoft Networks
- File and printer sharing for Microsoft Networks
- Internet protocol (TCP/IP)
- NIC software driver

As you see later in this chapter, it is the presence of Microsoft networking and TCP/IP together that places your computer at risk when it is connected to the Internet.

Until the arrival of broadband Internet, access security for the home user was of little concern. Security was simply a good lock on your front door. After you're connected to the Internet, the rules change. Unless you take a few basic steps, the door to your computer is still wide open. And unless you install a personal firewall, it will always be cracked. To see why this is the case you must first understand how the various Microsoft networking components fit together, as discussed in the following section.

Understanding How Microsoft Networking Is Implemented

The software configuration that makes up a Microsoft network can be viewed as existing at three separate and distinct levels. At the top level are three Microsoft software services that provide basic networking functionality, including the capability to connect to a Microsoft network and share its resources. These services are outlined as follows:

- Client for Microsoft Networks—A networking component that provides an interface to a home network and allows information to be redirected to and from a computer over that network.
- Microsoft Family Logon—An optional component available on Windows 98 and Me that is used to log on to Microsoft networks and access network resources.

■ File and printer sharing for Microsoft Networks—An optional component that allows your computer to share its files, folders, and printers with the rest of the network. By default, this option is disabled. However, unless you installed your own operating system, you should double-check to make sure that is has not been turned on, as shown later in this chapter.

The Client for Microsoft Networks provides a two-way connection to a Microsoft network. The Microsoft Family Logon provides a convenient means for logging on to local area networks. File and printer sharing is an optional networking component that allows you to provide shared access to the disk and printer resources on your computer. Although these three software components are key parts of a Microsoft home network, they are unnecessary if all you need to do is connect to the Internet. However, as has already been stated, the Client for Microsoft Networks and the Microsoft Family Logon are automatically installed when you set up your Internet connection, leaving your computer vulnerable to attack. Depending on who installed your computer's operating system, file and printer sharing may be installed and enabled as well.

The middle level of the Microsoft networking model consists of Microsoft-supported network protocols. TCP/IP is the protocol used to access the Internet and most other networks. As you learned in Chapter 3 "Firewalls Explained," TCP/IP addresses and transports data across networks such as the Internet. Other protocols, such as NetBEUI, can reside at this level as well.

NetBEUI is a simple and easy-to-implement protocol for managing communication on home networks. It requires no configuration and cannot be transported over your Internet connection.

The lower level of the Microsoft networking model consists of connections to various networks. Each of these connection types are outlined here:

■ Local area connection—A connection to a home network.

■ Dial-up connection—A connection to the Internet via a regular 56Kbps modem.

■ Broadband connection—An always-on cable or DSL connection to the Internet.

Trusting Microsoft Networks

By default, Microsoft networking is based on a networking model that assumes a certain degree of trust. As such Microsoft operating systems automatically configure or bind the software components located at every layer of the networking model

together, as shown in Figure 4.1. Although this might be acceptable for a home network, this level of trust is inappropriate for a computer with an always-on Internet connection.

FIGURE 4.1

By default, Microsoft operating systems allow all networking components to communicate and interact with one another.

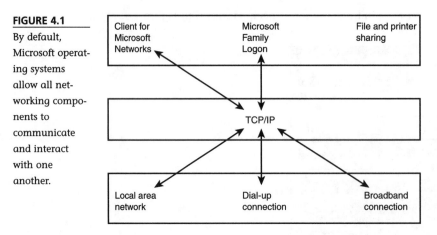

Client for Microsoft Networks

Microsoft Family Logon

File and printer sharing

TCP/IP

Local area network

Dial-up connection

Broadband connection

Binding is the process of connecting two network components so that they can communicate with one another. Unless two networking components are bound they cannot communicate. Therefore, reducing the number of network components that are bound can remove some of the security holes that Microsoft operating systems have when connected to the Internet.

You can view the network bindings for a particular Windows component from the Network dialog box by selecting and examining its properties. For example, the following procedure demonstrates how you can view the bindings for an Internet connection on a Windows 95, 98, or Me computer.

1. Click Start, Settings, and then Control Panel. The Windows Control Panel opens.

2. Double-click the Network icon. The Network dialog box opens, as shown in Figure 4.2.

3. Select the adapter representing your network connection and click Properties.

4. Select the Bindings property sheet, as shown in Figure 4.3.

As you can see, the Internet connection is bound to TCP/IP. If your Windows 95, 98, or Me computer is attached to a home network, you can view the bindings of your NIC card as shown:

1. Click Start, Settings, and then Control Panel. The Windows Control Panel opens.

2. Double-click the Network icon. The Network dialog box opens.

3. Select network adapter and click Properties. The Properties dialog box for the network adapter appears.

4. Select the Bindings property sheet, as shown in Figure 4.4.

FIGURE 4.2

Examining the networking components installed on a typical Microsoft computer.

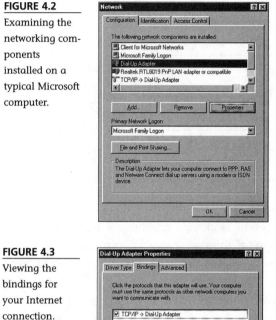

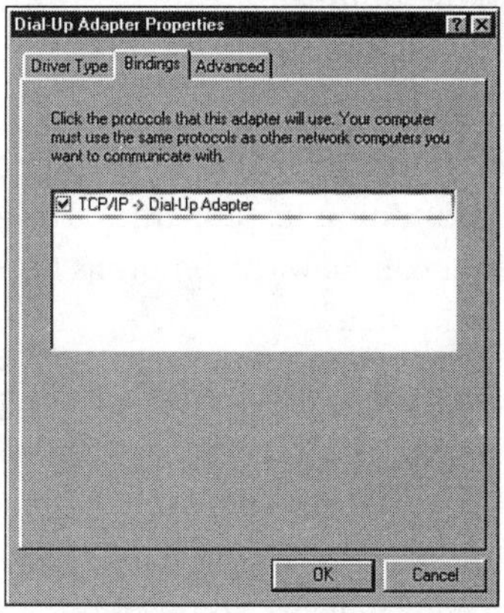

FIGURE 4.3

Viewing the bindings for your Internet connection.

As you can see, the NIC is also bound to your TCP/IP connection the same as the computer's Internet connection. By default, Microsoft operating systems bind everything at each layer to everything at adjacent layers in the networking model. This makes network configuration a whole lot easier but a lot less secure. Therefore, it is possible for someone on the Internet to hack into your computer via your TCP/IP connection and then access the home network to which your computer is attached.

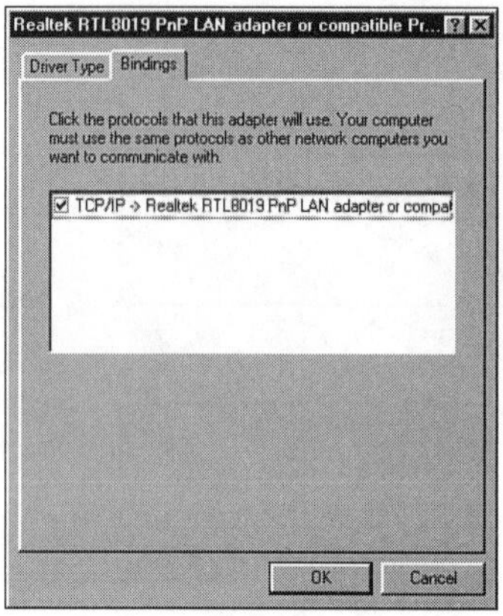

FIGURE 4.4

Viewing the bindings of a NIC on a home network.

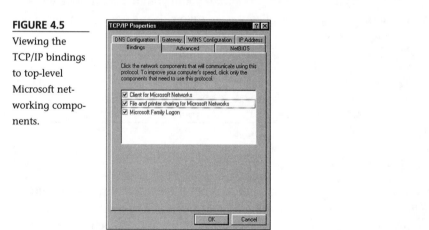

To view the bindings that exist between TCP/IP and the top-level Microsoft networking components on a Windows 95, 98 or Me computer, use the following procedure.

1. Click Start, Settings, and then Control Panel. The Windows Control Panel opens.

2. Double-click the Network icon. The Network dialog box opens.

3. Select either the TCP/IP component associated with the Internet connection or the one associated with the network adapter and then click Properties. The Properties dialog box of the selected TCP/IP component appears.

4. Select the Bindings property sheet, as shown in Figure 4.5.

FIGURE 4.5

Viewing the TCP/IP bindings to top-level Microsoft networking components.

As you can see, TCP/IP is bound to all the top-level Microsoft software components by default. This allows the computer to connect to the home network and access its network resources. If you are also running a home network, Microsoft's file and

printer sharing need to be enabled on each computer to allow them to share their resources with other network computers, as shown in Figure 4.6.

FIGURE 4.6

Viewing Microsoft's default network bindings for a computer connected to the Internet and a home network.

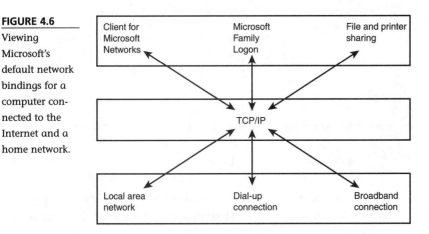

If the dial-up and broadband bindings were disabled, the network connections depicted in Figure 4.6 would be secure by virtue of the fact that the connection to the Internet has been disabled. But as soon as you connect to the Internet, the rules change, especially when you have a broadband connection.

Because file and printer sharing and your Internet connection are bound to TCP/IP, it opens the way for an intruder to attempt to access your local disk drives. It's even possible for a hacker to access a home network if your computer is connected to one because your Internet connection and your local area network are both bound to TCP/IP by default.

Microsoft operating systems beginning with Windows 98 display a message when TCP/IP is first installed warning of the dangers of leaving it bound to an Internet connection and offering to turn it off. However, unless you install TCP/IP yourself, you will never see this message and chances are good that your computer is exposed.

Closing Down Your NetBIOS Ports

As was stated previously in this chapter, the Client for Microsoft Networks is automatically installed on your computer anytime the operation system detects a connection to some kind of network. Even if you do not have a home network, the Microsoft operating system will install the default Microsoft networking components because an Internet connection is also considered to be a network connection.

When the Client for Microsoft Networks is installed, Microsoft automatically opens TCP ports 137, 138, and 139. It does not matter whether you have a home network; Microsoft installs them anyway. Microsoft uses these ports, along with a protocol called NetBIOS, to facilitate communications on Microsoft networks. It is through these ports that resources such as folders, disk drives, and printers are shared on networks (including the Internet). It is through these ports that network computers share information about their shared resources as well. This provides any network computer with the capability to query the computer for information about itself. These ports and their services are listed here:

- 137–NetBIOS Name Service
- 138–NetBIOS Datagram Service
- 139–NetBIOS Session Service

Unfortunately, NetBIOS does not require any authorization from anyone on the network (home or Internet) and therefore provides several pieces of information upon request, including:

- The name of the currently logged on user
- The computer's name
- Home network workgroups that the computer is a member of

These pieces of information tell hackers something about you and give them a starting point for launching an attack. For example, if you name your computer after a character on a TV show then perhaps your passwords, if you have them, are based on other TV characters. The information that NetBIOS provides can also act as a lure that draws the attention of hackers. To protect yourself, consider giving your computer a name that is as uninteresting as possible.

If the computer that you use to connect to the Internet is also connected to a home computer, you should also assign uninteresting names to any shared resources on it.

Protecting Printers and Disk Drives from Internet Intruders

If you do not have a local area network in your home, there is no reason for you to leave the Client for Microsoft Networks, Microsoft Family Logon, and file and printer sharing installed on your computer. They serve no other purpose than to support a local area network connection. Simply removing them will make your system more secure. Removing them will also shut down NetBIOS ports 137–139.

As an extra little bonus you'll find that removing these networking components frees up a small amount of memory and can even help your computer to boot faster.

As Figure 4.7 shows, the only networking connection left will be between TCP/IP and either a dial-up or broadband connection, depending on which one you use to connect to the Internet.

FIGURE 4.7

Only TCP/IP and your Internet connection need to be bound together for all your Internet applications such as Internet Explorer to work.

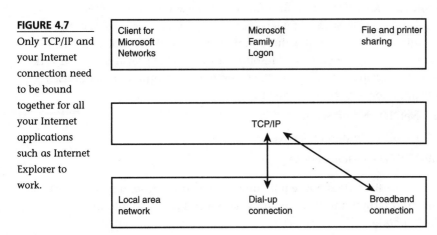

If you do not have a home network, you should consider removing the Microsoft networking components. The following procedure outlines the processes of removing these three Microsoft networking components from a Windows 95, 98, or Me computer.

1. Click Start, Settings, and then Control Panel. The Windows Control Panel opens.

2. Double-click the Network icon. The Network dialog box opens.

3. Select the Client for Microsoft Networks and click Remove.

4. Select the Microsoft Family Logon and click Remove.

5. Click OK.

File and printer sharing, if installed, will automatically be removed when Client for Microsoft Networks is removed.

Configuring Communications for Home Networks

If you have a home network, you need to provide for communications between each network computer while trying to reduce the risk posed by your Internet connection. This means that you need to leave your Microsoft networking components installed on your network computers. To reduce your exposure, you should manually unbind

all top-level binding with TCP/IP so that TCP/IP can only communicate with its Internet connection and not with other Microsoft top-level networking components.

If you do not unbind your TCP/IP bindings and you are running Microsoft file and printer sharing, you are leaving your computer wide open. There are dozens of free scanners available on the Internet. Some of these scanners are specifically designed to search ranges of IP addresses looking for computers that expose ports 137–139.

If you know how to share a folder or drive, as demonstrated in Chapter 11, "Home Networks and Internet Connection Sharing," you know how easy it is to access them over a network. Remember that when you are connected to the Internet you are also connected to a network over which you have no control. If you have not applied passwords to protect your shared resource, anyone who has scanned your computer and discovered that it is not protected can map your network drives. On Windows 95, 98, and Me computers, this gives hackers complete control to do anything that they want, including reading, copying, renaming, and even deleting your files.

> You might have heard that you can add a $ to the end of a shared resource's name to make it invisible to prying eyes. Well, this is not true. Adding a $ to the end of a shared resources name only makes it disappear from the view of other network when they are browsing the networking with the My Network Neighborhood. Hacker tools found out on the Internet can see all your shares, whether they have a $ appended to their names or not.

Even if you have password-protected shares, you are still in big trouble because most shared passwords can be easily broken using any of dozens of freely available password cracking programs found on the Internet. Even worse, Microsoft does not provide you with any warning when someone is running a password-cracking programming against your shared network resources.

> A personal firewall with built-in intrusion detection can block password crackers and notify you when an attack has occurred.

> If you absolutely must share resources over a home network, try to avoid sharing entire disk drives and limit the number of shared resources as much as possible.

Most people do not create passwords for home networks because of the inconvenience of having to type the password every time you want to access a resource. Using the same password to protect every shared resource is not good either because, after it's cracked, it leaves everything wide open. Your only alternative is to create a unique password for every shared resource, and not just any password will do. Because password-cracking programs have the capability to break passwords that

include common names and words, you need to create passwords that have the following characteristics:

- They are lengthy
- They are cryptic (not easy to guess)
- They include numbers, upper- and lowercase letters, and special characters

> **Tip**
>
> It is also a good idea to set up a schedule for regularly changing your password. This way, if a hacker cracks it, he or she will have access to it for a more limited period of time.

Unfortunately, passwords can be hard to remember. And when you have more than a few of them, it gets even harder. In addition, people also have a tendency to name shared resources with descriptive names that identify their contents. Although this makes it easy to locate things, it also makes it easy for hackers to hone in on interesting targets. Therefore, shared names should be as uninteresting as possible.

If you do have a home network, you should use the following procedure to remove unnecessary network bindings to TCP/IP on Windows 95, 98, or Me computers.

1. Click Start, Settings, and then Control Panel. The Windows Control Panel opens.

2. Double-click the Network icon. The Network dialog box opens.

3. Select either the TCP/IP component associated with the Internet connection or the one associated with the network adapter and then click Properties. The Properties dialog box for the selected TCP component appears.

4. Select the Bindings property.

5. Clear each of the selections to the top-level networking components and click OK.

6. Close the Network dialog box and restart the computer when prompted.

Now that you have cleared your TCP/IP bindings, you need to provide each computer on your network with a way to communicate with one another. An easy way to achieve this is to keep the reduced set of TCP/IP bindings shown in the previous example and to load and install the NetBEUI protocol on all your home network computers. Logically, your network bindings would then look like those depicted in Figures 4.9 and 4.10.

Figure 4.8 shows how the network binding appears on the network computer that has the Internet connection. As you can see, both TCP/IP and NetBEUI are installed. However, both are bound to different resources and there is no binding path between the two.

FIGURE 4.8

Using NetBEUI as your local area network protocol instead of TCP/IP.

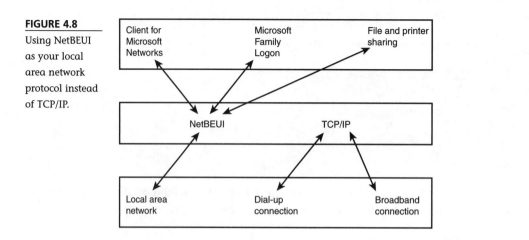

Figure 4.9 shows how the network binding appears on the rest of the network computers. As you can see there is no sign of TCP/IP.

FIGURE 4.9

NetBEUI is an excellent local area network protocol that requires no configuration to install or deploy.

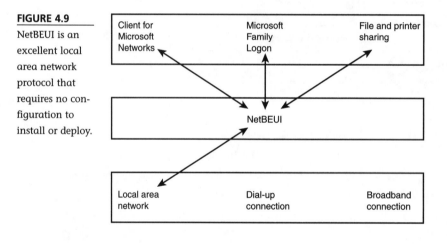

Note

Another home networking solution is to purchase a hardware personal firewall and use it to protect your TCP/IP-based home network from the Internet. More information on this option is available in Chapter 11.

The following procedure demonstrates how to install the NetBEUI protocol on Windows 95, 98, and Me computers.

1. Click Start, Settings, and then Control Panel. The Windows Control Panel opens.

2. Double-click the Network icon. The Network dialog box opens.

3. Click the Add button. The Select Network Component Type dialog box appears, as shown in Figure 4.10.

FIGURE 4.10

Installing a new local area network protocol.

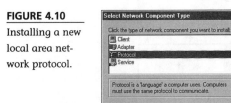

4. Select Protocol and click Add. The Select Network Protocol dialog box appears, as shown in Figure 4.11.

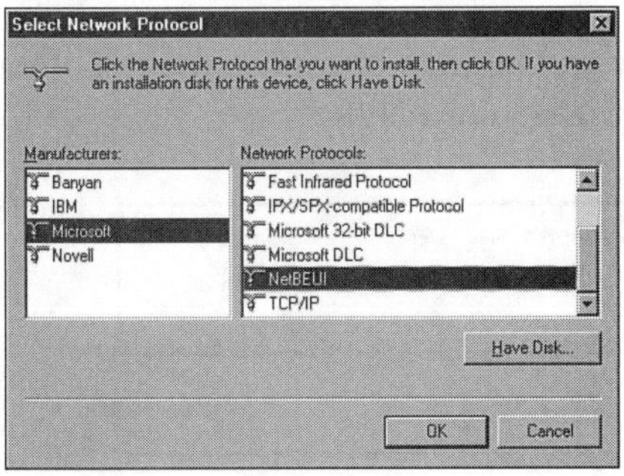

FIGURE 4.11

Selecting the Microsoft NetBEUI protocol.

5. Select Microsoft from the Manufacturers list.

6. Select NetBEUI from the Network Protocols list.

7. The Network dialog box reappears. Click OK. Windows begins to install NetBEUI. Insert the Windows CD if requested.

8. Click Yes when prompted to restart your computer.

Improving Your Security

Up to this point in the chapter you've learned how to make your computer more secure by either removing unnecessary Microsoft networking components or changing their configuration to one that is safer when you have a home network. This section addresses another way to improve your computer's security: by upgrading your operating system.

If you are running Windows 95, 98, or Me, you might want to consider upgrading to Windows 2000 Professional or Windows XP Home Edition when they become

available in later 2001. Windows 2000 Professional and XP Home Edition provide support for a significantly more secure file system that provides the following capabilities:

- The capability to require user authentication before getting access to a computer's resources
- Strong file system permissions that can be used to govern access to specific resources such as files, folders, and entire disk drives
- The capability to encrypt files so that only the person that encrypted them can decrypt and access them

Implementing Usernames and Passwords

Unlike Windows 95, 98, and Me, Windows 2000 and Windows XP both allow you to implement the requirement of usernames and passwords without which you or a hacker are denied access to your computer and its file system. These operating systems can also be configured to disable a user account in the event that a hacker tries to run a password-cracking program against it. For example, you can configure an account lockout after a few missed attempts at guessing or cracking a password.

User account passwords need to be carefully thought out and should never be made up of common names or words. Default accounts, created when the operating system is installed, should be renamed. This includes the Administrator and Guest accounts. Leaving these two account names unchanged just makes it easier for hackers to find them.

Windows 2000 Professional and Windows XP Home Edition also allow you to share folder and disk resources. If you do not have a home network, you should not have any shares set up, and if you do, you should remove them. If you do have a home network, you need to apply all the same strategies for modifying bindings and applying strong share passwords as you do on Windows 95, 98, and Me systems.

NTFS Security

The Windows operating system that you use has a great deal to do with how secure you computer is. Different Windows operating systems provide support for different files systems, as shown in Table 4.1.

Table 4.1 Microsoft Operating Systems File System Support

O/S	Windows 95	Windows 98	Windows NT	Windows 2000
FAT	Yes	Yes	Yes	Yes
FAT32	OSR2 only	Yes	No	Yes

Table 4.1 (continued)

O/S	Windows 95	Windows 98	Windows NT	Windows 2000
NTFS 4	No	No	Yes	Yes
NTFS 5	No	No	Requires SP4	Yes

Windows 95, 98, and Me are all designed to work with versions of the FAT file system. A *file system* is a mechanism that an operating system uses to organize, store, and retrieve information from disk drives.

The FAT file system is a 16-bit file system that stores files using eight character filenames with an optional three-character file extension. There is no built-in mechanism for securing files stored on FAT drives. FAT32 is a 32-bit version of FAT that provides support for long filenames (up to 256 characters). Like FAT, FAT32 is not a secure file system. Therefore, if you are running Windows 95, 98, or Me when you are connected to the Internet, the files stored on your hard drive are potentially vulnerable.

Windows NT, 2000, and XP, on the other hand, support the NTFS file system, which is significantly more secure than the FAT file system. NTFS provides the operating system with the capability to secure files, folders, and entire disk drives using security permission. When properly applied, NTFS allows access to files based on these permissions. This places a greater challenge to hackers because even if they gain access to view the contents of your disk drives, they can still be blocked from opening, modifying, or deleting files.

Anyone trying to access a file on a Windows 2000 or XP system must first have the appropriate permissions. This means that if a hacker can access your computer and does manage to crack one of its user accounts, he or she will still be blocked from files that the account does not have permission to access.

You can apply security permissions by right-clicking a Windows resource, such as a file or folder, selecting Properties, clicking the Security property sheet, and then clicking the Permission button. This opens the resource's Properties dialog box, as demonstrated in Figure 4.12.

To give a user or group of users access to the resources, select them from the list of accounts and click Add. When you return to the Security property, select the permissions that you want to assign to the account and click OK.

In order for hackers to get access to a resource on a Windows 2000 or XP system, they have to crack the password of a user account that has the appropriate set of permissions. If the hacker attempts a brute force dictionary attack on Windows 2000 and XP user accounts, the operation system will automatically disable the accounts when too many incorrect attempts have been made.

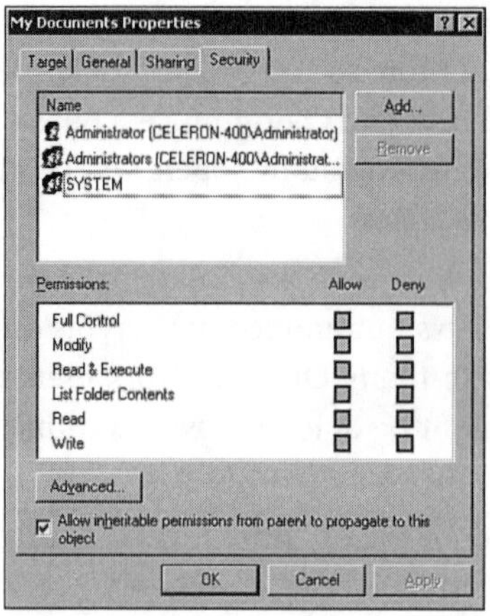

FIGURE 4.12

Configuring file permissions on a Windows 2000 computer.

Compare this security model to the one employed by Windows 95, 98, and Me, in which a hacker only needs to crack the password assigned to a given resource (which is not disabled by a brute force password crackers is run against it), and you can see that upgrading your operating system can make your computer a lot more secure.

But before you run off and buy Windows 2000 Professional or Windows XP Home Edition, you should be aware of a few drawbacks. Neither of these operating systems is free and both require a great deal more resources from your computer than do Windows 95, 98, or Me. Unless you have purchased your computer within the last few years, you might not be able to make the jump to one of these operating systems without a significant hardware upgrade or the purchase of a new computer.

The minimum hardware requirements for these two operating systems are listed in Table 4.2.

Table 4.2 Microsoft Operating Systems Hardware Requirements

O/S	Windows 98	Windows Me	Windows 2000	Windows XP
Memory	16MB	32MB	64MB	64/128MB
CPU	486	Pentium 150	Pentium 133	Pentium 233/300
DISK	175MB	480MB	650MB	1.5GB

Encrypting Your Files

Another feature provided by the Windows 2000 and Windows XP operating systems is the *Encrypted File System* (EFS). EFS is available only if you formatted your hard

disk using NTFS. EFS allows you to encrypt individual files, folders, or even entire hard drives. Encrypting a file makes it more secure because only the person who encrypted it can decrypt it. Of course, the encryption process adds a little overhead, which can slow things down just a bit when you are opening and closing files. However, you will probably never notice this.

After encrypted, your file, folder, or disk drive looks and acts the same as it always did because from that point on Windows automatically decrypts and re-encrypts them as necessary when you work with them. Other network users and Internet hackers who map your hard drive might be able to browse a listing of your encrypted files but should not be able to open them.

Although you can encrypt an individual file or entire hard disk drives, Microsoft generally recommends encrypting at the folder level. When you encrypt a folder, any files that you add to it are automatically encrypted.

You should probably encrypt your My Documents folder in addition to any other folders where you store sensitive information. In addition, you should also encrypt the Windows Temp folder because Windows sometimes places copies of files that you are working with in this directory.

Use the following procedure to encrypt the My Document folder on a Windows 2000 system.

1. Right-click the My Document folder and select Properties. The My Documents properties dialog box appears.

2. Click the General property sheet and select the Advanced button, as shown in Figure 4.13.

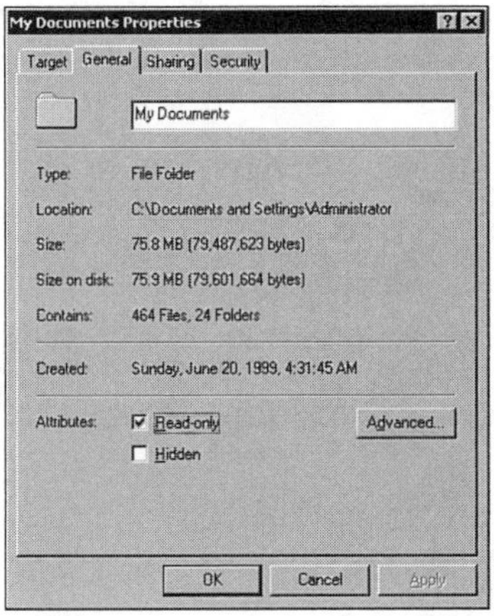

FIGURE 4.13

The General Property sheet of the My Documents Properties dialog box.

3. The Advanced Attributes dialog box appears, as shown in Figure 4.14.

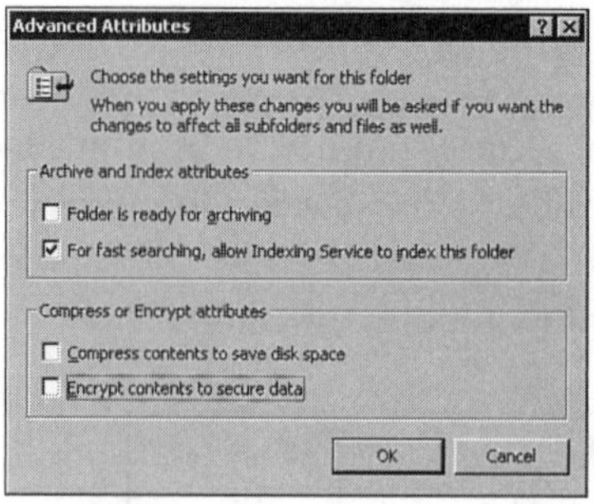

FIGURE 4.14

Encrypting the
Windows 2000
My Documents
folder.

FIGURE 4.14

Encrypting the
Windows 2000
My Documents
folder.

4. Select the Encrypt contents to secure data option and click OK.

5. Click OK when you return to the General property sheet.

6. The Confirm Attribute Changes dialog box appears asking whether any sub-folders found within the My Documents folder should be encrypted, as shown in Figure 4.15. To be safe, you should secure everything. Select Apply changes to this folder, subfolders, and files, and click OK.

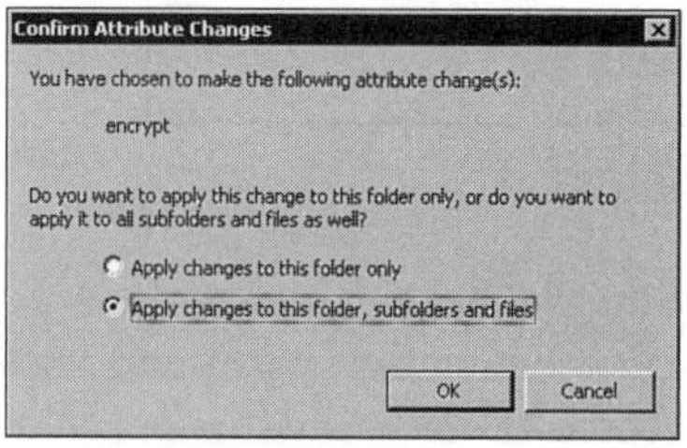

FIGURE 4.15

Applying
encryption to a
folder's contents,
including any
subfolders.

To verify that Windows 2000 has encrypted the folder and its contents, log off and then log back on as a different user and attempt to access a file in the My Documents folder.

Why You Should Still Get a Personal Firewall

If, after reading this chapter and changing the configuration of your home computer or home network, you feel like you are pretty secure, be warned that you are not. Just because you have disconnected Microsoft's networking components from your TCP/IP connection does not mean that you are going to be bulletproof when surfing the Internet. All that you have done is remove some of the targets that hackers look for. There are still other ways that hackers can get at your home computer. These include ways that have already been covered in this book, such as Trojan horses and worm programs, that after implanted on your computer expose you to a

wide range of problems. Other types of attacks can be embedded inside normal Internet applications.

Over the last few years a number of security holes have been uncovered in applications such as Microsoft's NetMeeting that allow hackers to infiltrate you computer system. Figure 4.16 depicts the way that TCP/IP provides communications with software programs installed on your computer and the Internet.

FIGURE 4.16

Any Internet application provides a hacker with a possible opportunity to threaten your computer or home network.

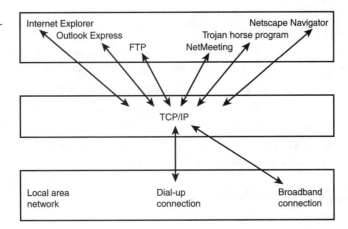

In many cases, you can protect yourself from these types of threats by keeping your operating system and applications up to date. This can be done by frequently visiting Microsoft's Update Web site for your operating system and the Web sites of the developers of your Internet applications. However, most people do not have the time to implement this level of diligence. So for now at least, the only way to achieve any level of safety for your always-on Internet connection is to get yourself a good firewall. Most firewalls include a year's worth of free updates that you can instruct to firewall to automatically download and apply in order to ensure that your personal firewall is as up to date and strong as it can be.

HARDWARE
FIREWALLS

*T*his chapter introduces you to a hardware device known as a Broadband EtherFast cable/DSL router. In addition to several other functions, these devices provide the services of a personal hardware firewall. This chapter shows you how to install and configure a personal hardware firewall using the Linksys BEFSR41 EtherFast cable/DSL router as an example.

In addition to physical setup, you will see how the firewall is configured using a standard Web browser. You also learn how to configure the logging of both inbound and outbound firewall traffic and how to access and view these logs.

- Learn how to install and configure a typical personal hardware firewall
- Learn how to apply a password
- Learn how to hide your TCP/IP ports
- Lean how to block IP addresses on your home network from connecting to the Internet
- Find out how to set up logs that record all inbound and outbound IP addresses, ports, and URLs

Hardware Firewalls

Today's personal hardware firewall is an external device that performs a number of services. It connects your computer and your cable or DSL modem and filters all inbound and outbound Internet traffic. These devices are typically called cable/DSL routers. Their list of features usually includes the following:

- Router—Manages the flow of traffic between two separate networks. In this case, the traffic is between your computer or home network and the Internet.
- Hub—Allows multiple home computers to be connected into a local area network. A hub supports one connection at a time that must be shared by all network computers.
- Switch—Allows a temporary dedicated connection established between two home computers to speed throughput and make games and multimedia content transfer faster. A switch allows multiple simultaneous network connections allowing multiple computers to communicate simultaneously.
- Firewall—Protects your computer or home network from external attack.

After they are properly installed and configured, these devices will represent the only visible connection to the Internet. These devices typical cost between $100–$250 and can connect between one and five computers to build a home network that can also share its Internet connection, although hums with more than five ports are now readily available. Because this is the only visible network device, your cable or DSL provider is unable to detect the number of computers connected to it, thus saving you the additional monthly expense of sharing the connection with more than one computer. This savings alone can easily pay for the device within a year or two depending on the number of computers that you share the connection with. More information on how to share your Internet connection and build a home network is provided in Chapter 11, "Home Networks and Internet Connection Sharing."

These networking devices do not require any additional software to be installed on your computer. They are equipped with a built-in firmware (software programmed into the devices chip set). You can configure the devices using any Internet Explorer or Netscape Communicator Internet browser starting at version 4 or above.

The BEFSR41 EtherFast Cable/DSL Router

The picture of the Linksys BEFSR41 EtherFast cable/DSL router, shown in Figure 5.1, is available at www.linksys.com and illustrates the operation of a typical hardware firewall.

FIGURE 5.1

The Linksys BEFSR41 EtherFast cable/DSL router allows you to connect up to four computers into a home network and to share a single hide-speed Internet connection using built-in firewall protection.

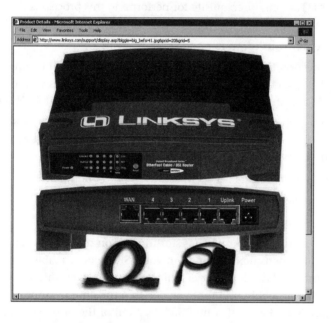

On the front of the BEFSR41 is a series of display lights that indicates the status of the device and each of its connections. On the lower-left is a power indicator. Three rows of lights indicate the status of each individual connection. The three indicators at the end of the rows indicate the status of the device connection to your cable or DSL modem. The *link* indictor indicates when a successful connection is established. The *Act* indicator shows when data is passing through the device. *Diag* indicates when the device is running a self-diagnostic test. This test runs whenever the device is first powered on.

On the back of the device you will find its power jack and six connection ports. On the far left is the WAN port. This port is used to connect the device to your cable or

DSL modem using a RJ-45 twisted-pair cable. The next four ports are used to connect between one and four computers and to build a home network, which can also share the Internet connection. The last port connects the device to another network hub. This allows you to expand the size of a home network.

Installing the Hardware Firewall

The following procedures outline the process of installing the BEFSR41 EtherFast cable/DSL router to work with a single home computer. Although specific to this router, this procedure can also be used as a generic description for installing other such devices. The only prerequisite for performing this process is that your home computer must have TCP/IP, which should already be the case.

1. Power off your computer and cable modem.

2. Connection the BEFSR41 to your cable or DSL modem by unplugging the end of the RJ-45 twisted-pair cable that currently connects your computer to your cable or DSL modem and plugging it into the BEFSR41's WAN port.

3. Connect the BEFSR41 to your computer by plugging a new RJ-45 twisted-pair cable into one of the open ports on the back of the BEFSR41 and your computer's Ethernet card.

4. Turn on the BEFSR41 by connecting its power adapter.

5. Power on your cable or DSL modem.

6. Power on your computer.

7. When you computer finishes starting, log on and open your Internet browser. What happens next depends on your ISP. If you are able to connect to the Internet and display your default home page, everything is done. However, you will probably find that you get an error similar to the one shown in Figure 5.2. Most cable and DSL ISPs monitor the number of active Internet connections from each of their customers using each connecting computer's MAC address (which you were required to provide when setting up your Internet connection). The BEFSR41 has its own MAC address and because your ISP does not recognize it, it is being blocked. To get around this you can change the BEFSR41's MAC address to match the one that you registered with your ISP. Continue to step 8 to change the BEFSR41's MAC address.

8. You can configure the BEFSR41 using your Web browser by typing **192.168.1.1** in your browser's URL field and pressing Enter. The Enter Network password dialog box appears, as shown in Figure 5.3.

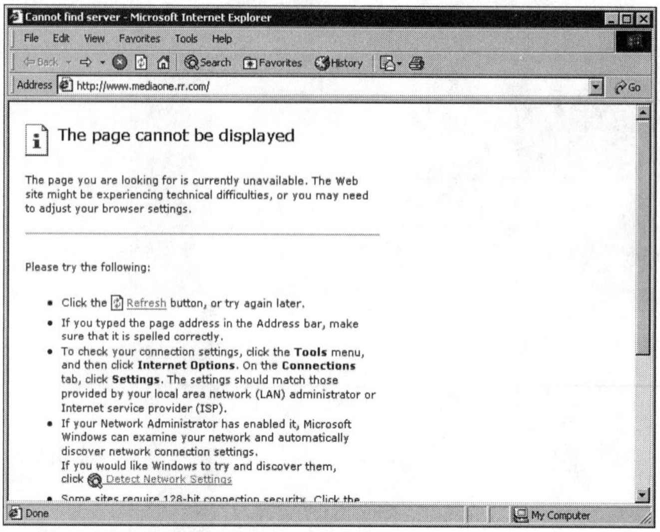

FIGURE 5.2

The cable or DSL ISP has blocked the DEFSR41's connection based on its MAC address.

FIGURE 5.3

The BEFSR41's configuration is protected with a password.

9. The BEFSR41's configuration is automatically secured using a password. The initial default password is `admin`. Leaving the User Name field blank, type **admin** in the Password field, and click OK.

10. The Linksys SETUP page is displayed, as shown in Figure 5.4.

11. Click the Advanced tab at the top of the display and then select MAC Address Clone, as shown in Figure 5.5.

12. Type in the MAC address of your computer's Ethernet card. This is the same MAC address that you registered with your ISP. Click Apply.

Note

If you do not remember your computer's Ethernet MAC address, open a command prompt on your computer and type **winipcfg** on your Windows 95 or 98 computer or **ipconfig /all** on your Windows Me, NT 4, 2000, or XP computer and press Enter.

13. The BEFSR41's MAC address is changed and the message shown in Figure 5.6 appears. Click Continue.

FIGURE 5.4

The main Linksys SETUP page allows you to view and change network configuration settings.

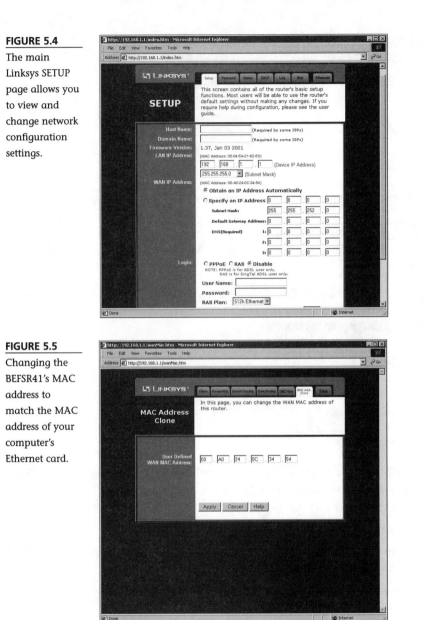

FIGURE 5.5

Changing the BEFSR41's MAC address to match the MAC address of your computer's Ethernet card.

14. Reset your cable or DSL modem by powering it off and on.

15. Restart your computer.

Your computer should now be ready to connect to the Internet.

FIGURE 5.6

You have successfully changed the BEFSR41's MAC address.

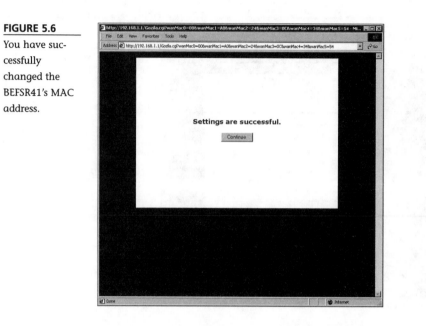

Configuration via the Web Browser

As you saw in the previous section, cable/DSL routers are configured by typing their default IP address into your Web browser and pressing Enter. In the case of the BEFSR41, this address is 192.168.1.1.

Establishing Basic Configuration Settings

By default the cable/DSL routers are configured to accept a dynamically assigned IP address from your ISP. Most ISPs assign IP addresses dynamically; however, if your ISP assigned you a static or non-changing IP address, you have to fill out the information in the Linksys SETUP page, as shown in Figure 5.7.

The Host Name and Domain Name fields allow you to type host and domain names if provided by your ISP. Usually, however, these fields are left blank. The Firmware Version field displays the version level of the router's firmware. The LAN IP Address sections display the router's MAC address, the IP address, and the subnet mask assigned to the router. These settings should be left as is.

Note

Hardware devices can have security problems. It's a good idea to occasionally check the vendor's Web site for your hardware firewall and make sure that you have the current version of their firmware installed. More information on upgrading firmware is provided later in this chapter.

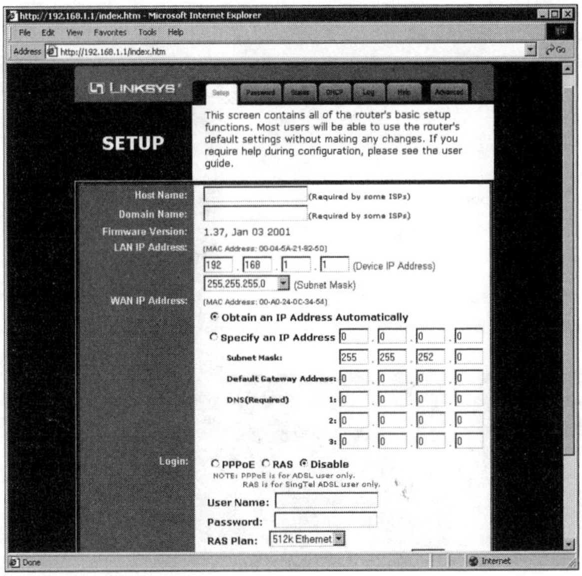

FIGURE 5.7

Configuring a static IP configuration.

The WAN IP Address section is set by default to Obtain an IP Address Automatically. To specify a static configuration assigned to you by your ISP, select the Specify an IP Address option and fill in the remaining fields with the information that was provided to you by your ISP.

Some DSL connections use the Point-to-Point protocol over Ethernet or PPPoE to establish connections instead of DHCP. PPPoE is a secure protocol that requires a username and password to establish a connection. If your DSL ISP uses this protocol, select PPPoE and type in your assigned username and password. Some other DSL ISPs provide connections using Remote Access Service or RAS. If your ISP uses this option, select RAS and type your username and password and then select either 256K or 512K from the RAS plan drop-down list. Otherwise, leave the default option of disable selected.

You can select the Connection on Demand and Max Idle Time options to configure the router to automatically disconnect from the Internet when you are not using your connection. The Max Idle Time field enables you to specify the number of minutes of inactivity that must pass before this features kicks in. This option provides a complete firewall block of Internet activity initiated from the Internet. However, as soon as you start an Internet application, the Internet connection is automatically re-established.

PPPoE Internet connections can time out over time. The Keep Alive option is designed to prevent this by transmitting a few packets at predetermined intervals so that your ISP will think that you are still using your connection.

Changing Your Password

It is important that you change the cable/DSL router password to prevent others from altering your configuration settings. Otherwise, anyone with access to your computer or home network can make changes by typing the router's IP address and typing admin as the password.

The Password page shown in Figure 5.8 allows you to change the router's password. Simply type a new password in both Router Password fields and click Apply.

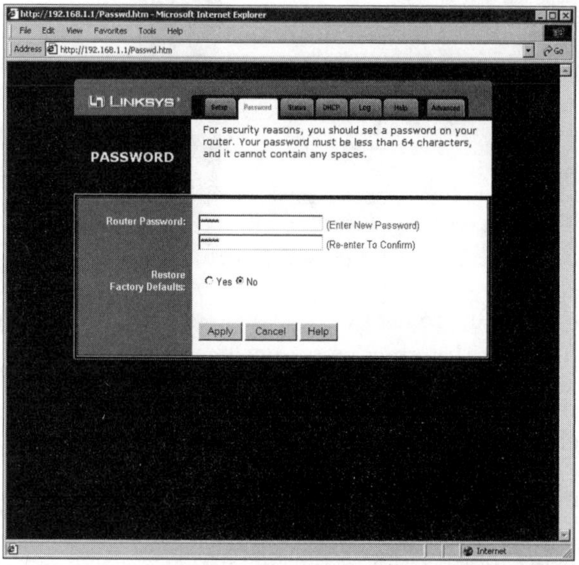

FIGURE 5.8

Changing the password prevents unauthorized configuration changes to your hardware firewall.

 Caution

The Restore Factory Default option will undo any changes that you have made to the BEFSR41 EtherFast cable/DSL router. You then have to start over to reconfigure the router. Use this option if you are having problems with the device and are unable to troubleshoot the nature of the problem. This will undo any custom configuration changes and allow you to start over.

Checking the Status of Your Router

The Status page, shown in Figure 5.9, displays the router's current configuring settings and reflects the choices that you made on the Setup page. Host Name shows your assigned hostname (if applicable). Firmware Version shows the current version of the router's software. Login displays the current login status (PPPoE, RAS, or Disable).

FIGURE 5.9

Viewing the
router's current
configuration
settings.

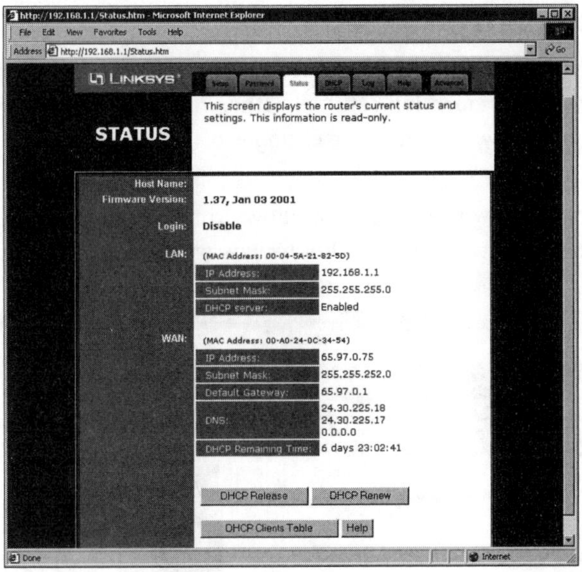

The LAN section shows the router's local IP address settings, whereas the WAN section shows the IP address information assigned by your ISP.

At the bottom of the page are the following three options:

- DHCP Release—Tells the router to notify your ISP that you want to release your current IP address.

- DHCP Renew—Requests a new IP address assignment from your ISP.

- DHCP Clients Table—Displays a listing of all clients on a local home network; including their names, IP addresses, and MAC addresses. This option is discussed more in Chapter 11.

Configuring Your DHCP Service

The DHCP page, shown in Figure 5.10, controls the router's DHCP service, which by default is enabled.

The DHCP Server option allows your router to assign all IP addresses to any computers on a home network. By default, this option is enabled. Even if you have just one computer, it's best to leave this default option enabled. The Starting IP field allows you to specify the starting IP address range that you want to use. The maximum possible range is from 192.168.1.2—192.168.1.253. This means the router can theoretically support a home network that consists of more than 250 computers. The default setting is 192.168.1.100. If you have a single computer attached to the

router, its default IP address is 192.168.1.100. More information on how IP addresses are assigned on home networks is available in Chapter 3, "Firewalls Explained," and Chapter 11. The button at the bottom of the page provides a link to the DHCP clients table.

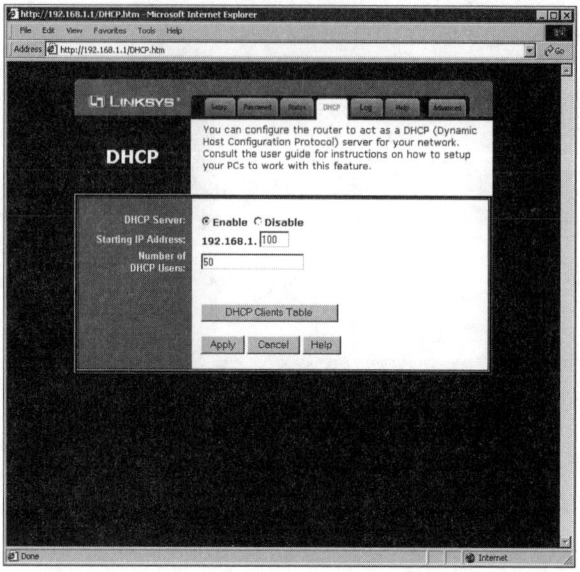

FIGURE 5.10
Configuring the router's built-in DHCP service.

Setting Your Router/Firewall Logs

The Log page, shown in Figure 5.11, lets you establish logs for storing both inbound and outbound Internet activity. Recorded information includes the following:

- The IP address and ports associated with all inbound traffic
- The URLs and ports used by your computer or other computers on a home network when connecting to the Internet, as well as the IP address of the local computer that made the connection

By default, the Access Log option is disabled. If you enable it, you will need to also specify the IP address of a local computer where the log files will be created. You can view all inbound traffic by clicking Incoming Access Log. Likewise, you can view outbound traffic by clicking Outgoing Access Log.

Figure 5.12 shows an example of the Incoming Log table. As you can see, it lists the IP address of the Internet computer trying to make a connection and the port number where the connection was attempted. In this example, the activity looks suspicious because it appears that a computer is attempting to methodically probe the computer's ports. This was in fact the case, however, the probe, shown in this exam-

ple, was initiated on purpose using a free Internet port scanning service offered at grc.com. More information on port scans is available in Chapter 9, "How Secure Is Your Computer?"

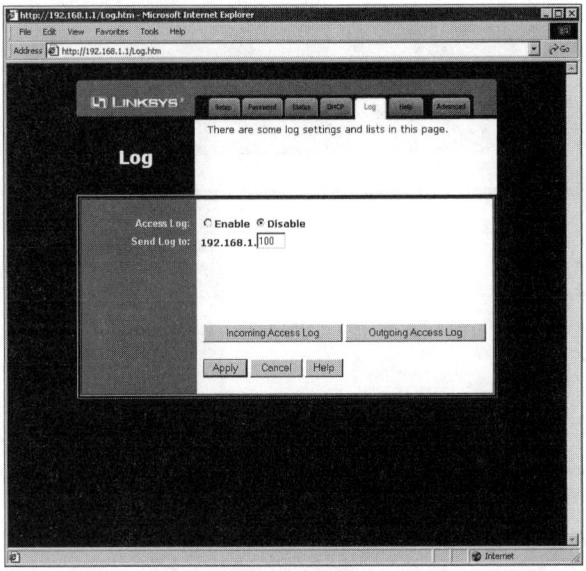

FIGURE 5.11

Setting up logs to record inbound and outbound traffic as it passes through the firewall.

FIGURE 5.12

Viewing a report on inbound Internet traffic.

Figure 5.13 shows an example of the Outgoing Log table. As you can see, it lists the IP address of the local computer that made the Internet connection as well as the

Universal Resource Locator (URL) or the remote computer. Examples or URLs include www.microsoft.com and www.quepublishing.com. If the URL is not available, the IP address of the remote computer or Web site that was contacted is displayed. In the case of the example records listed here, all were HTTP requests to various Web servers. If the computers were part of a home network, you should also see the IP address and Web sites that other computers had accessed.

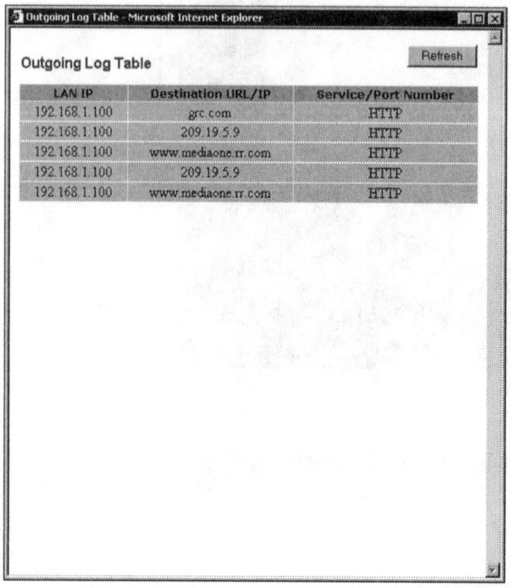

FIGURE 5.13

Viewing a listing of all the outbound Internet connections made by local computers.

Finding Help
=============

Help is available on most of the router's configuration pages. In addition, you can click the Help page, shown in Figure 5.14, to find links to additional resources. In the left column are links to pages with documentation on each of the router's configuration pages. On the right are links to additional resources located on the Internet, including a link to the Linksys Web site and a link to an online copy of the router's user manual.

Linksys provides updates for its router's firmware on its Web sites. Upgrades are free but you are discouraged from upgrading unless you are experiencing a specific problem that is addressed by the upgrade. You can apply an update after downloading it by clicking the Upgrade Firmware link on the Help page. This displays the Upgrade Firmware page shown in Figure 5.15.

Type the router's password in the Password field, specify the location of the update file in the File Path field, click Upgrade, and then follow the instructions presented to complete the firmware update.

FIGURE 5.14

Getting additional help.

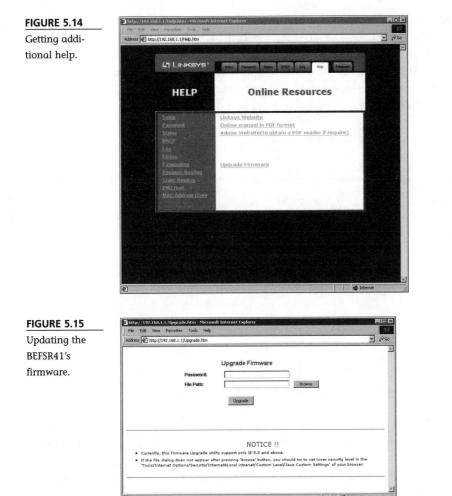

FIGURE 5.15

Updating the BEFSR41's firmware.

Other Cable/DSL Router Functions

If you click the Advanced tab after first opening the BEFSR41 configuration page, you'll see a new set of configuration pages, as shown in Figure 5.16. Most of these pages are used to configure advanced networking features, which are beyond the scope of this book. The exception to this is the MAC Address Clone page, which was discussed earlier in this chapter, and the Filters page, which is displayed in Figure 5.16.

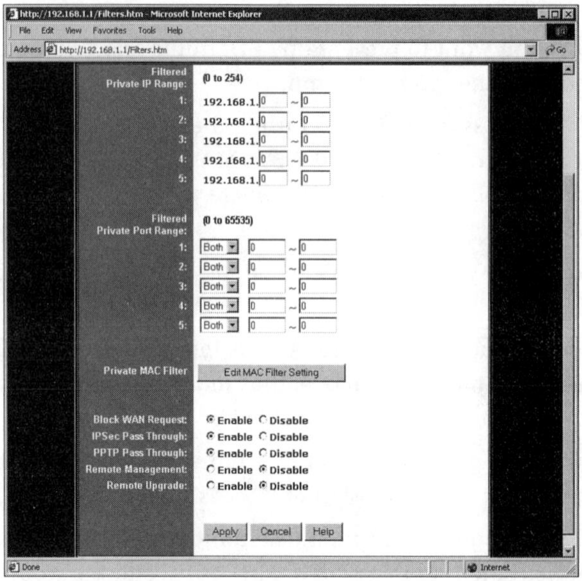

FIGURE 5.16

The Filters page enables you to configure a number of firewall options.

The Filtered Private IP Range section enables you to specify up to five ranges of IP addresses that are to be blocked from access to the Internet. Obviously, this option only applies when you have a home network and are allowing more than one computer to share your high-speed Internet connection. To block a single address, type the last part of its assigned IP address in both columns. To block a range of IP addresses, type the last part of the starting IP address range in the first column and the last part of the ending IP address range in the second column. For example, using this blocking feature, you can prevent specific computers from accessing the Internet. This way, if you have a home network but want to prevent the kid's computers from accessing the Internet, you can do so. The children will have to use mom's and dad's supervised computer for surfing the Internet.

Note   In order to block a computer's IP address, you must assign it a static IP address.

You can also block specific ports from being open by specifying up to five ranges of ports in the Filtered Private Port Range section. When specifying a port, indicate whether you want to block any of the following:

- **TCP**—Blocks the specified TCP port range
- **UDP**—Blocks the specific UDP port range
- **Both**—Blocks both TCP and UDP ports in the specified range

For example, FTP clients use ports 20 and 21 when communicating with FPT servers on the Internet. If you want to prevent any FTP traffic select Both and type **20** in the first column and **21** in the second column.

You can even filter access to the Internet using the MAC address on your network computer's Ethernet cards by clicking the Edit MAC Filter Setting option. This opens the MAC Access Control Table dialog box, where you can specify up to 50 individual MAC addresses.

In addition to the three previous filtering options, you can also enable or disable any of the following:

- Block WAN Request—This option blocks Internet pings of your computer and puts your ports into stealth mode, thus making them invisible form the Internet. This firewall option is enabled by default.

- IPSec Pass Through—This option determines whether IPSec traffic is permitted through the router. A discussion of IPSec is beyond the scope of this book.

- PPTP Pass Through—This option determines whether PPTP traffic is permitted through the router. A discussion of PPTP is beyond the scope of this book.

- Remote Management—This option determines whether you want to allow your router to be configured from the Internet. It is disabled by default.

- Remote Upgrade—This option determines whether you want to allow your router to be upgraded over the Internet. By default this option is disabled.

Using the Linksys BEFSR41 EtherFast Cable/DSL Router As a Personal Firewall

As you have seen throughout this chapter, only a subset of the features provided by cable/DSL routers can be categorized as relating to personal firewalls. Using the BEFSR41 as an example, Table 5.1 lists the personal firewall features provided by cable\DSL routers.

Table 5.1 Locating Hardware Personal Firewall Features

Personal Firewall Feature	Location
Basic setup	Setup page
Password security	Password page
Log management	Log page
IP filtering	Advanced Settings: Filters page
Port filtering	Advanced Settings: Filters page

Table 5.1   (continued)

Personal Firewall Feature	Location
MAC filtering	Advanced Settings: Filters page
Blocking WAN connection requests	Advanced Settings: Filters page
Cloning your computer MAC address	Advanced Settings: MAC Addr. Clone page

For maximum protection, you might want to consider running both a personal software firewall and a personal hardware firewall. Both firewalls will operate independently of one another and together provide the maximum possible protection. Chapters 6–8 provide you with everything that you need to know to choose and implement a software personal firewall.

Other Cable/DSL Routers

There are a number of competing products on the market that provide services similar to those provided by the Linksys BEDSR41 cable/DSL router. These devices are usually described as cable/DSL routers or gateways and typically support one or more connection ports. Table 5.2 provides a list of some of these competing products.

Table 5.2   Products That Act As Hardware Firewalls

Manufacturer	Model Number	Web Site	Description
Linksys	BEFSR11	www.linksys.com	1-port cable/DSL router
Netgear	RT311	www.netgear.com	1-port cable/DSL router
Netgear	FR314	www.netgear.com	4-port cable/DSL router
D-Link	DI-704	www.dlink.com	4-port cable/DSL router

If you already have a home network with an Ethernet hub, you can combine it with a single port cable/DSL router to allow all your network computers to share your high-speed Internet connection.

MCAFEE PERSONAL FIREWALL

*T*his is the first of three chapters dedicated to the coverage of software-based personal firewall products. This chapter focuses on the McAfee Personal Firewall from Network Associates. Coverage includes instructions on how to install and configure the personal firewall. You also learn about what McAfee does behind the scenes to protect your computer.

In addition to reviewing its major features, this chapter also points out some of the features lacking in this personal firewall. Of course, no discussion is complete without a review of the firewall logging and reporting capabilities.

- Learn how to install the McAfee Personal Firewall
- Learn how to use the configuration wizard to establish security policies
- Find out how to manually adjust configuration settings
- Learn how to manage Internet applications
- Learn how to read report logs

Overview of McAfee

The McAfee Personal Firewall is provided by Network Associates, which is located at www.nai.com. This personal firewall started as the ConSeal Private Desktop from Singal9 Solution, but was purchased by McAfee and renamed McAfee Personal Firewall in January 2000.

The McAfee Personal Firewall is a product targeted at the home user. It is designed to filter and block Internet traffic to and from your computer based on security policies that you set. This firewall has been designed for the non-technical user. Thanks to its configuration wizard, which starts right after you install the firewall, you only have to answer a few simple questions and the wizard will build all your security policies for you. Of course, if you prefer to dig deeper, you can view and manually change configuration policies to fine-tune your personal firewall to meet your own requirements.

> **Note**
>
> The McAfee Personal Firewall is one of two firewall products provided by McAfee. The other is the McAfee.com Personal Firewall. Although they share many of the same features, there is one significant difference. The McAfee.com Personal Firewall is delivered as a Web service over the Internet, whereas the McAfee Personal Firewall installs and runs like a typical Windows application.

This personal firewall manages your network traffic in two ways. First, it monitors all network traffic and blocks or allows it based on policies governing the use of network protocols. These policies represent the more technical side of the McAfee Personal Firewall. Fortunately, a strong set of policies comes pre-configured so you might not need to make any changes to these settings.

The second way that the personal firewall protects your computer is by allowing or blocking network traffic based on a list of trusted and blocked applications. Any application in the list that is trusted is permitted to communicate through the personal firewall. Any application on the list that is marked as blocked is not permitted through the firewall. Any time an application tries to communicate over the Internet

that is not in the McAfee Personal Firewall's list, the application is temporarily blocked and a pop-up dialog box appears asking whether you want to let the application communicate.

The McAfee Personal Firewall provides a number of advanced features that include:

- Blocking non-trusted applications
- Detecting Trojan horse programs
- Logging all monitored activity
- Reporting on all Internet sites that have been visited
- Preventing access to shared files and printers
- Identifying all active user connections

System Requirements

As of the writing of this book, McAfee Personal Firewall version 2.15 was available. Its official hardware requirements are listed here:

- 32MB of memory
- 6MB of hard disk space
- 486 or higher processor
- CD-ROM drive

Additionally, you need a dial-up, cable, or DSL connection to the Internet and one of the following operating systems:

- Windows 95 (running WinSock 2)
- Windows 98
- Windows Me
- Windows NT 4
- Windows 2000
- Windows XP

Note

WinSock or *Windows Sockets* is a component of Windows TCP/IP that supports communications between Internet applications. The McAfee Personal Firewall works with WinSock through an application-programming Interface based on Microsoft's second WinSock version, WinSock 2. Windows 95 comes with WinSock 1. To use the McAfee Personal Firewall on a computer running Windows 95, you need to download and install WinSock 2, which as of the writing of this book was available for free at
`www.microsoft.com/windows95/downloads`.

Installation and Setup

The installation of the McAfee Personal Firewall is a straightforward process. Before you begin, close any active programs, including those that are communicating with the Internet. Insert the McAfee CD in your CD-ROM drive and the CD's auto-run program should start. The following procedure outlines the steps required to complete the installation process.

1. The McAfee CD will automatically load. Select Install Firewall.

2. The McAfee Firewall Setup Wizard appears. Click Next to begin the installation process.

3. The McAfee license agreement appears. Read the agreement, shown in Figure 6.1, select "I accept the terms of the license agreement," and click Next.

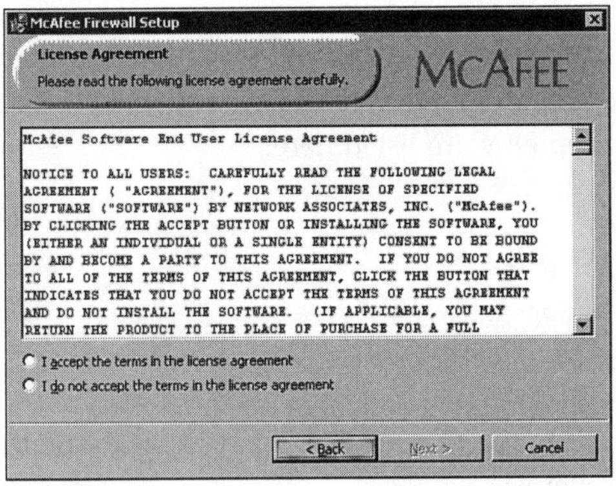

FIGURE 6.1

You must accept the terms of the McAfee license agreement in order to proceed with the installation of your personal firewall.

4. The Setup Type dialog box appears, as shown in Figure 6.2, asking you to choose between the following two options:

   ■ **Complete**—Installs all personal firewall components.

   ■ **Custom**—Allows you to select which components to install.

Select Complete and click Next.

5. The Post Installation Options dialog box appears, as shown in Figure 6.3, asking whether you want to view McAfee's README.TXT file at the end of the setup process. The Open README.TXT file option is selected by default. Leave this option enabled and click Next.

6. The installation process continues. A graphical status bar displays the progress of the personal firewall installation. A pop-up dialog box appears, shown in Figure 6.4, asking whether you want to start your personal firewall automatically when Windows starts. Click Yes.

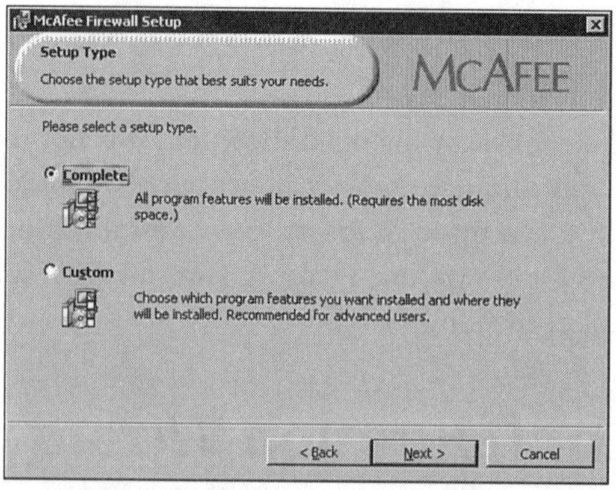

FIGURE 6.2

You can select between a complete install and a customized install.

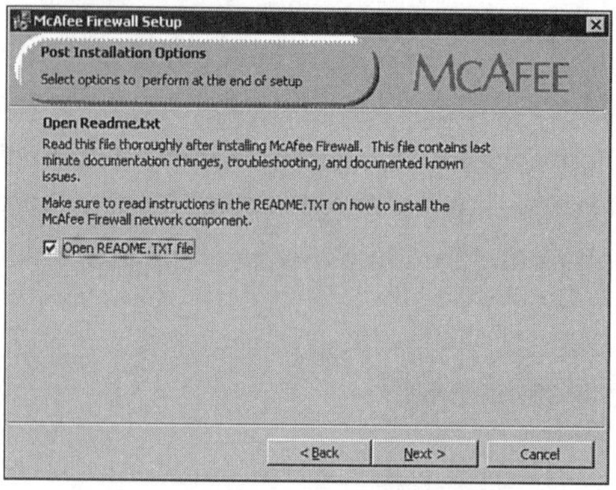

FIGURE 6.3

Although reading the README.TXT file is optional, it is strongly recommended.

FIGURE 6.4

Configuring the McAfee Personal Firewall to start automatically allows it to start before other applications, thus securing any communication attempts that these applications try to initiate.

7. Next, the Windows Notepad application starts and the text of the README.TXT file is loaded. Read the file and close Notepad when you are done.

8. The installation process completes and a dialog box appears asking you to click Finish.

Your McAfee Personal Firewall is now installed. However, it is not ready to be used. The McAfee Firewall Configuration dialog box now appears. This is the first of several dialog boxes that guide you through the process of establishing security policies that govern the operation of your McAfee Personal Firewall. This configuration process is covered in the next section.

Working with the Configuration Wizard

The McAfee Personal Firewall is designed so that you do not have to know much about networking in order to configure your network security policies. It accomplishes this task by presenting you with a series of questions to determine what you want it to do and then builds security policies based on your answers.

You are prompted to configure the McAfee Personal Firewall immediately after its installation. The following procedure outlines the steps involved in this process.

1. The McAfee Firewall Configuration dialog box appears, as shown in Figure 6.5.

FIGURE 6.5

Three levels of network control govern how the personal firewall handles filtered traffic.

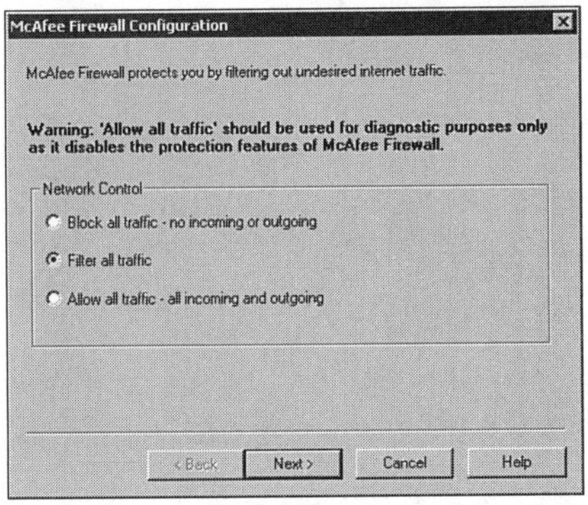

You are asked to select from one of three Network Control settings that tell the firewall what do to with the Internet traffic that it is filtering. These options are as follows:

- Block all traffic—no incoming or outgoing—Blocks any network traffic from passing through the firewall, which in effect prevents any Internet communication.

- Filter all traffic—Tells the McAfee Personal Firewall to filter traffic based on its security policies.

■ Allow all traffic—all incoming and outgoing—Allows all network traffic through the firewall—in effect lowering your defenses.

Filter all traffic is selected by default and is the only option that provides secure and usable Internet communication. Leave this option selected and click Next.

2. Next you are prompted to choose between two options that control the format of your McAfee Personal Firewall's logging activity, as shown in Figure 6.6.

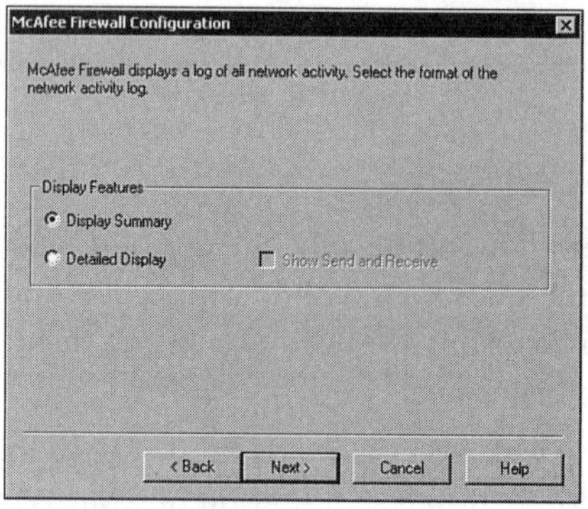

FIGURE 6.6

Determining how the McAfee Personal Firewall logs network activity.

McAfee Firewall Configuration

McAfee Firewall displays a log of all network activity. Select the format of the network activity log.

Display Features

⊙ Display Summary

○ Detailed Display   ☐ Show Send and Receive

< Back   Next >   Cancel   Help

The options are as follows:

■ Display Summary—Provides a moderate level of information designed to be read by home users.

■ Detailed Display—Provides detailed logging of network information with a level of complexity aimed at advanced users and network administrators.

By default, Display Summary is selected. If you select Detailed Display, you will also be given the option of selecting the Show Send and Receive option, which records the number of bytes sent and received. Leave the default option selected and click Next.

The Shown Send and Receive option requires additional overhead for every network packet that passes through the personal firewall and can somewhat degrade the performance of your computer. If you do not need this feature, disabling it might give your computer a small performance boost.

3. Next, you are prompted to select how the firewall starts, as shown in Figure 6.7.

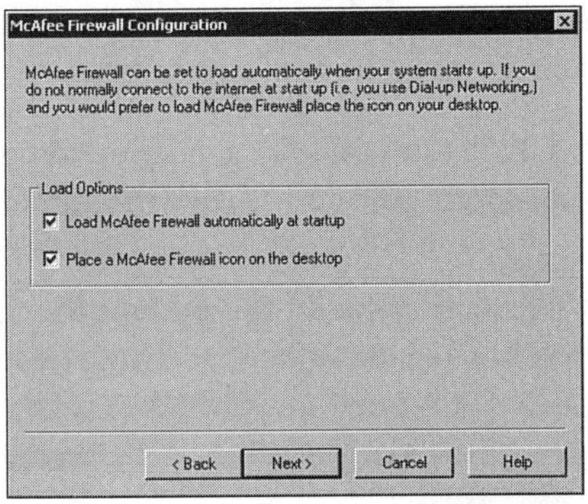

FIGURE 6.7

You can configure the McAfee Personal Firewall to load at system startup or allow for its manual execution by also placing an icon on the Windows desktop.

The available options are as follows:

- Load McAfee Firewall automatically at startup—Clear this option if you connect to the Internet using a dial-up connection and do not want your computer to incur the overhead of running the personal firewall when you are not connected.

- Place a McAfee Firewall icon on the desktop—Leave this option selected to place an icon for your personal firewall on your Windows desktop.

By default both options are selected. Click Next.

4. Next, the dialog box shown in Figure 6.8 appears. From here you can specify any applications that you want to allow or disallow through the firewall.

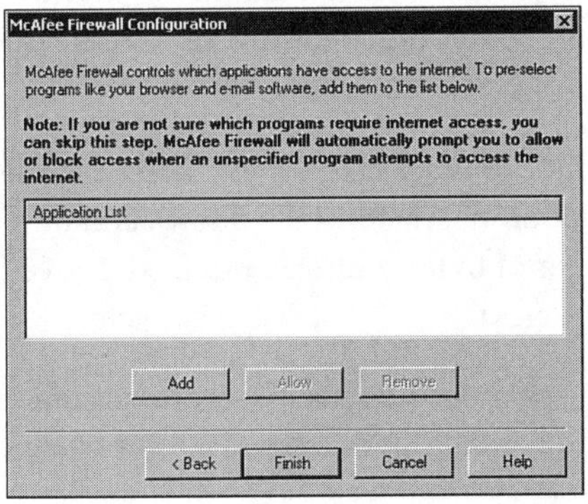

FIGURE 6.8

You can tell your personal firewall about any number of Internet applications and configure whether they are permitted to access the Internet.

5. Click Add. An Explorer-styled dialog box appears, as shown in Figure 6.9, which allows you to locate and select Internet applications.

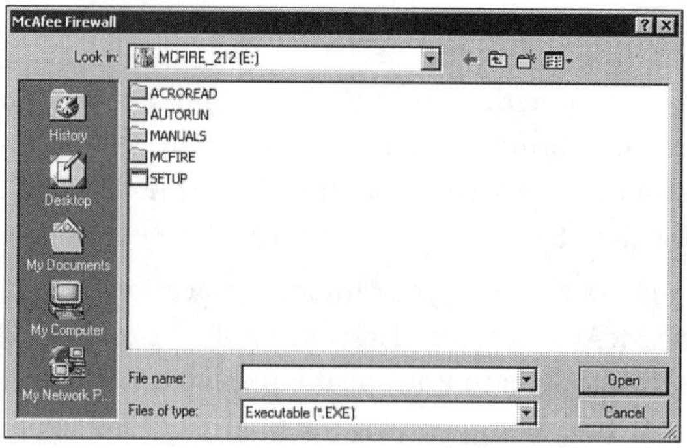

FIGURE 6.9

Specifying the name and location of Internet applications.

6. When you add an application to the list, a small screen icon initially appears beside it indicating that the application will be permitted to communicate through the firewall, as shown in Figure 6.10.

FIGURE 6.10

A small green icon identifies trusted applications.

7. To block the application from communicating through the firewall, select it and click Block. The icon to the left of the application changes to red, as shown in Figure 6.11.

FIGURE 6.11

A red icon identifies blocked applications.

When a blocked application is selected, the Block icon changes to the Allow icon. Continue adding applications to the list until you have added all the desired applications. Don't worry about missing any applications. The first time that an application not on this list attempts to communicate over the Internet, the firewall will catch it and prompt you as to whether the application should be permitted to communicate. The firewall then adds the application to the list based on your reply.

When you are done adding and configuring application access, click Finish. That's it; your firewall is now running and monitoring all your Internet traffic.

Normal Operation

After it's installed and configured, your McAfee Personal Firewall sits quietly in the Windows system tray monitoring all your network traffic and blocking or allowing communications based on your security settings. You can also find an entry for it on the Start menu by selecting Start, Programs, and McAfee Firewall.

Depending on how well you defined your initial application list, you might find that from time to time the McAfee Personal Firewall displays a pop-up dialog box, as shown in Figure 6.12, indicating that it has intercepted an application attempting to connect to the Internet. This dialog box asks you whether the application should be permitted to do so.

FIGURE 6.12

The McAfee Personal Firewall has intercepted an unidentified application attempting to connect to the Internet.

If you want to allow the application to communicate then click Yes. Click No to block the application. An entry is then added to the applications list. In the case of the example shown in Figure 6.12, the application trying to communicate is Microsoft NetMeeting.

Beyond these occasional pop-up dialog boxes you do not see or hear anything else from your personal firewall. However, you might want to work with it from time to time to adjust its security settings and view its activity logs. In addition to double-clicking its desktop icon or selecting it from the Start menu, you can work with your personal firewall using either of the following two options.

- Double-clicking the McAfee icon in the system tray—Opens the main McAfee Firewall dialog box where you can configure and work with the firewall's features.
- Right-clicking the McAfee icon in the system tray—Provides single-click access to a subset of the most commonly used firewall features.

Double-clicking the McAfee icon in the Windows System Tray opens the McAfee Firewall dialog box, shown in Figure 6.13.

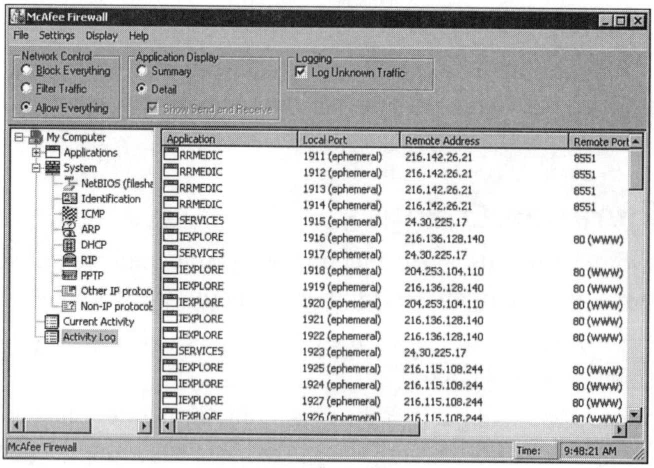

FIGURE 6.13

From the McAfee Firewall dialog box you can configure all firewall options and view recent log information.

The top portion of the dialog box displays the McAfee Firewall menus and provides access to Network, Application, and Logging configuration settings. The rest of the display provides access to a tree-like view of the firewall's configuration. The left side of the display shows the firewall's application and network settings and its activity logs. You can select any entry in the left pane to view detailed information about it in the right pane. For example, selecting the Activity Log displays the last 100 recorded application events in the right pane.

You can also work with the firewall by right-clicking the McAfee icon in the system tray and selecting from any of the options that appear in its context menu, as shown in Figure 6.14.

FIGURE 6.14

The McAfee Personal Firewall provides a number of options and views for you to work with.

The following section discusses the options found on the McAfee Firewall dialog box and its desktop context menu.

Saving Configuration Changes

The Save Settings option on the File menu allows you to save any configuration changes that you have made to the personal firewall immediately. By default, changes are saved only when the firewall is closed.

Securing Configuration Changes

The Password option on the File menu allows you to apply a password to your personal firewall configuration. Four submenu options are available:

- Enter—Allows you to enter the personal firewall's password and work with its configuration and logs file.

- Purge—Used to log out of the personal firewall after making configuration changes. If you do not use this option, you will remain logged in to the personal firewall for the remainder of your session.

- Set—Allows you to change the password assigned to the McAfee Personal Firewall.

- Required—Allows you to implement password protection of your firewalls settings.

When you elect to require a password to protect your personal firewall's configuration settings, the Set Password dialog box appears, as shown in Figure 6.15. Type a password in the Password and Confirm fields and click OK.

Apply the same rules for creating a strong personal firewall password as you follow when creating your personal passwords. For example, make them greater than eight characters long and include a combination of numbers, special characters, and upper- and lowercase letters without using any common words.

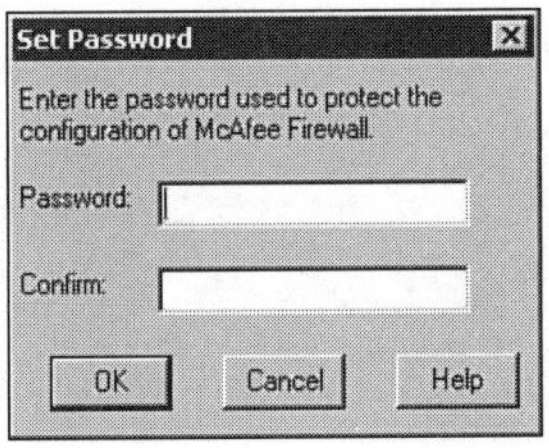

FIGURE 6.15

Protecting firewall configuration with a password.

Set Password

Enter the password used to protect the configuration of McAfee Firewall.

Password:

Confirm:

OK   Cancel   Help

After it's applied, the password prevents modification of personal firewall settings unless the correct password is supplied. McAfee's configuration file is called CPD.SFR and it is located in the same folder as the McAfee Personal Firewall source files, which by default is inside the Program Files folder.

If you are running Windows NT 4, 2000, or XP you should consider changing the per-missions on the McAfee folder so that only trusted individuals have access to it and to its configuration file. Because Windows 95, 98, and Me cannot secure their files and folders with NTFS security permissions, these users will simply have to be diligent and check their configuration file on a regular basis to ensure that it has not been modified.

Managing the McAfee Personal Firewall's Log File

The Log File option on the File menu allows you to specify the location where the personal firewall will record log information and specify the maximum log file size. It displays the McAfee Firewall—Log File dialog box shown in Figure 6.16.

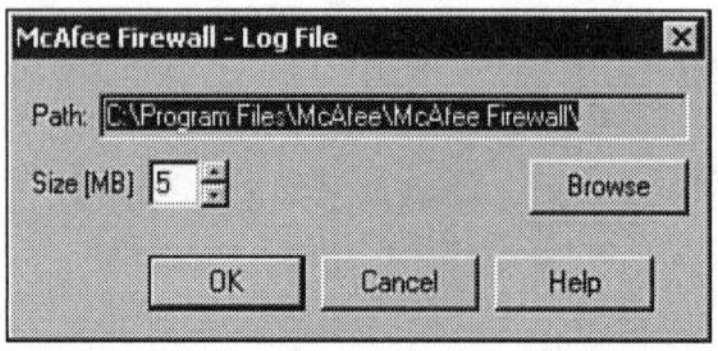

FIGURE 6.16

Configuring the location and size of the personal firewall's log file.

McAfee Firewall - Log File

Path: C:\Program Files\McAfee\McAfee Firewall\

Size (MB) 5

Browse

OK   Cancel   Help

By default, the log file is located in the same folder in which the McAfee source files have been installed and is limited to 5MB. You can change either of these options from this dialog box.

Starting the Firewall at System Boot

The Start automatically when Windows Starts option on the File menu lets you tog-gle the automatic startup of this application on and off. When enabled, a small checkmark appears to the left of the menu entry.

Closing the McAfee Personal Firewall

You use the Exit option on the File menu to close the McAfee Personal Firewall. Closing your personal firewall while still connected to the Internet is not advisable because it leaves your computer open to attack. Click Yes to close your firewall or No to leave it operational.

Configuring Application Settings

The Applications option on the Settings menu opens a dialog box that displays the McAfee Firewall Applications property sheet, as shown in Figure 6.17.

You use this dialog box to add and remove applications from the personal firewall's list of known Internet applications. To add a new application to the list, click Add,

locate the application, and click Open. By default, the application is trusted, as shown by the green icon to the left of its entry. You can mark it as non-trusted by selecting it and clicking Block. If you accidentally add the wrong application or want to remove an application from the list, select it and click Remove.

At the top of the property sheet is an option labeled Trust all applications. When selected, this option overrides all applications configuration information and permits all applications to communicate with the Internet. Under ordinary conditions this option should never be selected. However, if you are having trouble getting an application to work correctly, you might want to try this option. You then run your application again to see whether the personal firewall was somehow preventing its execution. When done running the test, be sure to unckeck the Trust All Applications option to restore your firewall's defenses.

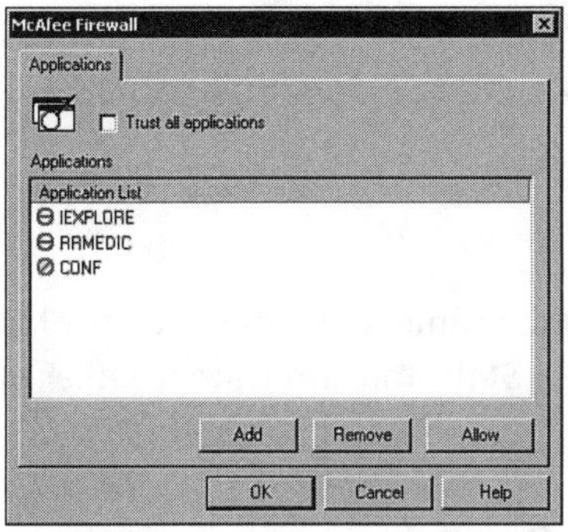

FIGURE 6.17

Modifying the list of known Internet applications.

System Settings

The System option on the Settings menu opens the System Settings dialog box, shown in Figure 6.18, which displays a list of network devices on your computer and allows you to select and configure how the McAfee Personal Firewall treats each one.

Each network connection is treated separately. This way, if you have an Internet connection and a home network, you can apply different security settings to each. For example, if you have a dial-up connection to the Internet and a local area network connection, you will see two entries in the Network Devices section and each device will have its own separate configuration. This allows you to apply tighter security settings to your Internet connection than to a home network connection. Check out Chapter 11 "Home Networks and Internet Connection Sharing" for more information on home networks.

To restore the network settings of your Internet connection back to their original settings, select the connection and click Restore Defaults. To change an existing setting, select it and then click Properties. Doing this will display its Properties dialog box.

FIGURE 6.18

Viewing system network devices.

Network settings apply to TCP/IP protocols and not to individual applications. The McAfee Personal Firewall can filter a number of TCP/IP settings, each of which is located on one of the property sheets on this dialog box, as outlined in the following sections. You can also configure each setting to report all allowed and all blocked traffic on a setting-by-setting basis.

NetBIOS Over TCP

The NetBIOS over TCP property sheet, shown in Figure 6.19, allows you to block NetBIOS ports 137–139, which are used to connect to other computer's shared resources and to shared resources on your own computer. By leaving the Allow other systems to reach my shares option cleared, you can block any attempts from the Internet over these NetBIOS ports. The Allow me to reach other systems' shares option is used to allow you to connect to other computers shared resources.

If you are configuring a local area network connection, you might want to enable these options so you can share your disk drives and printers with other local area network users and access their shared resources as well.

If you are configuring your Internet connection, you should leave these options cleared to prevent outsiders from getting at your disk drives. However, if you are already sharing your disk drives over the Internet with other users or accessing other people's shares drives—and you wish to continue doing so—you will have to enable these options. But, do so with great care. You are opening a hole that a hacker may try to use to access your disk drives. If you still want to share drives over the Internet, be sure you pick strong passwords and disable your Internet connection when you won't be using it for long periods of time.

Identification

The Allow Identification option on the Identification property sheet, shown in Figure 6.20, is selected by default and permits applications to publish your identity. This is sometimes required by e-mail systems and applications that use Internet Replay Chat or IRC. To increase your privacy, you might want to disable this option and see whether any of your applications are affected. If they are, you can always re-enable it.

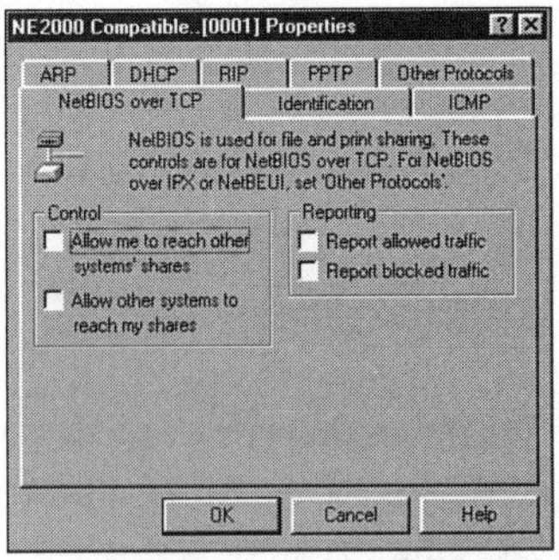

FIGURE 6.19

Configuring how
the personal
firewall deals
with NetBIOS
over TCP/IP
traffic.

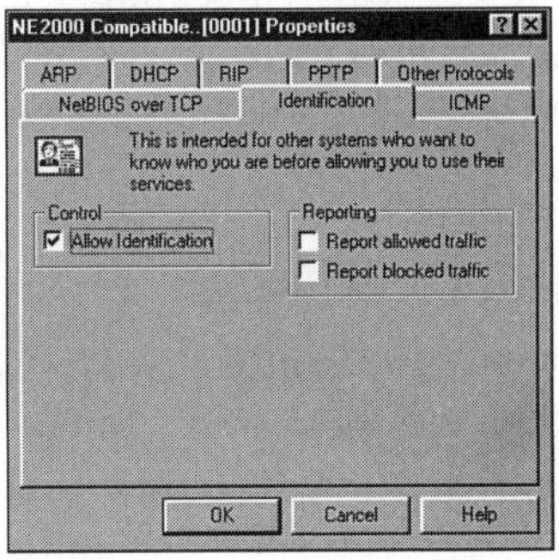

FIGURE 6.20

The Allow
Identification
setting is
required by
some Internet
e-mail systems.

Note IRC is an Internet service that allows two people on the Internet to communicate by typing text messages to one another.

ICMP

The Internet Control Message protocol (ICMP) property sheet, shown in Figure 6.21, is a maintenance protocol used by the TCP/IP PING command to test the capability to reach a remote computer. Unfortunately, it has been used by hackers to spoof a computer session and trick a computer into communicating with a computer that's impersonating another computer.

Your options are to allow, block, or limit ICMP packets. By limiting the number of ICMP packets, you might be able to leave the protocol enabled while limiting a hacker's capability to spoof you. By default the Block all ICMP option is selected.

ARP

The Address Resolution protocol (ARP) property sheet, shown in Figure 6.22, is used to help two computers using TCP/IP determine each other's MAC addresses. To date,

no one has reported a hacker using ARP to hack into a computer system. Because it is critical to the communication process it is enabled by default and should be left that way.

FIGURE 6.21

ICMP is a protocol that hackers can use to spoof or trick your computer into thinking that it is communicating with a different computer.

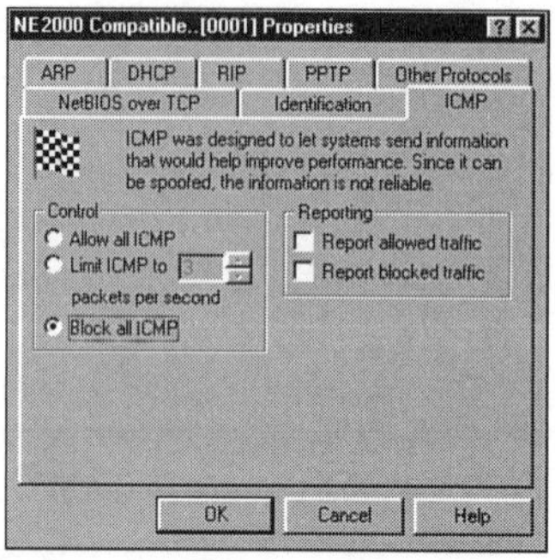

FIGURE 6.22

ARP is an Ethernet protocol that determines MAC addresses.

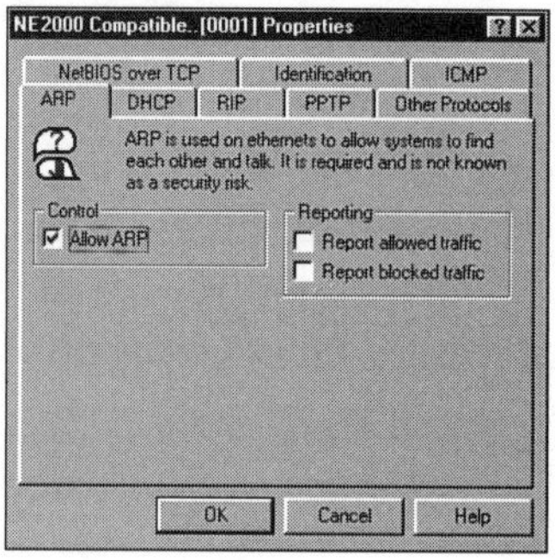

DHCP

The Dynamic Host Configuration protocol (DHCP) property sheet, shown in Figure 6.23, is used by ISPs to lease IP addresses to their customers so that they can connect to the Internet. You should enable this setting only for network devices that receive their IP addresses using DHCP. If your ISP uses DHCP to assign your computer its Internet IP address and you block it, your Internet connection will fail.

FIGURE 6.23

DHCP is a service used by most ISP to dynamically assign IP addresses to their customers.

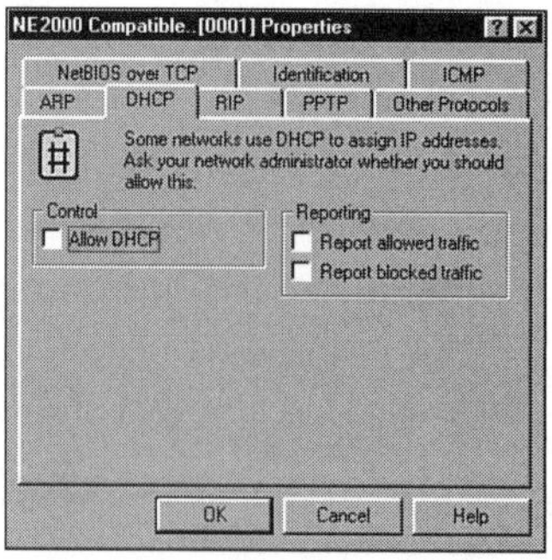

RIP

The RIP property sheet, shown in Figure 6.24, determines whether the RIP protocol, which is used by some network devices to route TCP/IP traffic across networks, is allowed to pass through the firewall. Unless your ISP requires the use of this protocol, you should leave it disabled.

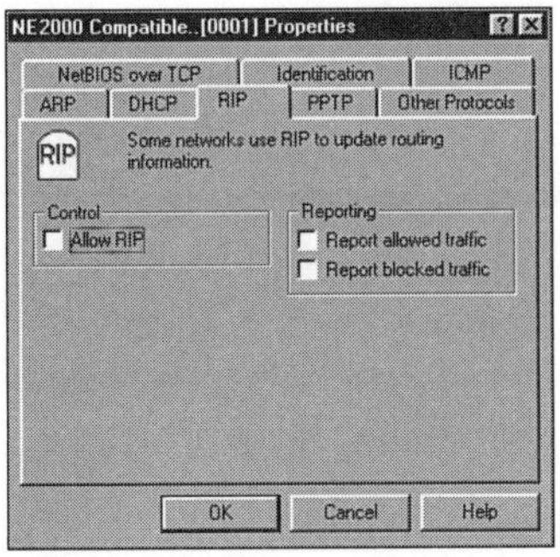

FIGURE 6.24

RIP is a router-level protocol used by some networks.

PPTP

The Point-to-Point Tunneling protocol (PPTP) property sheet, shown in Figure 6.25, establishes secure encrypted communications between two computers over the Internet. Unless you use the Internet to connect to a corporate network using PPTP, you should leave this setting disabled.

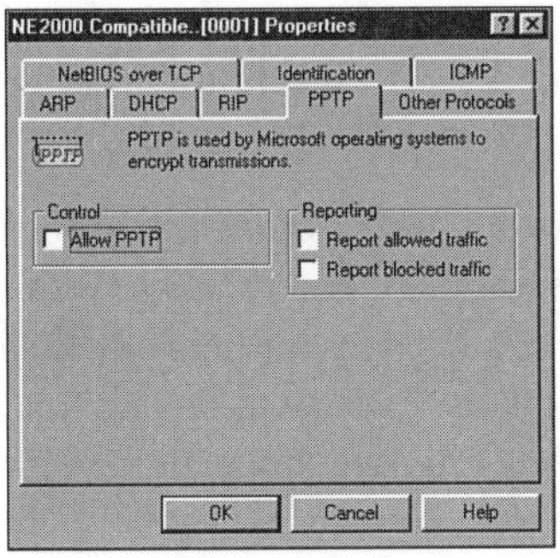

FIGURE 6.25

The point-to-point tunneling protocol establishes secure communications between two computers over the Internet.

Other Protocols

The McAfee Personal Firewall filters TCP/IP-based protocols and allows or blocks their communication based on your security policies. It can also block other non-TCP/IP protocols such as NetBEUI. These settings are configured from the Other Protocols property sheet, shown in Figure 6.26. The McAfee Personal Firewall cannot filter non-TCP/IP protocols and perform any detailed analysis of them. It simply

blocks all or allows all traffic for these protocols. To allow or block a given protocol, select it from the list of protocols and click one of the following options:

- Allow—Allows the selected protocol to pass through the firewall.
- Block Incoming Fragments—Blocks fragmented packets of the specified protocol.
- Log Allowed Traffic—Logs all Internet communications that are allowed to pass through the firewall.
- Log Blocked Traffic—Logs all attempted Internet communications that have been blocked by the firewall.
- Allow Protocols Other Than IP, ARP, and RARP—Allows other TCP/IP through the firewall.
- Log Non-IP Traffic—Logs all network traffic for non-IP protocols.

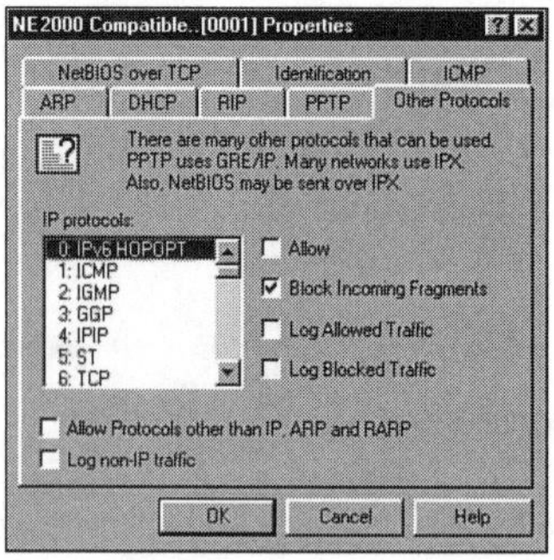

FIGURE 6.26

The McAfee Personal Firewall can also block other protocols in addition to TPC/IP.

Fragmented Packets

The Fragmented Packets option on the Settings menu option lets you toggle the blocking of incoming fragments on and off and determines whether they are logged. By default, incoming fragments are blocked and not logged.

Minimize to SysTray

The Minimize to SysTray option on the Display menu lets you toggle the setting on and off. When enabled, it tells the McAfee Personal Firewall to minimize in the system tray. When turned off, it tells the firewall to minimize to the Windows task bar.

Start in SysTray

The Start in SysTray option on the Display menu lets you toggle the setting on and off. When enabled, it tells the McAfee Personal Firewall to start minimizing in the

system tray. When turned off, the firewall displays the McAfee Firewall dialog box each time that it is started.

Help

The Help menu option opens the McAfee Personal Firewall's help system, as shown in Figure 6.27.

From here, all online documentation is organized into major categories. If you click the Index button, you'll see the standard Microsoft style help dialog boxes with Index and Find property sheets that allow you to search the help system based on keywords.

Block Everything

The Block Everything option in the network Control section allows you to block all inbound and outbound network traffic. It can be used when you know that you are going to be away from your computer for a lengthy period of time and need extra security.

Filter Traffic

The Filter Traffic option in the Network Control section allows you to turn your network and application policies back on so that you can surf the Internet while protecting your computer and its resources.

Allow Everything

The Allow Everything option in the Network Control section disables your firewall's network and application security policies and allows all network traffic to flow through your personal firewall. Unless you are trying to determine whether your firewall is inadvertently preventing the proper functioning of a application, you should never enable this option because it leaves you unprotected.

Reporting Summary Application Information

The Summary option in the Application Display section specifies that McAfee Personal Firewall should only record high-level summary information regarding application activity in its logs.

Reporting Detailed Application Information

The Detail option in the Application Display section specifies that detailed information should be recorded in the logs. This is particularly useful when you are attempting to track down suspicious activity.

Note   One option found on the McAfee Personal Firewall's context menu, but not on the McAfee Firewall dialog box, is the Record Application Traffic option. It's enabled by default and should be left this way. Without proper logging, you will not have a record of your personal firewall's activity and more importantly a record of activity of any applications running on your computer.

Working with Report Logs

The McAfee Personal Firewall can log three types of information depending on how it has been configured, as shown here:

- Application summary or detailed list
- Network traffic
- Unknown traffic

The McAfee Firewall dialog box provides a view of the activity log. The Current Activity view lists data for currently active applications and the Activity Log lists the last 100 application events. Neither of these logs provides access to network events. To view all logged McAfee Personal Firewall events, you need to examine the log file. By default, the log file is located in the same folder as the McAfee Personal Firewall source files (typically c:\Program Files\McAfee\McAfee Firewall). Log files have a

name of *yyyymm* where *yyyy* is the year and *mm* is the month of the information recorded in the log file.

By default, the log file is set to 5MB but you can change this size by right-clicking the McAfee Personal Firewall icon in the Windows system tray, selecting the Log File option, and specifying a new log size. If the log file fills up, application and unknown events will stop being logged. However, network events will continue to be recorded. It is therefore very important that you monitor the log file and ensure that its size is properly adjusted to accommodate the recording of all your events.

To give you an idea of the kind of information that you will see in the McAfee Personal Firewall log file and help you to understand its format, an excerpt of log file events along with a brief description is shown here.

The following message indicates that the McAfee Personal Firewall is starting:

```
Starting McAfee Firewall 2.1 on 2001/06/27 4:33:22 PM
```

This tells you when your firewall is started. You'll see this message recorded each time you restart your computer or when you have manually stopped and restarted you firewall. Next, you see a message indicating the location of the firewall's log:

```
C:\Program Files\McAfee\McAfee Firewall\\200106.log
```

Use the information in this entry if you want to find the log so you can make copies of it for later review. The following log entries identify the network devices that the firewall filters:

```
Devices:
Dial-Up Adapter [0000]
NE2000 Compatible..[0001]
```

The main thing to look for here is that all your network connections are identified. The following log entries indicate that the network devices are being activated. This time, each device is listed using a numeric number:

```
Attaching to devices:
0000
0001
```

The following entry identifies the location of your McAfee Personal Firewall security policies:

```
Ruleset file: C:\Program Files\McAfee\McAfee Firewall\CPD.SFR
```

A number of log file entries will then show the current status of a number of firewall settings. Review these log entries to be sure your firewall settings are correctly set. For example, the following entry shows that the Filter traffic network setting has been specified:

`Network Control: Filter`

The following entry shows that you will be prompted any time an application not in the firewall list of known applications tries to connect to the Internet. This will allow you to identify and block Trojan horse programs:

`Prompt before allowing applications communicate`

The next entry shows that you have selected to record summary information for application events:

`Summary display`

The next log entry shows that the Log Unknown Traffic setting has been enabled. This records network traffic for communications that you did not initiate:

`Log unknown traffic`

The following two statements show the current settings dealing with incoming packet fragments:

`Incoming fragments will be blocked.`
`Blocked incoming fragments will not be logged.`

The following log entries identify all Internet applications that have been defined to the personal firewall and their trusted or blocked status. Review this list to make sure you have correctly identified all the applications you want your firewall to allow or block:

`Allowed Applications:`
`IEXPLORE`
`Blocked Applications:`
`(none)`

You also see a number of log entries that identify your network settings. This information is written as a long table with columns for each network protocol. The information for each monitored network device is presented separately. Several pieces of information are reported about each device, including the status of each protocol (either `allowed` or `blocked`), and whether allowed or blocked packets are logged (choose `y` or `n`).

```
System Settings:
Device                          ARP     DHCP     Identification ICMP
RIP
    OtherIP  PPTP      NonIP    Shares          (Others)
Dial-Up Adapter [0000]                   allowed  allowed  allowed       blocked
allowed
    allowed  allowed  allowed  allowed          allowed
Log allowed packets             n       n        n             n
```

```
n            n
             n        n        n              n
Log blocked packets           n        n        n              n
n            n
             n        n        n              n
NE2000 Compatible..[0001]      allowed  blocked  allowed     blocked
blocked
    blocked  blocked  blocked  blocked       blocked
Log allowed packets           n        n        n              n
n            n
             n        n        n              n
Log blocked packets           n        n        n              n
n            n
             n        n        n              n
```

The next log entry displays the name of the computer:
MYCOMPUTER

The IP addresses assigned to each networking device are then listed. In this example, you see two IP addresses. One IP address is assigned by an ISP for an Internet connection and the other belongs to the computer's home network connection.
Assigned IP addresses are:
24.168.255.207
169.254.254.247

The following message indicates that the McAfee Personal Firewall has completed its initialization and is now filtering network traffic. This tells you when your firewall's security is in effect.
----------------- McAfee Firewall is running --------------------

Over time, you might make configuration changes to your firewall's settings. As you do, entries recording these changes are placed in the log. For example, the next entry indicates that the Application logging level has been changed from Summary to Detailed.
Show Detail

The following entry shows that the Show Send and Receive setting for the Detail logging option has been enabled as well.
Show send and receive

Whenever an Internet application is started, an entry is recorded in the log. For example, the following entry indicates that Internet Explorer has been stored on the computer and that the McAfee Personal Firewall has been configured to allow it to

communicate through the firewall.

```
IEXPLORE running (it will be allowed)
```

The next two log entries represent a sampling of some of the entries that you might see recorded in your log. In this case, these entries show that a connection was made to www.mediaone.rr.com. The format of these entries is broken down as follows:

- Date
- Time
- Application name
- Local port number used
- The IP address of the remote computer
- The port used by the remote computer
- The service running on the remote system
- The length of the session
- The number of bytes sent
- The number of bytes received

```
2001/06/28 4:40:09 PM: IEXPLORE port 1268 (ephemeral) - 24.30.203.14 port
80
     (WWW), lasting 3 second(s), 229 bytes sent, 223 bytes received.
2001/06/28 4:40:15 PM: IEXPLORE port 1269 (ephemeral) - 24.30.203.14 port
80
     (WWW), lasting 1 second(s), 288 bytes sent, 864 bytes received.
```

The next entry shows that Internet Explorer has been closed:

```
IEXPLORE has stopped
```

The following entry appears when you close your firewall:

```
----------------- McAfee Firewall is stopping --------------------
```

This final entry shows that the McAfee Personal Firewall is no longer running or protecting your Internet connection:

```
Stopping McAfee Firewall on 2001/06/27 4:46:21 PM
```

Limitations

Overall, the McAfee Personal Firewall proves itself to be a solid and reliable personal firewall. It monitors network traffic and can allow or block access based on trusted applications and network settings. However, there are a few features missing in this

personal firewall that are found in some competing products. For example, there are no intrusion-detection capabilities. Unless you make a habit of examining your firewall's log, and most people do not, you have no way of knowing when your systems have been probed by a port scanner.

In addition, there is no mechanism for allowing or blocking communication with specific IP addresses or ranges of IP addresses.

If you have or plan to build a home network, you'll need to look elsewhere for your personal firewall because the current version of the McAfee Personal Firewall does not support Microsoft's Internet connection-sharing capability.

Testing the McAfee Personal Firewall

After installing and configuring your McAfee Personal Firewall, you should test it to make sure that it is running and protecting your computer as expected.

Start Internet Explorer, Netscape Communicator, or one of the other applications that you have configured as trusted and see whether you can connect to the Internet. Once you are successful with this test, start an application that has been listed as non-trusted. If all works as expected, the application will not be able to make the connection and will display an error message.

If all is going well so far, try starting an Internet application that you have not added to the McAfee Personal Firewall's list of known Internet applications. You should see a pop-up dialog box appear asking whether you want to allow or block the application. Make the appropriate selection. Next, right-click the McAfee icon in the system tray and select Application Settings and make sure that the application has been added to the list appropriately.

If all these tests seem to be working correctly, it's time to run an Internet scan of your computer's defenses and see how well it will protect your computer.

Refer to Chapter 9 "How Secure Is Your Computer?," for a demonstration of how to run a free Internet scan against your computer. In addition, Appendix B, "Other Web Sites That Will Test Your Security," provides a number of free Internet sites that you can use to further test your Internet security.

BLACKICE DEFENDER

*T*his is the second of three chapters dedicated to the coverage of software-based personal firewall. This chapter focuses on BlackICE Defender from Network ICE. Coverage includes instruction on how to install and configure the BlackICE Personal Firewall. You learn about what goes on under the covers and what makes this personal firewall different from the others covered in this book. In addition to a review of BlackICE's features, this chapter also identifies some areas where there is still room for improvement.

- Learn how to install BlackICE Defender
- Learn how to change its default configuration settings
- Learn how to gather information about intruders
- Learn how to configure and work with BlackICE Defender's alerts

Overview

The BlackICE Defender Personal Firewall is provided by Network ICE, whose Web site is located at www.networkice.com. This personal firewall is aimed at home users with dial-up, DSL, and cable modem connections.

This personal firewall operates differently from the other personal firewalls examined in this book. Instead of blocking specific applications and protocols, BlackICE Defender uses a detection and analysis engine that examines the contents of every incoming and outgoing packet and performs a structural analysis to determine whether it poses any threat to your computer. BlackICE Defender attempts to identify the nature of every attack against your computer and can provide you with detailed information about the type of attack and what it did to respond to it. When the firewall determines that the computer is under attack, it performs a series of actions, including:

- Stopping firewallthe attack by blocking the hacker's IP address
- Performing a back trace and building an evidence file containing as much information as possible about the attacker
- Notifying you of the attack using both graphical and audio alerts

BlackICE Defender Firewall blocks an attacker's IP address from accessing your computer for 24 hours. After that, the block is removed. This way, access to a legitimate Web server is not permanently blocked as a result of an attempt by a hacker to spoof the server's identity. If, after analyzing the event, you decide that you want to permanently block the IP address, you can do so.

You can also specify IP addresses of trusted computers. If you have a home network that uses TCP/IP as its protocol, you can set up the other networked computers as trusted systems, allowing network traffic to flow freely between your home computers. After a trusting computer is defined, it is allowed to pass through your firewall without having any of its data packets checked. Use this option with caution.

A back trace firewallis an attempt on the part of BlackICE Defender to retrace the path that network packets take to reach you from their senders. Using the address information contained within the data packets, the firewall attempts to retrace them

to their sender and gather as much information as possible about the hacker, including his or her

- IP address
- MAC address
- Hostname

This information firewall and anything else that it can collect is then recorded into an evidence file. Unfortunately, evidence files require a special application to read. They also require a good deal of network experience to interpret their contents. Evidence files are not intended to be read by the home user but rather to be passed on to your ISP when reporting hacker activity.

BlackICE Defender presents a detailed real-time graphical analysis of network activity to help you gauge the level of network activity occurring at various intervals.

Unlike many other personal firewalls, the BlackICE Defender Personal Firewall installs without running a configuration wizard that asks questions about how it should configure the firewall's security policies. Instead it automatically installs a default set of security policies. Of course, you are permitted to later review and change them as required to meet your own security requirements.

BlackICE Defender provides four security settings. Each setting provides a different level of protection:

- **Paranoid**—This firewallsetting blocks all unsolicited incoming traffic and might cause problems when browsing Web sites that provide interactive content. This setting can also disrupt instant messaging and streaming audio/video.
- **Nervous**—This setting blocks all unsolicited incoming traffic with the exception of some interactive content. This permits most streaming audio and video through the firewall.
- **Cautious**—This setting blocks unsolicited incoming traffic that attempts to communicate with network or operating systems services.
- **Trusting**—This security setting does not block any traffic and leaves all TCP/IP ports open and exposed.

BlackICE Defender is composed of two parts:

- **Detection and analysis engine**—Filters all network traffic and protects the computer from attack.
- **Summary Application**—Provides an interface for viewing firewall and network activity and configuring firewall settings.

The Summary Application provides access to network events. From here, you can view information about

- Attacks on your computer
- General network activity
- Information collected about attackers
- BlackICE Defender's actions

Note As of the writing of this book, Internet Security Systems acquired Network ICE. Although the BlackICE Defender Personal Firewall is sure to be a major player in the personal home firewall market, it's possible that its name or home Web site might be changed.

System Requirements

As of the writing of this book, the current version of BlackICE Defender is 2.1. Its official hardware requirements are listed here:

- 16MB of memory
- 10MB of hard disk space
- Pentium processor
- CD-ROM drive

Note BlackICE's 16MB memory requirement is fine for Windows 95, 98, and NT Workstation. However, operating systems such as Windows Me and Windows 2000 Professional have greater memory requirements. Windows Me requires a minimum of 32MB while Windows 2000 Professional requires 64MB. To run BlackICE Defender on one of these operating systems you must at least meet the operating system's minimum memory requirements.

In addition, you need a dial-up, cable, or DSL connection to the Internet and one of the following operating systems:

- Windows 95
- Windows 98
- Windows Me
- Windows NT 4 with Service Pack 4 or higher
- Windows 2000 with Service Pack 1 or higher
- Windows XP

Installation and Setup

The first step in preparing to install BlackICE Defender is to close any active programs, including those that might be communicating with the Internet. Insert the BlackICE Defender CD into your CD-ROM drive. In a few moments, its auto-run program will start. The rest of the BlackICE Defender installation process is outlined here:

1. The BlackICE Defender CD automatically loads.

2. The BlackICE setup program begins to execute and extract files needed by the installation process. Within a few moments, you'll see the InstallShield Wizard for BlackICE appear. Click Next.

3. The BlackICE License Agreement appears. You have to accept its conditions in order to install the firewall. Read the agreement and then click I ACCEPT.

4. You are then prompted to type the BlackICE Defender License number that was supplied with your copy of the software. Type the license number exactly as shown, including capitalization, and then click Next.

5. Next, you are prompted to confirm the destination folder where BlackICE Defender will be installed. The default location is C:\Program Files\Network ICE\BlackICE. Click Browse to specify an alternative location. When you're ready, click Next.

6. You are then prompted to select the program folder where BlackICE Defender's icons will be stored. The default is Network ICE. You can also select from several alternative folders or type a new program folder name. After you have made your selection, click Next.

7. A dialog box appears displaying a summary of all the settings that you have specified. Make sure that everything looks correct and then click Next.

8. The installation process then completes. A dialog box appears with an option asking if you would like to view the README file that came with BlackICE Defender. The option is selected by default. Click Finish.

9. A Notepad window opens and displays the BlackICE Defender README file. Examine its contents and then close it.

BlackICE Defender is now installed and protecting your computer. You should see a small BlackICE Defender icon in your Windows system tray in the lower-right corner of the screen.

In addition, if you click Start, Programs, and then Network ICE you should see the following components:

- BlackICE Defender QuickStart Guide
- BlackICE README
- BlackICE Utility
- Install Adobe Acrobat Reader

Configuring BlackICE Defender

As mentioned earlier in this chapter, BlackICE Defender does not provide a configuration wizard like many other personal firewalls. Instead it installs itself with a default set of security settings. You can view and change these settings at any time.

BlackICE Defender settings are viewed from its BlackICE Setting dialog box, as shown in Figure 7.1. This dialog box consists of a number of property sheets, each of which maintains the configuration for a particular aspect of the personal firewall.

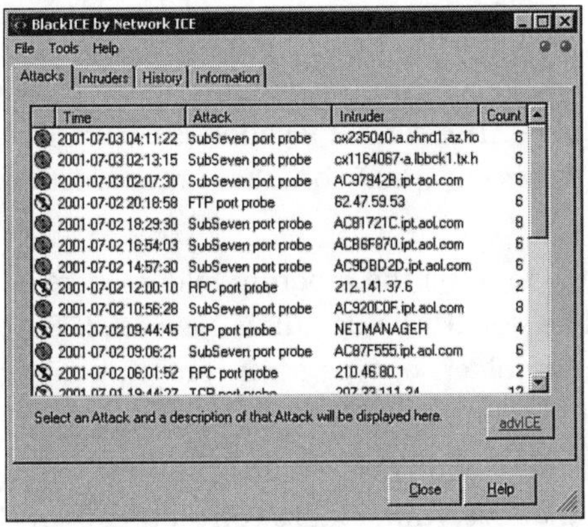

FIGURE 7.1

The firewall's configuration settings are managed using the property sheets on the BlackICE by Network ICE dialog box.

You can open this dialog box in either of two ways. One way is to click Start, Programs, Network ICE and then BlackICE Utility. This starts the Application Summary interface. From here, you click the Edit BlackICE Setting option on the Tools menu. The other way is to right-click the BlackICE Defender icon in the Windows system tray and select Edit BlackICE Setting from the pop-up menu that appears, as shown in Figure 7.2.

FIGURE 7.2

You can access any BlackICE Defender feature by right-clicking its icon in the system tray.

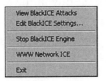

Protection Settings

The Protection Property sheet, shown in Figure 7.3, allows you to select one of the firewalls four-security levels. As discussed in more detail earlier in this chapter, these levels are Paranoid, Nervous, Cautious, and Trusting.

The default security level is Cautious.

There also are three additional options at the bottom of the property sheet. These are:

- **Enable Auto-Blocking**—Allows the BlackICE Defender to block the IP address from which a serious threat originates.

- **Allow Internet file sharing**—This setting allows your computer to share its folders and disk drives with other people on a home network or over the Internet.

- **Allow NetBIOS Neighborhood**—Allows NetBIOS to announce information about your computer to other computers.

By default, the last two options are disabled. Unfortunately, if you leave these settings in their default state, your computer cannot share its resources with other computers on a home network. Even worse, if you enable these options, you expose your computer to the entire Internet.

The answer to this problem is to use the NetBEUI protocol as the local area network protocol on your home network, as explained in Chapter 11, "Home Networks and Internet Connection Sharing."

Log Settings

The Packet Log property sheet, shown in Figure 7.4, allows you to tell the firewall how to manage the logging of network traffic. When enabled, BlackICE Defender logs all network traffic. Whenever a log fills up, a new one is opened. This process repeats until the maximum number of logs is filled, at which time the firewall begins to overwrite the oldest log.

You can configure any of the following settings:

- **Logging enabled**—Allows you to enable and disable log files. The default setting is disabled.

- **File prefix**—Allows you to provide a prefix name to the firewall's log files. The default prefix is log. For example, when enabled, the first log file created is named log000.enc.

- **Maximum size**—Specifies the maximum file size of a log file. When the limit is reached, a new log file is started. The default size is 0KB.

- **Maximum number of files**—Specifies the maximum number of log files that will be created before the firewall will begin overwriting log files. By default this value is set to 10.

BlackICE Defender's logs are stored as sniffer files using the same formation as evidence files. These files are not legible when viewed with text editors. Instead, you must use a sniffer file application to analyze the log's contents. Unfortunately, even then you'll need a great deal of network administration experience to understand them.

FIGURE 7.4

You can configure whether your firewall keeps log files and specify both their size and number.

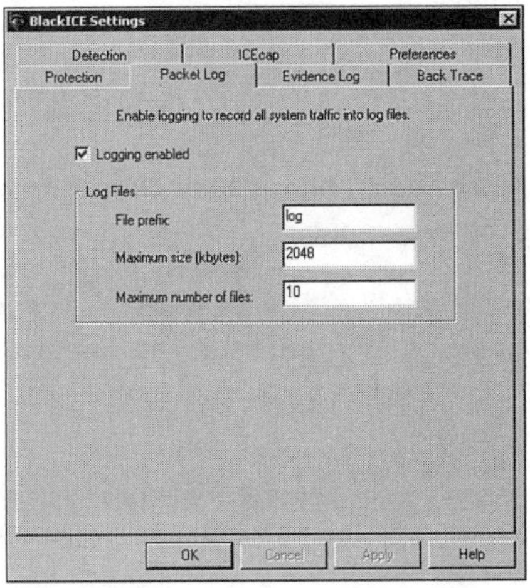

Evidence Log Settings

The Evidence Log property sheet, shown in Figure 7.5, allows you to tell the firewall how to manage the creation of evidence logs. Evidence logs are created when BlackICE Defender determines that an attack has been launched against your computer.

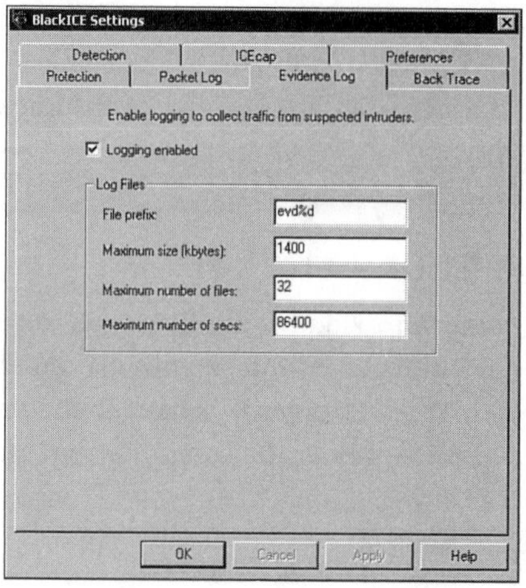

FIGURE 7.5

The firewall can be configured to collect detailed information about the hackers that attack your computer.

When enabled, you will find these files in the same folder as BlackICE Defender's source files, which is usually C:\Program Files\Network ICE\BlackICE. These log files have an .enc file extension and can only be read using a sniffer application.

In addition to protecting your computer or home network, one of the most important things a personal firewall can do is provide you with good logging information. Packet and evidence logs require special programs to decode them and network administration experience to understand them. You can give these logs to your ISP when reporting an attack, but they otherwise are not of much help to most users. Fortunately, as you see later in this chapter, BlackICE Defender provides detailed logging information in a format that is understandable to the home user from its Application Summary Interface.

The following settings can be configured on this property sheet:

- **Logging enabled**—Allows you to enable and disable log files. The default setting is enabled.

- **File prefix**—Allows you to provide a prefix name to the firewall's log files. The default prefix is evd%d. EVD stands for evidence and the %d is a variable that is replaced with the system date each time a log file is created.

- **Maximum size**—Specifies the maximum file size of a log file. When the limit is reached, a new log file is started and the old log file is saved. The default size is 1440KB.

- **Maximum number of files**—Specifies the maximum number of log files that are created before the firewall will begin overwriting log files. By default this value is set to 32.

- **Maximum number of secs**—The amount of time, in seconds, that the firewall captures network data when creating an evidence file. This setting allows you to limit the amount of disk space that's consumed by a single evidence file.

Gathering Information About Your Attacker

The Back Trace property sheet, shown in Figure 7.6, allows you to tell the firewall how to collect information about hackers who attack your computer. A *back trace* is a procedure used by the firewall to trace data packets back to their source and gather as much information as possible about the computer that sent them.

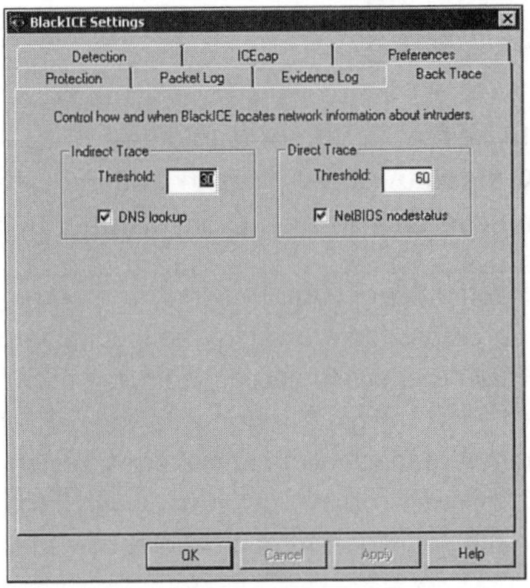

FIGURE 7.6

Telling BlackICE Defender how you want to go about collecting information about hacker attacks.

Two types of back traces can be performed:

- **Indirect**—Traces data packets back across the Internet but never attempts to probe the hacker's computer. This type of trace is invisible to the hacker.

- **Direct**—Traces data packets back across the Internet and gathers more information about the hacker. This type of trace can be detected if the hacker is running his or her own firewall and can provoke further attacks.

The indirect trace option includes a suboption that allows it to perform a DNS lookup. DNS servers are found on the Internet and large networks and can sometimes be used to look up the name assigned to a computer. The direct trace has its own suboption. When enabled, the NetBIOS node status option tells BlackICE Defender to perform a NetBIOS query against the hacker's computer.

Threshold settings determine when a back trace is performed. By default, a security event with a level of 30 or higher will invoke an indirect trace. Similarly, a security event of 50 will invoke a direct back trace.

BlackICE Defender automatically assigns a severity value to each attack. Four broad categories of events are defined, each of which represents a different range security threat, as shown in Table 7.1.

Table 7.1 BlackICE Defender Security Event Levels

Event Category	Severity	Description
Critical	75–100	An attack designed to harm your computer or its contents.
Serious	50–74	An attack designed to access information on your computer.
Suspicious	25–49	A non-threatening activity such as a port scan that might indicate a possible pending threat.
Informational	0–24	A non-threatening network event.

Managing Specific IP Addresses

The Detection property sheet, shown in Figure 7.7, allows you to specify IP addresses that the firewall should trust or attacks that should be ignored. Trusting an IP address allows all traffic from that IP address to pass through the firewall unchecked. Telling the firewall to ignore a specific type of attack from a specific IP address allows you to filter out network traffic flagged by the firewall as dangerous when in fact it is not. For example, you might want to exclude any port scans from your ISP.

Each IP address is listed on a separate line. Each entry displays the IP address to trust, the name of an attack to trust, and its attack ID. The attack ID is a number assigned to each known type of attack by BlackICE Defender.

To add a new IP address to the list, click Add; to modify an existing entry, click Modify. To delete an entry, click Delete and click Yes when prompted for confirmation.

Both the Add and Modify options open the Exclude from Reporting dialog box,
shown in Figure 7.8.

This dialog box provides the following options:

Addresses to Trust

- **All**—Select this option to specify an attack that is to be ignored from all IP
  addresses.

- **IP**—Type a specific IP address to trust.

- **Add Firewall Entry**—Tells the firewall to allow all communication from
  the specified IP address.

Attacks to Ignore

- **All**—Select this option to ignore all attacks from the specified IP address.

- **Name**—A drop-down list of known attacks. Select one to be ignored.

■ **ID**—Instead of specifying an attack using the drop-down list in the Name field, you specify it by selecting the ID that BlackICE Defender has assigned to the attack.

The ICEcap Property Sheet

The ICEcap property sheet, shown in Figure 7.9, is disabled. ICEcap is a Network ICE product that is designed to run on corporate networks and to consolidate information from computers running BlackICE Defender onto a single server where it can be correlated and examined.

FIGURE 7.9

ICEcap is a Network ICE product designed to consolidate information from firewalls running on corporate networks.

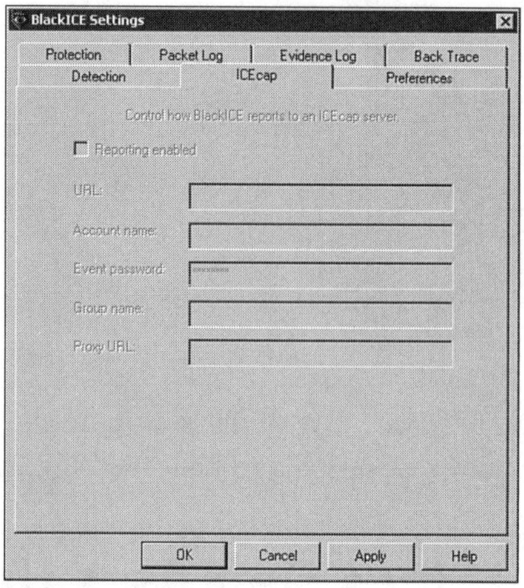

Establishing Interface and Alert Settings

The Preference property sheet, shown in Figure 7.10, configures settings that control how the firewall notifies you about alert conditions, how it checks for updates, and how it displays tooltips.

The Prompts section lets you decide whether confirmation dialog boxes will be displayed when you make configurations changes. The Show tooltips option enables the display of tooltips when the firewall is started.

The Update Notification section allows you to specify whether BlackICE Defender checks the Network ICE Web site for updates. The Interval for Checking options allows you to specify how often the check is performed.

The Attack Notification section lets you specify whether graphic or audio alerts are used to notify you. In addition, you can specify the severity levels required to initiate an alert.

Your options are:

- Critical
- Critical and serious
- Critical, serious, and suspicious

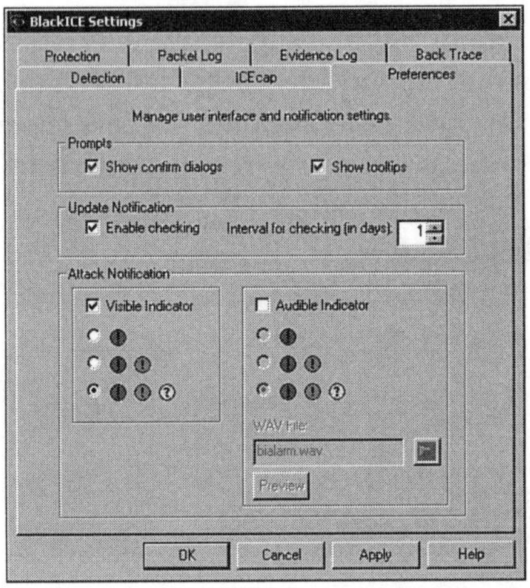

FIGURE 7.10

Configuring notification options.

The WAV file option allows you to specify a WAV file to be played when an audio alert is triggered. The Preview button allows you to hear the WAV file.

Keeping BlackICE Defender's Defenses Up to Date

From time to time, Network Ice provides updates to BlackICE Defender. These updates keep your firewall as strong as possible and allow it to defend against the most recent types of attacks that have been reported. You can set up your firewall to automatically check for available updates or you can manage this process manually. Unless you are in the habit of performing regular maintenance on you computer and its software programs, I recommend that you set things up to let BlackICE Defender take care of this chore for you.

Automatically Updating Your Personal Firewall

You can configure the firewall to monitor the Network ICE Web site and report when an update is available for download by using the following procedure:

1. Right-click the BlackICE Defender icon in the Windows system tray and select View BlackICE Attacks.

2. Click the Edit BlackICE Settings option on the Tools menu.

3. Select the Preferences property sheet.

4. Select the Enable checking option in the Update Notification section and specify an interval, in days, that you want the Web site to be checked.

The interval that you set to tell BlackICE Defender to check for updates is automatically reset if you restart your computer. Therefore, if you do not leave your computer on overnight, you have to remember to manually check for updates to your firewall.

BlackICE Defender notifies you that an update is available by displaying the Ni icon in the upper-right corner of the BlackICE by Network ICE dialog box, as shown in Figure 7.11.

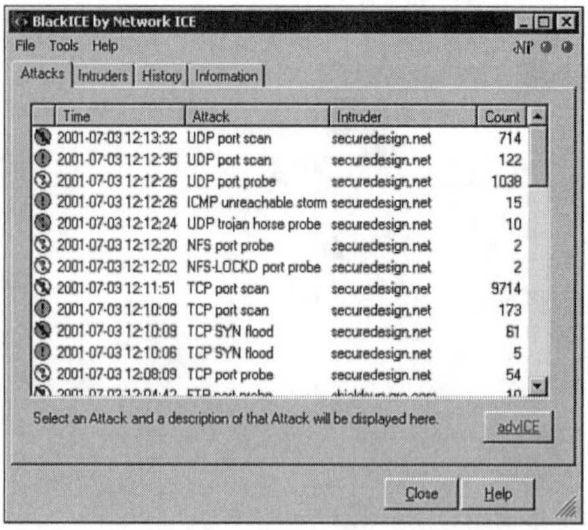

FIGURE 7.11

A new update is available for the BlackICE Defender personal firewall.

You can download and apply the update by clicking the Ni icon. Your Internet browser will start and connect to the Network ICE Web site. You will then be prompted to either save the update file or open it from its current location.

If you click the option to download and save the update file, you need to run it after the download completes in order to update your firewall. If you select the option to open the update file from its current location, the BlackICE Configuration Wizard loads and displays the Welcome to BlackICE Defender maintenance setup dialog box as soon as the update file finishes downloading.

The following procedure describes the steps involved in updating your firewall:

1. The Welcome dialog box displays a message identifying the version of BlackICE Defender being run on your computer, as shown in Figure 7.12. Click Next to begin the update process.

FIGURE 7.12

The Welcome to BlackICE Defender maintenance setup dialog box.

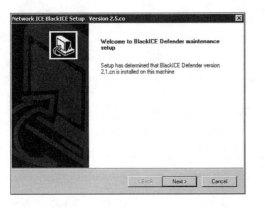

2. You are then prompted to apply the upgrade as demonstrated in Figure 7.13. Select the upgrade option and click Next.

FIGURE 7.13

Applying the upgrade to Defender BlackICE.

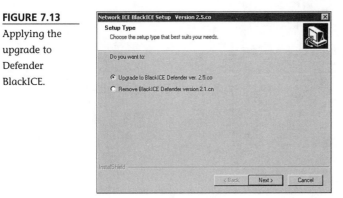

3. You are prompted to confirm the upgrade. Click Yes.

4. If the BlackICE Defender License Agreement appears, click I ACCEPT.

5. When prompted, click Finish.

That's it. Your BlackICE Defender personal firewall is now stronger than ever.

Manually Updating Your Personal Firewall

If you prefer, you can perform the process of updating the BlackICE Defender Personal Firewall manually. If you are going to handle things manually you probably ought to make a note to yourself to check for updates every 2-3 weeks. The procedure for doing so is outlined here:

1. Right-click the BlackICE Defender icon in the Windows system tray and select View BlackICE Attacks.

2. Click the Download Update option on the Tools menu.

3. Your Internet browser will start and connect to the Network ICE Web site. If an update is available, you will then be prompted to either save the update file or open it from its current location. From this point, the installation process is the same for an automatic update.

| If your firewall is already at the current update level, you will see a Web page stating that you are already running the most current version of BlackICE Defender. In addition, you'll see your license key and the software version of your firewall.

Normal Operation

After it's installed and configured, your BlackICE Defender firewall sits quietly in the Windows system tray monitoring all your network traffic and blocking or allowing communications based on your security settings. You will also find an entry for it on the Start menu by selecting Start, Programs, and Defender BlackICE.

Working with Report Logs

After BlackICE Defender is installed and properly configured, you are ready to begin working with your personal firewall. The easiest way to do this is by right-clicking the BlackICE Defender icon in the Windows system tray. The following options are available:

- View BlackICE Attacks
- Edit BlackICE Settings
- Advanced Firewall Settings
- Stop BlackICE Engine
- WWW Network ICE
- Exit

Each of these options is described in the sections that follow.

View BlackICE Attacks

The BlackICE Defender Application Summary program provides you with detailed reporting information regarding network and firewall activity and provides a type of online log. Functionally, the Application Summary program is organized into four property sheets:

- **Attacks**—Provides information about attacks and other suspicious network activity targeted at your computer.

- **Intruders**—Provides information gathered about computers that initiate attacks or suspicious network activity targeted at your computer.

- **History**—Provides a graphical view of network traffic and hacker activity on your computer.

- **Information**—Provides BlackICE Defender license and support information.

At the top of the dialog box is its menu system. It is composed of four menus:

- **File**—Contains an Exit option, which allows you to close the Application Summary program.

- **View**—Contains options that allow you to freeze the display so that you can focus on a particular event. Also allows you to filter the display to show any combination of critical, serious, suspicious, and informational events.

- **Tools**—Contains options for managing the firewall's settings, starting and stopping the firewall engine, clearing the attack list, performing a manual update, and configuring advanced firewall settings.

- **Help**—Provides access to the BlackICE Defender's help system, online support, and the Network ICE Web site.

In the upper-right corner are two circle icons. The left icon represents outbound traffic and the icon on the right represents inbound traffic. These icons blink when traffic is passing through the firewall. A solid light indicates a continuous stream of traffic. Both lights are color-coded to indicate the type of system activity passing through the firewall:

- Gray icon—No traffic is occurring.

- Green icon—Normal network traffic is occurring.

- Yellow icon—Suspicious traffic is passing through.

- Orange icon—Traffic aimed at accessing data on your computer is being intercepted.

- Red icon—Traffic attempting to do harm to your computer is being intercepted.

Depending on the level of network traffic, you might find that working with the dialog box is difficult because it can update so frequently that you will have trouble focusing on a particular event. You can use the Freeze option located on the View menu to temporarily suspend the updating of events. When you are done, you can unfreeze the display by selecting Unfreeze from the Tools menu.

Over time, you might find that the number of events displayed becomes difficult to work with. You can click the Clear Attack List option on the Tools menu to delete the events from the display.

Analyzing Attacks on Your Computer

You can view a list of all the attacks that BlackICE Defender has recorded against your computer on the Attacks property sheet, shown in Figure 7.14.

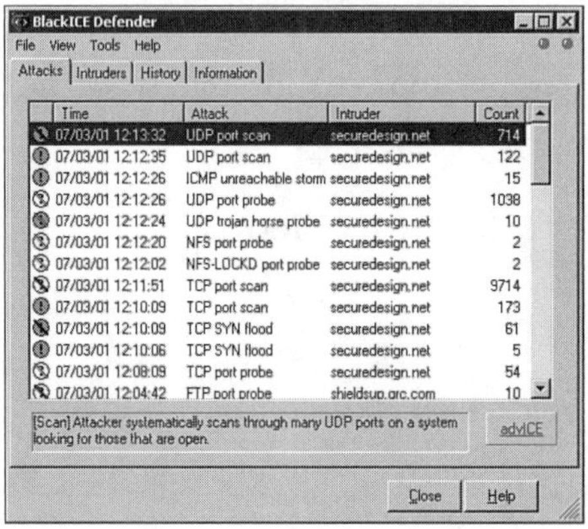

FIGURE 7.14

The Attacks property sheet provides detailed reporting on all recent attacks on your computer.

Information is displayed in columns, which are configurable. By default, information is sorted by time and then by severity. You can click any column heading to sort using an ascending sort order. Click on the column a second time to reverse this sort order. The default columns of data that are displayed include:

- **Severity**—An icon representation of the severity of the event and the firewall's response to the event.
- **Time**—The date and time that the event occurred.
- **Attack**—The type of attack.
- **Intruder**—The name (if available) or IP address of the attacker.
- **Count**—The number of times in a row that the attack occurred.

BlackICE Defender displays an icon in the Severity column representing its interpretation of the danger imposed by an attack. Table 7.2 displays these icons and their values.

Table 7.2   BlackICE Defender Severity Icons

Icon	Color	Description
⬤	Red	Critical
◉	Orange	Serious
◉	Yellow	Suspicious
◉	Green	Informational

BlackICE Defender overlays severity icons with the icons shown in Table 7.3 to indicate its response to attacks.

Table 7.3   BlackICE Defender's Response Icons

Icon	Attack Status
◥	Blocked
◢	Unsuccessful
○	Status Unknown
◎	Possible
⬤	Successful

There are four actions that you can take against any event by right-clicking it. These actions are:

- **Ignore Attack**—Provides two suboptions, which allow you to tell the firewall to either ignore this particular type of attack or to ignore this attack when launched against the intruder that initiated it.

- **Block Intruder**—Tells the firewall to block the intruder who launched the attack for any of the following intervals: an hour, day, month, or forever.

- **Trust Intruder**—Tells the firewall to add the intruder who caused the event to its list by either trusting or accepting all network traffic from the intruder's IP address or by ignoring all attacks from the IP address.

- **Clear Attack List**—Allows you to clear all events from the display in the event that it becomes too cluttered to be useful.

In addition to viewing information about an attack, you can also view information about the intruder who launched the attack by double-clicking any attack. This

causes the view to switch over to the Intruder's property sheet where information is available on the hacker who initiated the event.

You can add or remove columns for display from the Attacker's property sheet by right-clicking any column heading and selecting Columns. The Columns dialog box appears. To remove a column from the display, deselect its entry. To add a column, select any of the available columns from the list.

BlackICE Defender displays a brief description of any selected attack at the bottom of the property sheet. You can find more information on any attack by selecting it and clicking advICE. When clicked, this button starts your browser and loads a Network ICE Web page with detailed information about the attack and advice on what you might be able to do about it.

Examining Intruder Information

The Intruder's property sheet allows you to view detailed information collected about the Internet computers that have initiated events against your computer, as shown in Figure 7.15.

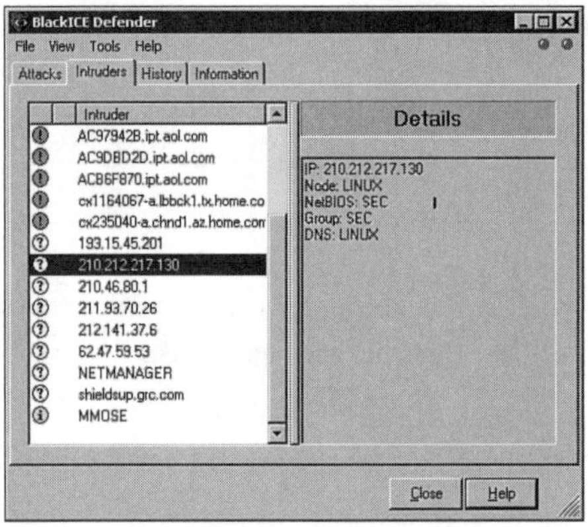

FIGURE 7.15

Viewing information about your intruders.

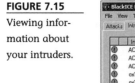

By default, all information on this property sheet is sorted by intruder name and then by severity. You can click any heading once to sort on it and twice to reverse its sort order. In addition, you can right-click any column heading and select the Columns option to add and remove columns from this property sheet.

When you select an intruder entry, all information collected about that intruder is displayed in the right pane. This information includes the intruder's IP address, NetBIOS name, DNS name, and MAC address.

You can right-click an intruder in the left pane and select to either block or trust the intruder using the same options presented on the Attackers property sheet.

Studying Network and Hacker Activity

The History property sheet provides you with a view of hacker and network activity, as shown in Figure 7.16. This way you can view attacks and look for patterns of occurrences. You can get detailed information about any attack by clicking a point in the attack or clicking the network traffic graphs. This causes BlackICE Defender to jump to the Attacks property sheet and display the attack that occurred at the point in time you selected.

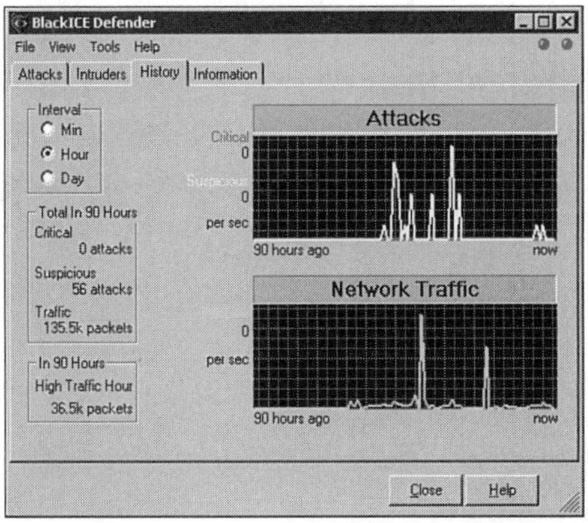

FIGURE 7.16

Graphically analyzing attacks launched against your computer.

The Interval section allows you to determine the time interval used to represent data in both graphs. The Total In 90 Hours section breaks down attacks into the following categories:

- Critical
- Suspicious
- Traffic

The In 90 Hours section displays the highest number of attacks occurring during any specified interval (such as in 90 hours).

Viewing Information About the Firewall

The Information property sheet displays license and support information, as shown in Figure 7.17. It also displays information about the version of BlackICE Defender

that you are running, including the features, fixes, and changes that have been added to the release.

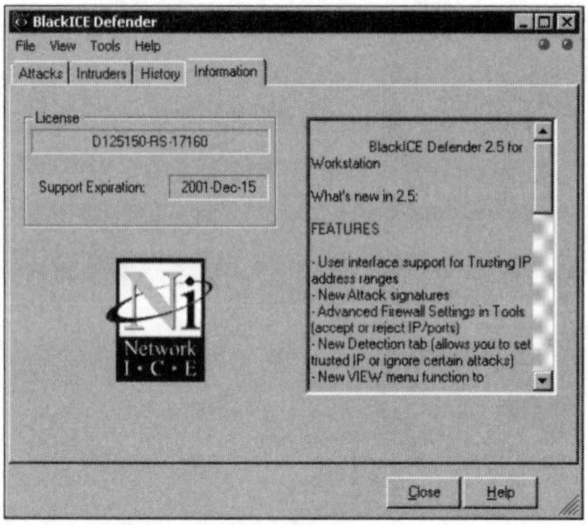

FIGURE 7.17

Viewing licensing and support information about BlackICE Defender.

Advanced Firewall Settings

The Advanced Firewalls Settings option found on the Application Summary Tools menu provides access to a dialog box where you can administer IP addresses and port settings. Figure 7.18 shows the IP Address property sheet on this dialog box. Its information is presented in several columns, which include:

- **Icon**—A green icon indicates a trusted IP address and a black icon shows a block IP address.
- **Owner**—Shows who created the entry.
- **Address**—The IP address being blocked.
- **Start Time**—The time that the block began.
- **End Time**—The time that the lock is set to expire.
- **Name**—The name, if available, associated with the IP address.

The display can be sorted by any column by clicking its heading. In addition, you can right-click any column heading to add and remove columns from the display.

You can also right-click any entry and select from the following options:

- Unblock Only
- Unblock and Accept
- Unblock, Accept, and Trust
- Modify

FIGURE 7.18

Administering advanced firewall settings.

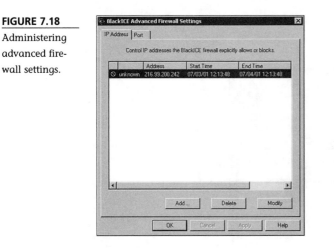

In addition, you can click the Add, Delete, or Modify buttons to add, remove, and change the entries in the IP Address list.

The Port property sheet, shown in Figure 7.19, displays a list of all the TCP/IP ports settings. By default, there are no entries in this list. This property sheet allows you to set a permanent or temporary block of any TCP or UPD protocol. To block a port, click Add. You can later change the entry by clicking Modify or remove it from the list by clicking Delete. When adding an entry you will be prompted to type the name representing the block, the port number to be blocked, the protocol type (such as TCP or UDP), and whether you want a temporary or permanent block.

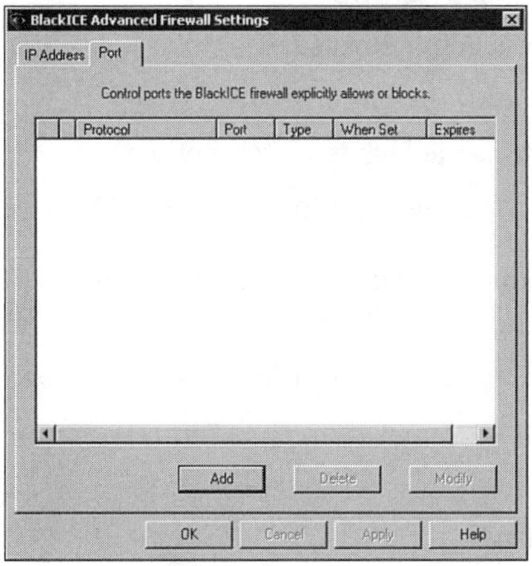

FIGURE 7.19

Blocking specific TCP and UDP ports.

Stop BlackICE Engine

The Stop BlackICE Engine option on the BlackICE Defender icon's context menu lets you stop the BlackICE Defender analysis and detecting engine. Stopping the BlackICE Defender engine leaves your computer completely unprotected while it is connected to the Internet. This option should be used with extreme caution. However, you might want to use this option if you have an Internet application that just will not seem to run in order to determine if BlackICE Defender is somehow interfering with the application.

After the program is stopped, the BlackICE Defender icon in the Windows system tray displays a red line over the icon. You can restart the program by right-clicking the icon and selecting Start BlackICE Engine.

You can also stop the BlackICE Defender engine from the Summary Application by clicking the Tools menu, selecting BlackICE Engine, and then Stop BlackICE Engine.

WWW Network ICE

Selecting the WWW Network ICE option on the BlackICE Defender icon's context menu starts your Internet browser and loads the Network ICE Web page (www.networkice.com), where you can find more information about BlackICE Defender and other products and services provided by Network ICE.

Exit

Selecting Exit from the BlackICE Defender icon's context menu closes the Application Summary program. It does not however, turn off BlackICE Defender. To restart the Application Summary program, select Start, Programs, Network ICE, and then the BlackICE Utility.

BlackICE Defender's Limitations

BlackICE Defender provides your computer with a very strong defense when you are connected to the Internet. It is easy to install and provides pre-configured security rules that allow it to begin working right away. In addition, it provides features not found in many other personal firewalls, including intrusion detection and the capability to back-trace and gather information about hackers who have tried to break into your computer.

However, there are a few missing features in this personal firewall that are usually found in competing products. For example, BlackICE Defender does not allow you to block specific applications from accessing the Internet. It is therefore possible for a cleverly written Trojan horse program to sneak onto your hard disk and disclose your personal information.

In addition, it does not allow you to provide different security settings for home network and Internet connections. Therefore you cannot disable TCP/IP file and printer sharing for your Internet connection without also disabling it on your home network. However, you can always load the NetBEUI protocol on each computer on your home network and share resources that way. For more information about sharing resources using a home network, refer to Chapter 11.

Testing the BlackICE Defender Personal Firewall

After installing and configuring your BlackICE Defender Personal Firewall, you should run a few tests to make sure that it is working and that your computer is being protected.

Begin by starting Internet Explorer or Netscape Communicator and making sure that you can still connect to the Internet. If your browser works, start your other Internet applications and make sure that they work as well.

Next, run a free Internet scan against your computer and see how well your computer is protected. Refer to Chapter 9, "How Secure Is Your Computer?," for instructions on how to run a free Internet security scan. Also, look in Appendix B, "Other Web Sites That Will Test Your Security," to find a list of different Web sites that provide free Internet scanning services. All in all BlackICE Defender is a solid personal firewall that does an excellent job of protecting personal computers. Its built-in analysis and detection engine provides it with more inherent intelligence than most other firewalls. However, of the three software personal firewalls covered in this book, it requires the most technical knowledge to fully utilize all its capabilities.

ZONEALARM

*T*his is the last of three chapters that cover software-based personal fire-walls. This chapter focuses on the ZoneAlarm Personal Firewall from Zone Labs. You learn how to install and configure the firewall and learn how it operates.

You also look at how ZoneAlarm lets you establish a different set of security settings for both home network and Internet connections and how you can configure alerts and automatically lock down your system when you are not using it. You also learn how to apply system and application security settings and interpret the contents of the ZoneAlarm log file.

- Learn how to configure alert notification
- Find out how to configure the ZoneAlarm log
- Find out how to automate the lock down of your computer
- Find out how to adjust security settings
- Learn how to identify trusted applications
- Find out how to enable the firewall to automatically check for updates

Overview

The ZoneAlarm Personal Firewall is provided by Zone Labs (www.zonelabs.com). This personal firewall is free for personal and non-profit use although a small fee is required when the firewall is used for business purposes. It can protect dial-up, DSL, and cable connections.

ZoneAlarm is one of two personal firewalls provided by Zone Labs. The other is ZoneAlarm Pro, which provides all the features found in ZoneAlarm plus other features, such as fine-grained security settings that also add a level of complexity to the product. This chapter focuses its attention on ZoneAlarm.

ZoneAlarm protects you from Trojan horse programs by intercepting any application that tries to connect to the Internet. You are notified of each event via a graphical alert, which allows you to decide whether the application can proceed. When you first install ZoneAlarm, you will find that it keeps you busy responding to alerts. However, it will not take it long to quiet down and learn the applications that you do and do not want to allow.

You can use ZoneAlarm to protect both your Internet connection and your home network. Its does this by defining two security zones: a local zone and an Internet zone. It provides three security settings, which you can apply separately to each zone, as follows:

- Low
- Medium
- High

A simple slider adjusts the security settings for each zone. As you change security levels, a description of the effects of the changes is displayed to help you understand how your personal security will be affected.

By default, ZoneAlarm applies a medium setting when securing a home network connection and a high security setting when protecting an Internet connection.

ZoneAlarm makes extensive use of pop-up dialog boxes to communicate with you while it operates. In addition, you can configure the firewall to record event information in a log file for later review and analysis.

System Requirements

As of the writing of this book, the current version of ZoneAlarm is 2.6. Its official hardware requirements follow:

- 8MB of memory
- 3MB of hard disk space
- 386 or higher processor (486 recommended)

To run Zone Alarm on any Windows operating system, your computer must meet the minimum memory requirements for the operating system. For Windows 95, 98, and NT I'd recommend at least 16MB. For Windows Me you'll need a minimum of 32MB. Windows 2000 Professional will demand no less than 64MB.

In addition, you need a dial-up, cable modem, or DSL connection to the Internet and one of the following operating systems:

- Windows 95 with WinSock 2
- Windows 98
- Windows Me
- Windows NT 4 with Service Pack 3 or higher
- Windows 2000
- Windows XP

Installation and Setup

You can get a free copy of ZoneAlarm from www.zonelabs.com. The name of the download file is zonalm26 (the last two characters represent the version number). The current version of ZoneAlarm as of the writing of this book is 2.6 and its installation program requires approximately 2.76MB.

The first step in preparing to install ZoneAlarm is to close any active programs, including those that are communicating with the Internet. The installation process consists of two parts. The first part involves information gathering that will be used to configure ZoneAlarm and the second part is the actual installation. Both of these processes are outlined here:

1. Double-click the ZoneAlarm Setup icon.

2. The ZoneAlarm Installation Welcome dialog box appears, as shown in Figure 8.1. Click Next.

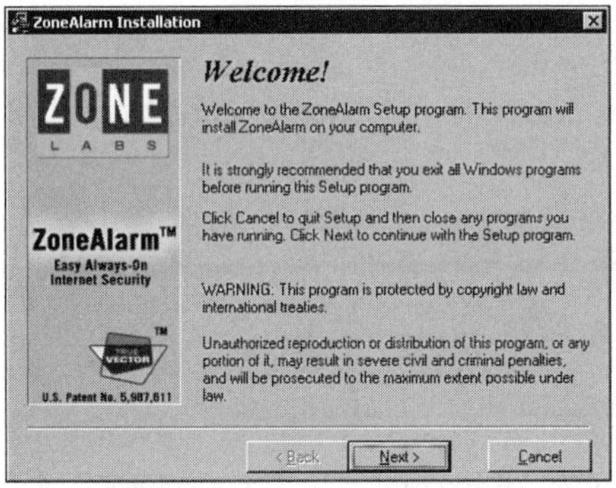

FIGURE 8.1

The ZoneAlarm
Installation
Welcome screen.

3. The Product Information dialog box appears displaying basic information, as shown in Figure 8.2, including system requirements, information regarding the installation and uninstallation of ZoneAlarm, and how to start the application. Review the information provided and then click Next.

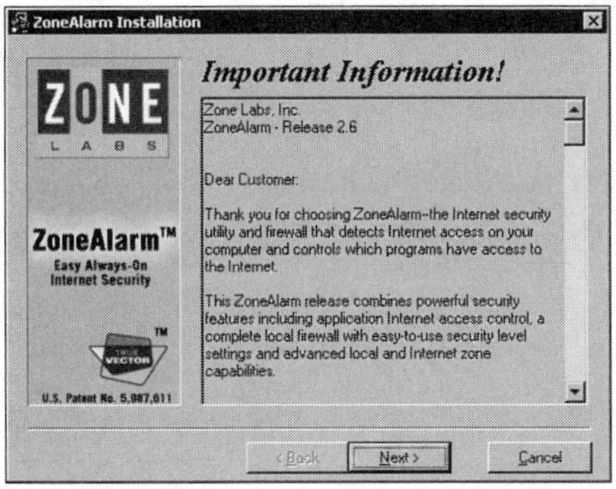

FIGURE 8.2

Reviewing
ZoneAlarm
basics.

4. Next, you are prompted to type your name, company name, and e-mail address, as shown in Figure 8.3.

You can also select from the following two options:

- I want to register ZoneAlarm so I can download updates.
- Inform me about important updates and news.

Complete the form and click Next.

FIGURE 8.3

Register for free
updates and
news about
ZoneAlarm.

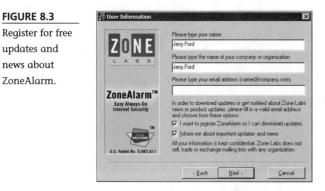

5. The ZoneAlarm License Agreement appears, as shown in Figure 8.4. You
   must accept the terms of this agreement in order to install ZoneAlarm. Click
   Accept.

FIGURE 8.4

Viewing the
ZoneAlarm
License
Agreement.

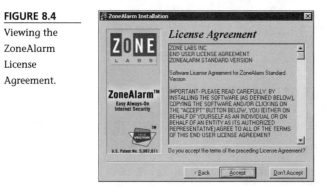

6. The Select Destination Directory screen appears, as shown in Figure 8.5. It
   displays the amount of available disk space and the amount that will be
   available after the installation. To change the installation folder, click
   Browse. Click Next.

FIGURE 8.5

Selecting the
folder where
ZoneAlarm will
be installed.

7. The installation process then looks for an Internet browser and, if it finds one, offers to configure the firewall to permit it to communicate with the Internet, as shown in Figure 8.6. Select Yes to permit the communication and click Next.

FIGURE 8.6

Configuring automatic Internet access for your Internet browser.

Configure Your Browser

For your convenience, ZoneAlarm can automatically detect your Web surfing components and give them permission to access the Internet (recommended).

These components are:
- your default Web browser
- Microsoft Windows Services and Controller app

ZoneAlarm maintains all other settings from previous installations (if applicable).

☑ Yes, please give these components permission to access the Internet.

< Back   Next >   Cancel

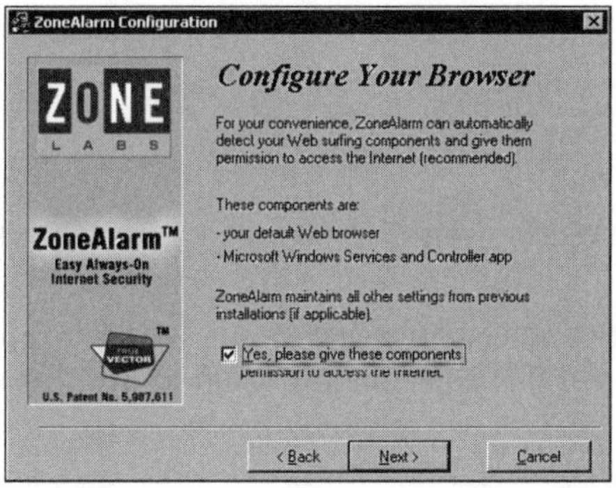

Note

If you do not configure access for your Internet browser now you can always set it up later.

Note

If you are a Windows 2000 user, you are also prompted to permit the Microsoft Windows Services and Controller app to traverse the firewall.

8. The Ready to Install! dialog box appears. Click Next.

9. The setup process begins installing ZoneAlarm files onto your computer. The User Survey dialog box, shown in Figure 8.7, appears. Fill out this form and click Finish.

FIGURE 8.7

The installation completes after you fill out ZoneAlarm's user survey.

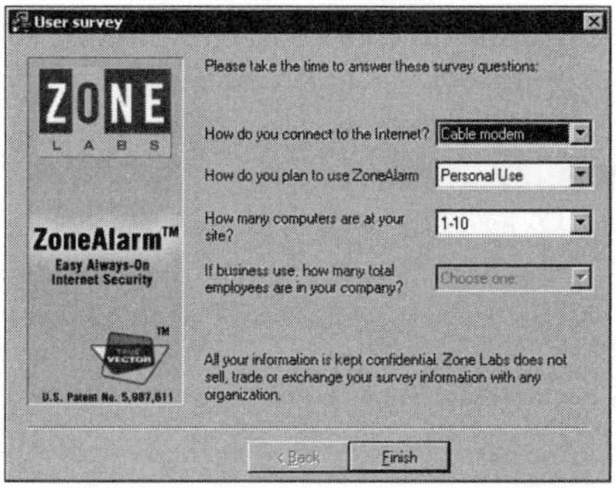

Please take the time to answer these survey questions:

How do you connect to the Internet? | Cable modem ▼

How do you plan to use ZoneAlarm | Personal Use ▼

How many computers are at your site? | 1-10 ▼

If business use, how many total employees are in your company? | Choose one ▼

All your information is kept confidential. Zone Labs does not sell, trade or exchange your survey information with any organization.

< Back   Finish

10. Setup is now complete. A pop-up dialog box appears asking you if you want to start ZoneAlarm. Click Yes.

Getting Started with ZoneAlarm

The first thing that you will see after starting ZoneAlarm for the first time is the ZoneAlarm—Getting Started dialog box, as shown in Figure 8.8.

FIGURE 8.8

Taking a brief tour of ZoneAlarm's features.

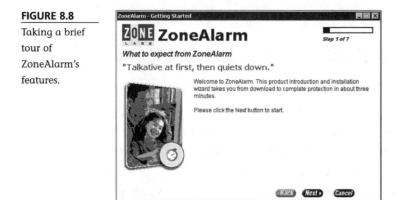

Clicking Next steps you through a total of seven screens, each of which tells you a little bit about working with ZoneAlarm. Click Next to continue or Cancel to dismiss this dialog box.

The next thing that you'll see is the ZoneAlarm Tips dialog box, as shown in Figure 8.9.

FIGURE 8.9

Viewing ZoneAlarm's tips.

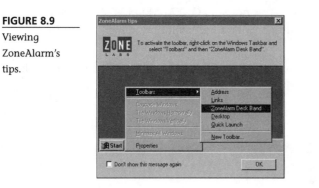

These tips appear every time that ZoneAlarm starts unless you select the Don't show this message again option at the bottom of the dialog box. Click OK to close the dialog box.

In addition to the ZoneAlarm main dialog box, you will see a ZA icon in your Windows system tray. When Network or Internet traffic occurs, the ZA icon changes into a graphic icon that flashes red and green to indicate activity, as shown in Figure 8.10.

FIGURE 8.10

The ZoneAlarm icon in the Windows system tray switches between a ZA and a graphic indicator whenever traffic occurs.

In addition to seeing the ZoneAlarm icon in the system tray, you'll find the following items listed on the Windows Start menu by clicking Start, Programs, and Zone Labs.

- **Readme**—The ZoneAlarm README file.
- **Uninstall ZoneAlarm**—A link to ZoneAlarm's uninstall utility.
- **ZoneAlarm Tutorial**—A link to the ZoneAlarm—Getting Started dialog box.
- **ZoneAlarm**—The ZoneAlarm executable program.

Working with ZoneAlarm

The ZoneAlarm executable program is named ZONEALARM.EXE. Unless you changed its default location during installation, you'll find it in c:\Programs Files\Zone Labs\ZoneAlarm.

To open the ZoneAlarm main dialog box, shown in Figure 8.11, double-click its icon in the Windows system tray or click Start, Programs, Zone Labs, and then ZoneAlarm.

FIGURE 8.11

The ZoneAlarm main dialog box.

The main ZoneAlarm dialog box is composed of five sections, each of which contain an icon and a link:

- **Graphs**—A dynamic set of bar graphs representing network traffic. The top two bar graphs indicate current upload and download traffic. The bottom two bar graphs show traffic over an extended period of time.

- **Padlock**—Allows you to toggle your system into a locked status, preventing any communication with the Internet. You can, however, exempt applications from this lock. A green bar under the lock indicates that it is open and its length indicates how much time is left before its automatic lock kicks in. A red bar indicates that the lock is closed and its length shows how long the lock has been active.

- **Stop**—Provides you with an emergency button for instantly shutting off all access to the Internet. All Internet traffic is affected by this option without exception.

- **Applications**—Displays a collection of icons representing active applications currently communicating with the Internet.

- **ZoneAlarm Logo**—Provides a link to Zone Labs' Web site, where help is available.

Beneath each icon is a button that opens ZoneAlarm panel where you can view and configure firewall settings. Each of these buttons is summarized in the following list:

- **Alerts**—Provides daily statistics and controls log settings.

- **Lock**—Allows you to establish an automatic lock for your firewall that activates after a predefined period of inactivity.

- **Security**—Lets you set up and configure a security zone for your Internet connection and a home network.

- **Programs**—Lets you view and manage which applications are permitted through the firewall.

- **Configure**—Lets you configure ZoneAlarm to automatically start at system startup and to check for updates.

When you minimize the ZoneAlarm main dialog box, it shrinks to the Windows task bar. But if you click the close button, the ZoneAlarm tips dialog box appears advising you that you can shut down ZoneAlarm by right-clicking its icon in the system tray and selecting the Shutdown ZoneAlarm option. After dismissing the dialog box by clicking OK, ZoneAlarm is minimized onto the system tray.

Select the Don't show this message again option to prevent the ZoneAlarm tips dialog box from appearing the next time you click the close button.

Managing Internet Alerts and Firewall Logging

Clicking the Alerts button on the main ZoneAlarm dialog box opens the Internet Alert panel, shown in Figure 8.12. This panel is divided into three sections. The Today's Summary section provides statistics on the number of bytes sent and received for the current day.

FIGURE 8.12

The Internet Alerts panel lets you configure alerts and log settings.

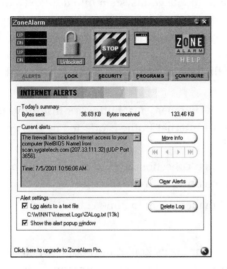

The Current Alerts section displays a scrollable listing of alerts that have occurred on your computer. To the right are four navigation buttons that allow you to jump ahead or back one alert or to jump to the beginning or end of the alert list. Above the navigation control is the More Info button. When clicked, this option opens your browser and passes the selected alert's information to the Zone Labs AlertAnalyzer, where it is analyzed and further explained, as demonstrated in Figure 8.13. While some of ZoneAlarm's alerts are self-explanatory, many require additional information to understand. I recommend that when you first install ZoneAlarm that you use this option a lot. This will help speed up your learning curve and provide you with more insight as to how the personal firewall works.

Below the navigation buttons is the Clear Alerts button, which allows you to clear all alert entries.

At the bottom of the Internet Alert panel is the Alert Settings section. Here, you can configure whether ZoneAlarm maintains a log file or displays pop-up alert messages. Both of these options are explained in greater detail later in this chapter. To the right of these configuration options is the Delete Log button, which you can use to delete the ZoneAlarm log file when it becomes too large.

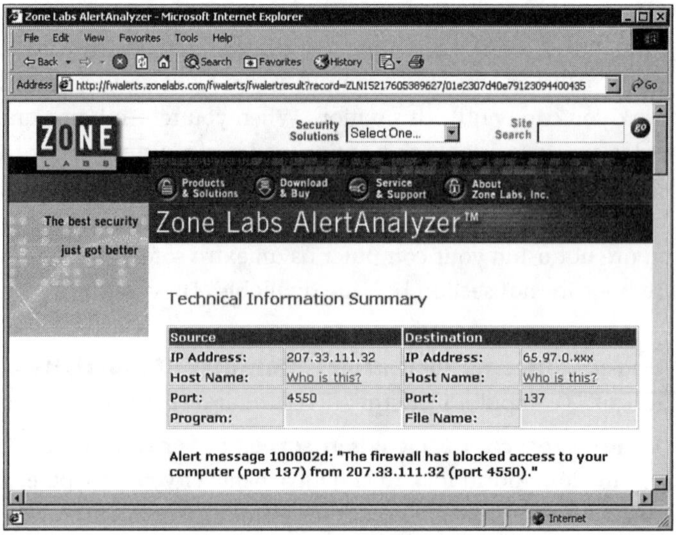

FIGURE 8.13

You can click More Info to open your Web browser and get more information about an alert from the Zone Labs Web site.

Working with Internet Lock Settings

Clicking the Lock button on the main ZoneAlarm dialog box opens the Internet Lock Settings panel, shown in Figure 8.14. This panel is divided into two sections. The Lock Status section displays the status of the ZoneAlarm lock (either open or locked) and whether the lock is enabled or disabled.

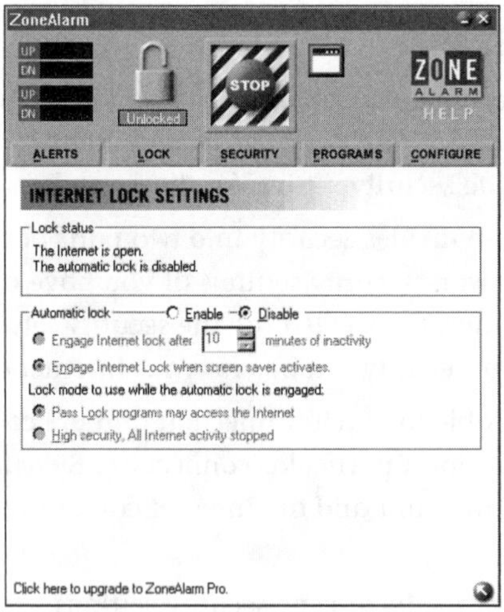

FIGURE 8.14

The Internet Lock Settings panel lets you enable and disable your personal firewall.

The Automatic Lock section is disabled by default. When you lock your computer, all Internet traffic is blocked, incoming and outgoing, regardless of your personal fire-

wall security settings. You can use this option to implement the strongest possible security on your computer any time you are going to be away from your computer for a lengthy piece of time. For example, if you leave your computer on when you are at work you can enable this option. When you return home and begin to surf the Internet, you can disable this option and begin surfing under the protection of your personalized configuration options. If you have elected to set ZoneAlarm's security setting to its lowest possible settings, I'd recommend enabling this setting any time you are not using your computer as an extra safety measure. When enabled, all the settings in that section become available. These settings include the following:

■ **Engage Internet lock after __ minutes of inactivity**—Automatically locks the computer's Internet access after a specified period of user inactivity.

■ **Engage Internet lock when screen saver activates**—Allows you to set up the ZoneAlarm lock to engage whenever your computer's screen saver runs.

■ **Pass lock programs may access the Internet**—Allows you to specify that programs configured to bypass the lock can do so when the lock is on. Individual programs can be configured from the Programs panel using the Pass Lock setting.

■ **High security; all Internet activity is stopped**—Tells ZoneAlarm to block all Internet activity when the lock is engaged.

Configuring Security Settings

Clicking the Security button on the main ZoneAlarm dialog box opens the Security Settings panel, shown in Figure 8.15. This panel is divided into two sections. The Security Level section displays the security setting for the firewall.

The ZoneAlarm Personal Firewall divides security into two parts or zones, allowing you to configure your home network security settings (if you have one) separately from your Internet security settings. On the left are the security settings for a home network and on the right are the security settings for your Internet connection.

Three security settings are available for each connection and are configured by dragging the security bar up or down for a particular connection. By default, the local (home) security setting is set to medium and the Internet connection setting is set to high.

The following list defines each of the local zone security settings.

■ **Low**—Makes your computer visible to other home network computers and permits file and printer sharing. When the Lock icon is enabled, this setting

only blocks application traffic as specified on the ZoneAlarm programs panel.

■ **Medium**—Makes your computer visible to other home network computers and permits file and printer sharing. When the Lock icon is enabled, this setting blocks all traffic.

■ **High**—Makes your computer invisible to other computers on the home network and blocks all file and printer sharing.

The following list defines each of the Internet zone's security settings:

■ **Low**—Makes your computer visible on the Internet and allows file and printer sharing.

■ **Medium**—Blocks NetBIOS services but still permits file and printer sharing. This will block scanners that look for NetBIOS ports 137 – 139 from querying your computer for information about any shared file and print resources that you may have without disabling your file and print capability.

■ **High**—Makes your computer invisible on the Internet, blocks NetBIOS services, and prevents file and printer sharing.

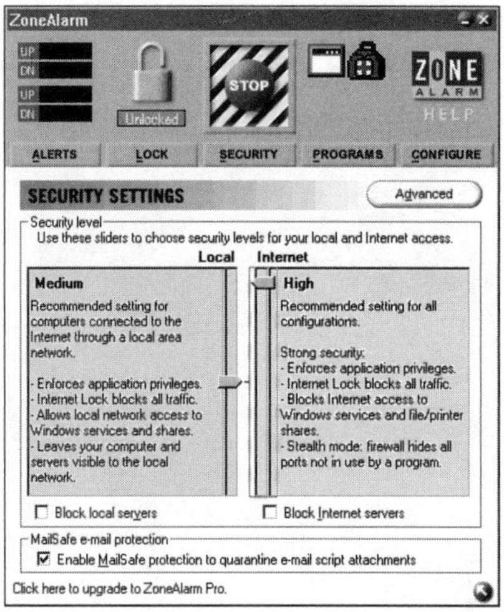

FIGURE 8.15

The Security Settings panel lets you configure security for your Internet connection and your home network.

Beneath the local and Internet security settings are options for blocking servers. Blocking local servers prevents an application from acting like a server when communicating over a home network. Blocking Internet servers prevents an application from acting like a server when communicating over the Internet. An application acts like a server when it provides a service to another requesting computer. For example, if you install Microsoft's Personal Web Server on your home computer and

use it to create your own Web site, your computer would then be able to function as a small Web server that accepts incoming connection requests to view your Web pages from other Internet users.

At the bottom on the Security Setting dialog box is the Enable MailSafe protection to quarantine e-mail script attachments option. When selected, this option tells ZoneAlarm to prevent the opening of e-mail attachments written in VBScript. VBScripts are sometimes used to transport computer viruses and Trojan horse programs within e-mail attachments. When enabled, ZoneAlarm changes the file extension of a VBScript program to .zl. This gives you the opportunity to contact the sender of the e-mail to determine if the attachment is legitimate before opening it.

The Advanced button, located in the upper-right corner of the Security Settings panel, opens the Local Zone Properties dialog box. From there, you can define computers that are on your home network so that your computer can communicate with them. To add a definition of a home network computer, click Add and specify the computer's Name and IP address. To modify an entry, select it and click Properties. To delete a computer from the list, select it and click Remove. More information about working with ZoneAlarm on a home network is provided in Chapter 11, "Home Networks and Internet Connection Sharing."

Managing Your Internet Applications

Clicking the Programs button on the main ZoneAlarm dialog box displays a listing of all configured Internet applications—shown in Figure 8.16—that ZoneAlarm knows about.

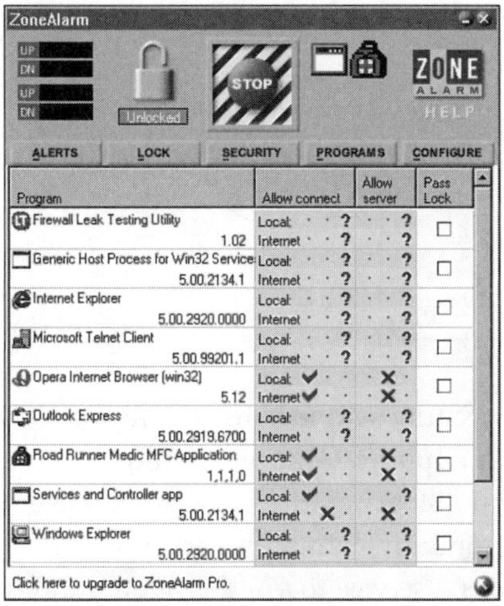

FIGURE 8.16

Viewing and administering your Internet applications.

Each time an Internet application runs, you are prompted to tell ZoneAlarm how to manage it. The information that is collected from you is then recorded here. Each Internet application is displayed in the Program column along with its version number. The Allow Connect column indicates whether the applications are permitted to connect to the local or the Internet zone. A green checkmark indicates that the application is allowed to communicate. A red X indicates that the application is blocked from communicating and a black question mark indicates that ZoneAlarm will query you the next time the application tries to run as to whether it is allowed to connect. You can use your mouse to change these configuration options by clicking the column fields for each application listed in the panel. For example, if you have elected to block an application's access to the Internet, you can restore it by clicking on the first column in the Allow Connection section for the application. This will place a green checkmark in that field showing that the application has been added to the approved list of applications.

You will probably want to allow most applications such as Internet explorer or Outlook Express to access the Internet. The main purpose behind this application blocking capability is to prevent Trojan programs from initiating secret connection to the Internet. Anytime an undefined application attempts to connect to the Internet, Netscape will notify you. If you are not sure what the application is or what it is trying to do I suggest that you tell ZoneAlarm to block it and then wait to see what happens. If everything continues to work correctly then it may be a Trojan application, which you can then delete. If another Internet application that you want to work with suddenly stops working it may be that the application that you blocked is a legitimate program that needs to be unblocked.

 Don't trust everything that you see. Some Trojan horse applications will give themselves a filename that matches the filename of a legitimate application, hoping to trick you into allowing it through your personal firewall. For example, if you see a ZoneAlarm alert asking for permission to let Internet Explorer through the firewall when you have already added the application to the approved list of applications you may really be looking at a Trojan horse.

The Allow Server column specifies whether the application can act like a server and accept incoming connections. The same three options allowed in the Allow Connect column are supported here. The Pass Lock column determines whether an application is permitted to bypass the ZoneAlarm lock when it has been activated.

You can manage an individual application by right-clicking it and selecting one of the following options.

- **Local Network**—This option lets you specify whether the selected application is allowed or disallowed or if you want to be asked the next time it runs.

You can also specify whether ZoneAlarm should allow, disallow, or ask you if the application can act like a server.

- **Internet**—This option allows you to apply the same settings used by the Local Network option to the Internet connection.

- **Pass Lock**—This option lets you toggle the pass lock setting for the application.

- **Changes Frequently**—This option allows you to identify a program that changes frequently. For example, you may use a shareware program that you downloaded from the Internet. If the program's author keeps improving it every few weeks and you keep downloading and installing it, it will be flagged as a changed program each time you run it because its file size will continue to change. Using this option you can save yourself the trouble of continually having to re-approve the application.

- **Remove xxxxxxx**—This option lets you delete the application entry from ZoneAlarm's application list.

Basic ZoneAlarm Configuration

Clicking the Configure button on the main ZoneAlarm dialog box displays a collection of configuration options, as shown in Figure 8.17.

FIGURE 8.17

Working with ZoneAlarm configuration options.

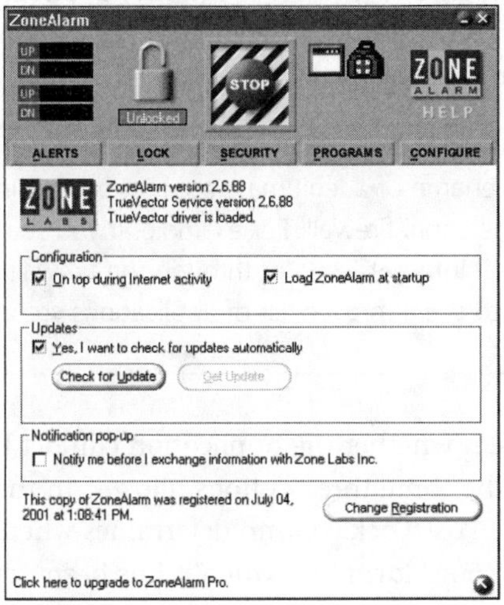

This panel is divided into three sections. The Configuration section provides the following options:

- **On top during Internet activity**—Causes the ZoneAlarm main dialog box to appear on top of other Windows when Internet traffic is occurring.

■ **Load ZoneAlarm at startup**—Tells ZoneAlarm to automatically start when your computer starts.

The Updates section allows you to configure ZoneAlarm to automatically check the Zone Labs Web site for updates. The Check for Update button lets you perform an immediate check. If an update is available, the Get Update button is activated. Click it to download the update.

The Notification Pop-up section allows you to specify whether you want to be notified when your firewall exchanges information with the Zone Labs Web site. The only time that ZoneAlarm contacts the Zone Labs Web site is when it checks for updates.

The last option on the panel is the Change Registration button. When clicked, it displays the Registration Information dialog box where you can change the name, company name, and e-mail address that you have registered with Zone Labs.

Working with the ZoneAlarm Desk Band Toolbar

ZoneAlarm automaticallyadds an option toolbar to the Windows toolbars collection when it is installed. This toolbar is called the ZoneAlarm Desk Band toolbar. You can use the following procedure to enable it.

1. Right-click an open area on the Windows task bar. A context-sensitive menu appears.

2. Select the Toolbars option. A submenu opens, as shown in Figure 8.18.

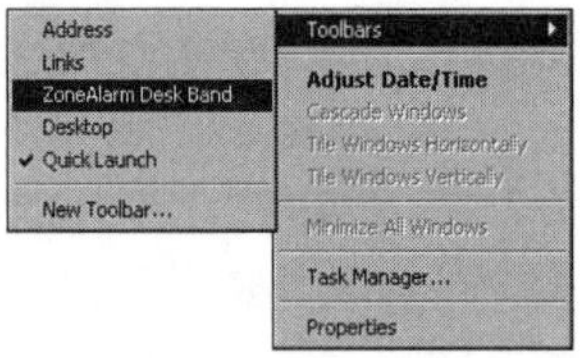

FIGURE 8.18

Configuring the ZoneAlarm Desk Band toolbar.

3. Select the ZoneAlarm Desk Band option. The toolbar appears on top of the Windows task bar, as shown in Figure 8.19.

FIGURE 8.19

The ZoneAlarm Desk Band toolbar.

The ZoneAlarm Desk Band toolbar provides single-click access to each of the icons on the ZoneAlarm main dialog box without taking up any space on the Windows desktop. I find that it provides very convenient access to ZoneAlarm and suggest that you use it at least for the first month or two after installing ZoneAlarm when

you'll probably find yourself interacting the most with the firewall. The first icon in the toolbar displays a graphic view of the current network activity. The next icon shows whether the firewall is in a locked status. When locked, a red X is superimposed on top of the lock icon when the lock is active. The third icon displays a red stop icon when the firewall stopped. An icon for each open Internet application appears next, followed by the ZoneAlarm icon.

ZoneAlarm's Alerts and Log File

ZoneAlarm can provide detailed information about events as they occur in two ways. It can log them to a file to maintain a running history of event information. It can also display event messages in the form of pop-up alerts as they occur. Each of these options is examined in the sections that follow.

Some people find enabling ZoneAlarm's popup alerts a bit irritating and turn them off as a result. I recommend against this. You will probably see a number of alerts in the first month or two after installing your firewall. However, once ZoneAlarm learns about all of your trusted applications things should quiet down a bit leaving only the more legitimate alert messages.

Working with ZoneAlarm's Log File

ZoneAlarm's log is configured from the Alerts Settings on the Alerts panel, as shown in Figure 8.20. From here, you can turn logging on and off and determine whether pop-up alerts display alert messages. In addition, the Delete Log button allows you to clear the log file when it becomes too large. I strongly recommend that you enable the logging of alerts and that you review your log on a regular basis.

FIGURE 8.20

ZoneAlarm's log is configured from the Alert Settings section of the Alerts panel.

Alert settings
☑ Log alerts to a text file
C:\WINNT\Internet Logs\ZALog.txt (13k)
☑ Show the alert popup window

(Delete Log)

Note
> You might want to make a copy of your log before deleting it. This will allow you to retain a log file history should you ever want to go back and research previous events.

The ZoneAlarm log is named ZALOG.TXT. On Windows 95, 98, and Me systems, the log is located in C:\Windows\Internet Logs. On Windows NT and 2000 systems, it is located in C:\Winnt\Internet Logs.

ZoneAlarm records three types of messages to its log:

- **FWIN**—Identifies a blocked incoming connection request.
- **FWOUT**—Indicates a blocked outbound connection request.
- **PE**—Identifies an application that is trying to connect to the Internet.

Some log messages include one or more TCP flags which provide additional information about the type of event that has occurred:

- **ACK**—The packet is an acknowledgement of data that was received.
- **FIN**—The packet represents a connection termination.
- **PSH**—The packet represents a "push" of data to an application.
- **RST**—The packet represents a connection reset.
- **SYN**—The packet represents a connection request.
- **URG**—The packet contains an urgent content.

When included as part of a log message only the first character of the TCP flag is shown. For example, (flags:A) indicates that the packet was an acknowledgement of data that has been received.

The following log examples are from a typical ZoneAlarm log. The first line identifies the version of ZoneAlarm that is being run.

```
ZoneAlarm Logging Client v2.6.88
```

The next line displays the operating system that is running.

```
Windows NT-5.0.2195--SP
```

Next you'll see a line that identifies the basic structure of a log entry.

```
type,date,time,source,destination,transport
```

From this point on, what you'll see in your ZoneAlarm log will vary based on your particular environment. For example, the following statement logs information about an application on the computer that tried to communicate with another computer on the Internet.

```
PE,2001/07/04,12:53:20 -4:00 GMT,Road Runner Medic MFC
Application,65.97.0.1:0,N/A
```

The previous example can be broken down as follows:

- **PE**—Identifies the type of log message.
- **2001/07/04**—Shows the date that the event occurred.
- **12:53:20**—Shows the local time that the event occurred.
- **-4:00 GMT**—Shows the GMT time that the event occurred.

- **Road Runner Medic MFC Application**—Identifies the application that triggered the event.
- **65.97.0.1:0**—Identifies the IP address and port number the application tried to use.
- **N/A**—No information was available for this field.

The next example shows a log entry where ZoneAlarm blocked an incoming connection request.

```
FWIN,2001/07/04,12:57:07 -4:00 GMT,24.30.225.31:0,65.97.0.75:0,ICMP
(type:3/subtype:3)
```

The previous example can be broken down as follows:

- **FWIN**—Identifies the type of log message.
- **2001/07/04**—Shows the date that the event occurred.
- **12:57:07**—Shows the local time that the event occurred.
- **-4:00 GMT**—Shows the GMT time that the event occurred.
- **24.30.225.31:0**—Identifies the IP address and port number of the Internet computer that triggered the event.
- **65.97.0.75:0**—Identifies the destination IP address and port number.
- **ICMP (type:3/subtype:3)**—Displays specific information about the TCP/IP transport protocol that was used to deliver the packet.

This final example shows a log message that includes a TCP flag parameter, which indicates a SYN type packet (for example, a connection request).

```
FWIN,2001/07/04,22:31:02 -4:00 GMT,207.33.111.34:44256,65.97.0.75:139,TCP
(flags:S)
```

Working with ZoneAlarm Alerts

In addition to log messages, you can configure ZoneAlarm to display message events in the form of pop-up alerts. You can enable alerting by selecting the Show the alert pop-up window option in the Alert Settings section of the Alerts panel.

ZoneAlarm alerts are composed of the following information:

- IP address
- Protocol and port
- Date and time
- TCP flag(s)

- Type of connection (incoming or outgoing)
- Application name version when available

ZoneAlarm creates two types of alerts: Program and Firewall.

Program Alerts

Program alerts report on the activity of software applications. There are four types of program alerts as listed here:

- New
- Changed
- Repeat
- Server

In addition, ZoneAlarm displays a More Info button with each alert that you can click to get more detailed information about the alert including advice on how to react to the alert. I recommend using this option anytime you are not sure what an alarm's message it telling you. It provides a great way to learn more about the inner workings of both your personal firewall and the Internet.

New Alerts

This type of alert is created the first time that an application attempts to access the Internet, as demonstrated in Figure 8.21. The alert prompts you to allow or deny the application access attempt.

FIGURE 8.21
ZoneAlarm creates a new alert any time an application tries to access the Internet for the first time.

Look under Technical Information to see the application's name and version number and the computer to which it is trying to connect. Click More Info to learn more about the alert. Clicking this button opens your Internet browser and the connection

to the Zone Labs Web site where the contents of the alert are analyzed and additional information provided.

To allow the application to make the connection, click Yes; to block it, click No. The Remember this answer the next time you use this program button allows you to tell the firewall to always allow the application to access the Internet.

Changed Alerts

This type of alert is very rare and might indicate a worm or Trojan horse program. I'd pay extra attention to one of these alerts if it appears. It appears only when the firewall detects a program trying to access the Internet that already is approved but that has been changed in some manner. Examples of changes include:

- A change in the program name
- A change in program file size or location
- A change in the program's version number
- A change in the program's executable name

Repeat Alerts

A repeat alert occurs when ZoneAlarm intercepts an application that has run before but that has not been configured as a permanently trusted application, as demonstrated in Figure 8.22. Here the application in question is named Road Runner Medic MFC.

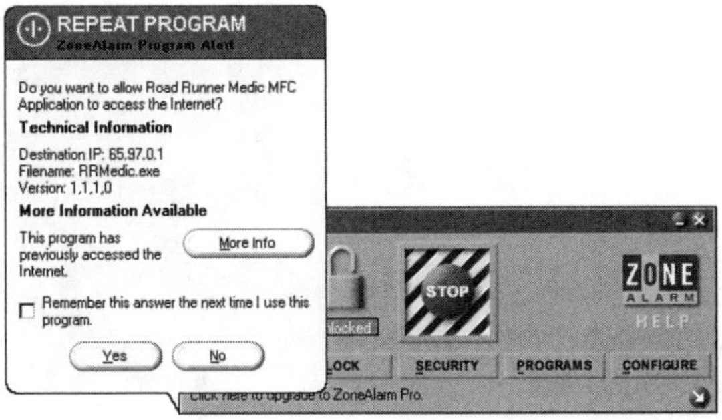

FIGURE 8.22

ZoneAlarm creates a repeat alert when it intercepts a known program that has not been configured for automatic access to the Internet.

Server Alerts

A server alert, shown in Figure 8.23, occurs when a program attempts to act like a server, meaning that it wants to accept connections from the Internet.

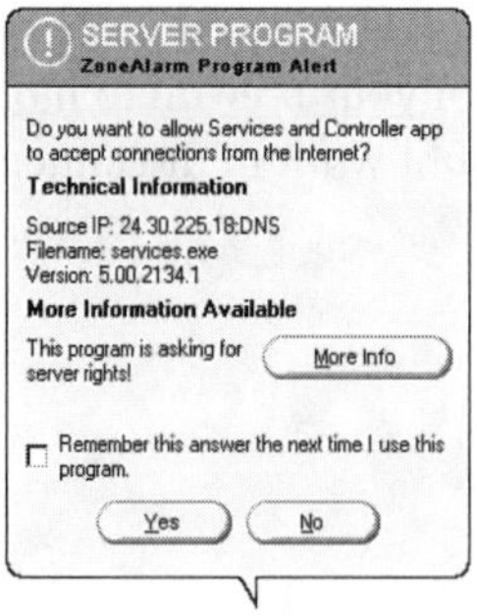

FIGURE 8.23
ZoneAlarm cre-
ates a server
alert for any
program that
wants to act as
an Internet
server.

Firewall Alerts

Firewall alerts look a lot like program alerts but provide information about incoming packets that appear threatening to your computer. There are two types of firewall alerts: Cautious and Urgent.

Cautious Firewall Alerts

A cautious alert indicates the occurrence of an event that is deemed as potentially
threatening but not immediately threatening to your computer. Figure 8.24 shows a
cautious alert. Its heading is displayed in orange. Its information includes the source
IP address and transport protocol as well as the date and time that the event
occurred.

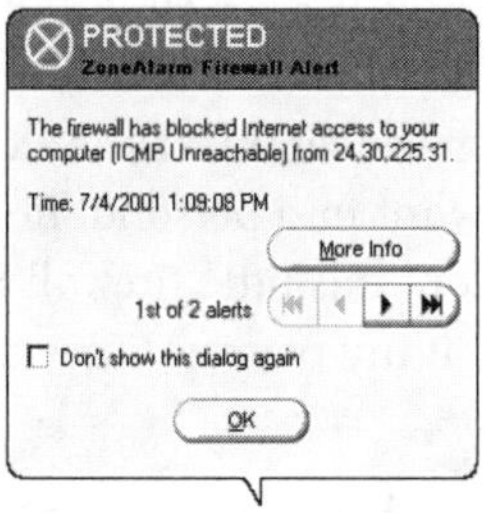

FIGURE 8.24
Cautious fire-
wall alerts are
warnings of
potential
trouble.

Urgent Firewall Alerts

An urgent alert appears with a red heading and indicates a more serious threat than
a cautious alert. For example, Figure 8.25 shows an alert that was generated as a
result of an Internet scan that was run against the local computer. It displays the
name and IP address of the scanning system and the protocol and port that was
scanned. A scan such as this may indicate a hacker trying to gather information
about your computer as a prelude to a more serious attack. The firewall has blocked
the scan so no further action is required on your part. However, if you begin seeing

repeated alerts reporting the same origination source you may be under an attack. You might want to increase the security level of your firewall to high if it is not already set to that setting. Optionally, you might want to disconnect from the Internet for a while.

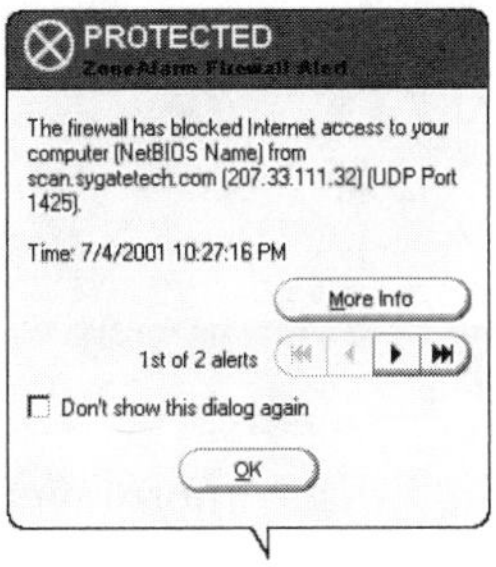

FIGURE 8.25

Urgent firewall alerts indicate immediate threats to your computer.

ZoneAlarm's Limitations

ZoneAlarm contains the most intuitive interface of any of the personal firewall products reviewed in this book. This makes it an excellent candidate for beginner users who may feel uncomfortable working with more technically oriented personal firewalls such as BlackICE Defender. In addition, it provides a strong defense against Internet hackers. It comes pre-configured with a set of security policies that Zone Labs considers appropriate for home users.

ZoneAlarm does not have a built-in configuration wizard. However, its intuitive interface and pre-configured security settings mitigate the need for such a tool.

Despite its small size and somewhat smaller set of features, ZoneAlarm manages to provide all the essential functions that you'll want in a personal firewall. In fact, with the exception of built-in intrusion detection, this little firewall has it all. Best of all ZoneAlarm is free for personal use making it my personal firewall of choice.

Testing Your Zone Labs Personal Firewall

After installing and configuring your Zone Labs Personal Firewall, you should test it to make sure that it is running and that it is protecting your computer appropriately. You can do this by starting your Internet browser and determining whether you can connect to the Internet. After you are successful with this test, start a different Internet application for the first time and see whether ZoneAlarm intercepts it. When it does, tell ZoneAlarm that you want to work with the application. You will likely see its icon appear in the Programs section of the ZoneAlarm main dialog box and it should work as expected from this point on.

Next, try another Internet application, one that you do not want to allow through the firewall. For example, if you have installed Microsoft's NetMeeting but do not plan on using it for a while or do not want your children using it, you can block it. When you start NetMeeting, ZoneAlarm will intercept it and allow you the opportunity to mark it as an application that should be prevented from communicating with the Internet. Verify that ZoneAlarm does block its access. You should get an error message from the application.

If you have any problems with one of the previous tests, try turning ZoneAlarm's security setting down a notch and see what happens. After everything is working correctly, try running an Internet scan against your computer to see how well ZoneAlarm's defenses stand up.

Refer to Chapter 9, "How Secure Is Your Computer?," for information about how to run and analyze the results of a free Internet scan. In addition, Appendix B, "Other Web Sites That Will Test Your Security," provides you with a number of free Internet sites where you can go to further test your Internet security.

HOW SECURE IS YOUR COMPUTER?

y now, you should have decided upon a personal firewall and installed and configured both it and your Windows operating system. It is now time to put your hard work to the test. This chapter steps you through the process of running three Internet security tests to help determine just how secure your Internet connection really is.

All these tests are free. To keep things simple and straightforward, this chapter uses three tests provided by the same Internet security Web site. The Web site is grc.com and it is provided as a service of the Gibson Research Corporation.

- ■ Learn how to run an Internet security scan and analyze its results
- ■ See how to run a scan that probes your TCP/IP ports
- ■ Learn how to run a test that simulates a Trojan horse

Testing Your Vulnerability to Internet Hackers

There is no way to know how secure your defenses are without testing them. This chapter helps you to do just that using two free Internet security scans and a software utility provided by the grc.com Web site. The first two tests run while the computer's personal firewall is disabled. This shows you the security vulnerabilities exposed by the computer under normal conditions. Windows 2000 Professional is used to run all tests in this chapter. This operating system is much more secure than any of the Windows 95, 98, or Me operating systems and will automatically start the computer off with higher security defense.

The second set of tests run after enabling a personal firewall. This chapter uses the ZoneAlarm Personal Firewall when conducting these tests; however, you can substitute any personal firewall.

The final test is a Trojan horse simulation using a free utility from grc.com called LeakTest. This little program attempts to breach your Internet security by breaking out from your computer to the Internet where it then connects to a server at grc.com and transfers a few harmless bytes of information.

Performing a Free Security Scan

Before initiating the first scan, disable your personal firewall. Because this chapter is using ZoneAlarm, you do this by right-clicking the ZoneAlarm icon in the Windows system tray and selecting Shutdown ZoneAlarm. You then click Yes when prompted for confirmation. Once your firewall is disabled, you can run the scan using the following steps:

1. Open your Internet browser and load the grc.com Web site.
2. After the site is loaded, click the Shields UP! link. This will open the Shields UP! main Web page. Scroll down until you see the Test My Shields! and Probe My Ports! options, as shown in Figure 9.1.
3. To perform a general test of your computer's defenses, click the Test My Shields! button.

Without an active firewall to protect your computer, the test will run very quickly, usually within a few moments. The first thing that you will see displayed is your IP

address and a message that asks you to stand by while the Shields UP! Web server tries to connect to your computer. If successful, the server will continue to probe your defenses in an effort to learn more about your computer and its shared resources.

As Figure 9.2 shows, the Shields UP! Server was able to connect to the computer using NetBIOS port 139.

FIGURE 9.1

The grc.com Web site provides two Internet security tests.

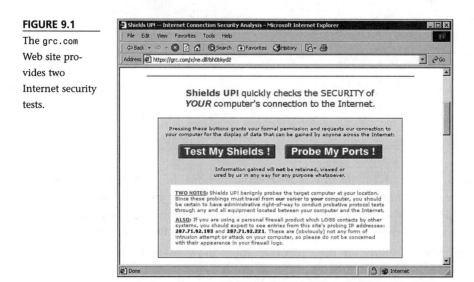

FIGURE 9.2

This computer, like most unprotected Windows computers, will accept a connection request from an unknown computer on the Internet.

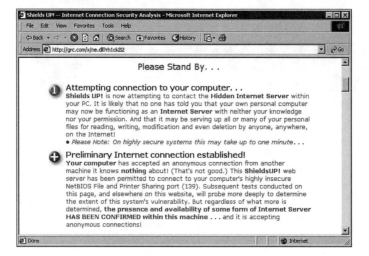

Next, a report of the rest of the security scan is displayed. Figure 9.3 shows that TCP/IP is bound to NetBIOS, allowing anyone on the Internet to view the computer and its shared resources.

FIGURE 9.3

When TCP/IP is bound to NetBIOS, your computer is more than happy to share information about itself with any computer on the Internet that cares to ask.

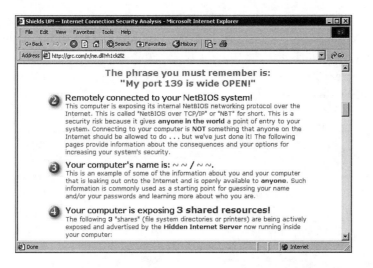

The scan was unable to determine the computer's name in this test. This is good because the less information that hackers can learn about you, the less information they will have when launching attacks. Unfortunately, the scan reveals that it was able to view all three of the shared resources belonging to the computer.

The next item displayed in the report is a graphical representation of the shared resources uncovered by the scan as shown in Figure 9.4. As you can see, Windows 2000 has protected these shared resources with a password. This might not be the case had this been a Windows 95, 98, or Me system.

FIGURE 9.4

All the computer's shared resources have been discovered, giving a would-be hacker targets to attack.

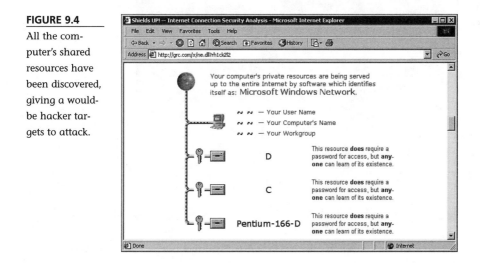

Next you'll see in Figure 9.5 that the MAC address of the computer's NIC has been uncovered as well. Even if your IP address changes over time, as is the case with dial-up connections, your MAC address remains constant, giving a hacker a means of identifying you.

FIGURE 9.5

Your NIC's MAC is a 48-bit number that uniquely identifies it from every other NIC.

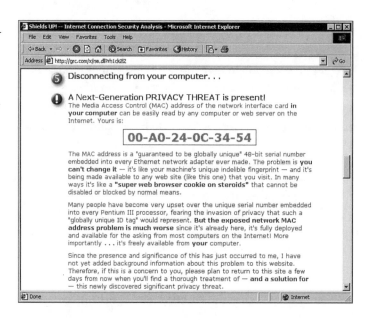

The last portion of the report, shown in Figure 9.6, provides a summary of the scan's results. The report states that the scan was able to connect to the computer and gain information about it. It also states that automated hacking tools can be used to roam the Internet and seek out targets that provide connections.

FIGURE 9.6

The final portion of the report provides a summary of the scan's results.

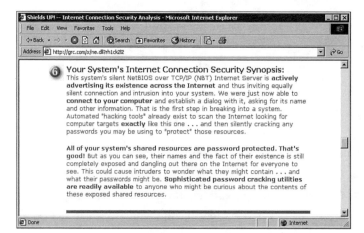

The report also warns that password-cracking programs may be used against your computer to attempt to break your passwords. Had this been a Windows 95, 98 or Me computer, it would have been especially vulnerable to such a password-cracking attack.

Port Probing

The results of the first Internet scan are less than encouraging because they show that the computer is ready to give away too much information about itself. To complete the analysis of the computer's defenses, run an Internet scan specifically designed to probe the computer's TCP/IP ports.

This can be done from the grc.com Web site by clicking the Probe My Ports! button on the Shields UP! Web page. This is by no means a complete port probe. It is a sampling of ports that are commonly left open. Refer to Appendix B, "Other Web Sites That Will Test Your Security," to find information about other Internet security Web sites that provide more exhaustive port-scanning services.

Figures 9.7 and 9.8 show the results of the port scan. All ports are closed except for port 139. The ports are listed as closed because there are no applications or services set up on this computer that use them. However, having port 139 open is bad enough to justify concern.

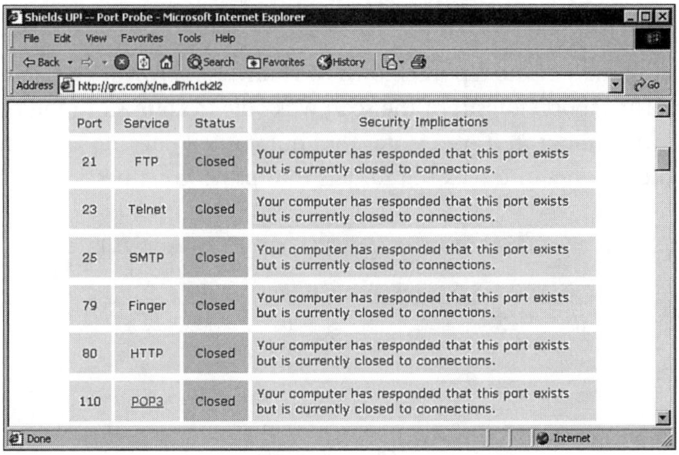

FIGURE 9.7

The ports shown in this list all have a status of closed.

The Shields Up! port scan labels ports using one of three statuses:

- **Open**—The port is open and accepting connections.
- **Closed**—The port is visible but is refusing incoming connection requests.
- **Stealth**—The port is invisible and cannot be detected from the Internet.

FIGURE 9.8

This list shows that the NetBIOS port 139 is wide open and accepting connection requests.

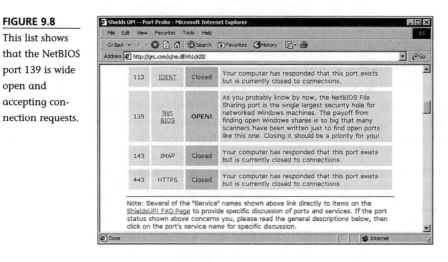

Open ports are exactly what Internet scanners are looking for and can quickly bring your computer to a hacker's attention. Closed ports are a definite improvement but still make their presence known. Port stealth can only be achieved using a personal firewall. If all the ports are running in stealth mode then your computer is invisible for all practical purposes.

Testing with Your Personal Firewall Up and Running

The next two tests are a repeat of the first two except that this time the computer's personal firewall is enabled. In the case of the ZoneAlarm Personal Firewall you can turn it back on by clicking Start, Programs, Zone Labs and then ZoneAlarm. All tests that follow use ZoneAlarm's default Internet security setting of High, as shown in Figure 9.9. Lowering this setting will, of course, lower the security protection provided by the firewall and potentially expose your computer to more threats.

FIGURE 9.9

By default ZoneAlarm configures its Internet security to its highest setting.

Rerunning the Internet Scan

When the first scan is rerun, the Shields UP! Internet scan takes considerably longer to run. This is because the computer's personal firewall is blocking the scanning service's attempts to penetrate your defenses. In fact, after about a minute, the scan is terminated and displays the results shown in Figure 9.10.

FIGURE 9.10

With the ZoneAlarm Personal Firewall in place, the scanning service was unable to establish a connection with the computer.

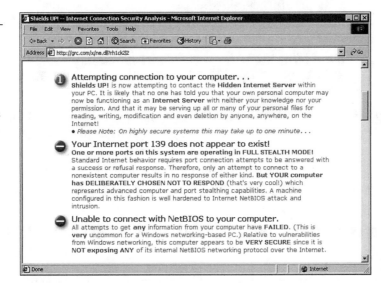

The report states that port 139, which had been open and accepting connections in the previous test, is not visible to the scanning service. In this test, the Shields UP! scanning services was unable to penetrate the personal firewall and gave the computer a very secure rating.

Probing Your Ports a Second Time

The fourth test involves a rerun of the Probe My Ports! Test with the ZoneAlarm Personal Firewall enabled. As you might expect, the results of this test reveal that none of the ports are open. In fact, all the computer ports were listed with a status of stealth this time, as demonstrated in Figure 9.11.

FIGURE 9.11

This time the computers ports ran in stealth mode and were invisible to the port scanner.

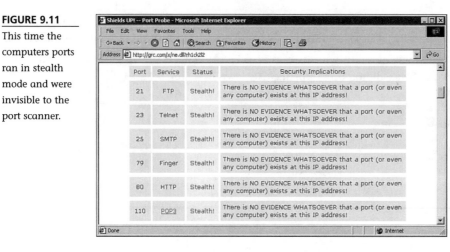

Testing Security from the Inside Out

So far, this chapter has discussed Internet security from the context of keeping the bad guys out of your computer. This is, of course, the correct strategy. But by itself, it's not good enough because sometimes the security breach lies within. A Trojan horse is a perfect example of a hacker tool that threatens your security from inside your computer. In the event that your personal firewall lets one sneak by and your antivirus scanner fails to detect such a program, you'll need a second defense.

This second line of defense is provided in the form of outbound traffic monitoring and filtering. For example, both the McAfee Firewall and ZoneAlarm monitor all application communications and block unauthorized applications running on your computer from initiating connections to the Internet. When an application attempts such a connection, it is temporarily blocked and you are notified and given the opportunity to decide whether access should be granted.

Note

BlackICE Defender operates under a different principle than the McAfee Personal Firewall and ZoneAlarm. Instead of filtering specific TCP/IP protocols and applications, it analyzes every data packet looking for potential threats. This firewall is designed to block any known threat and supports the establishment of trusted and non-trusted applications. The LeakTest utility, discussed in this section, is not flagged by BlackICE Defender as a security threat because it does not actually perform any threatening activity.

To determine whether your personal firewall is vulnerable to Trojan horse attacks, download the free LeakTest utility from `grc.com` located at `grc.com/lt/leaktest.htm`. LeakTest is a very simple tool that allows you to emulate a Trojan horse program.

LeakTest works by acting like an FTP client that attempts to establish a connection using port 21. If successful, it passes a few bytes of information to a server at grc.com.

After you download it, you can run LeakTest by double-clicking it. The Firewall Leakage Tester dialog box appears, as shown in Figure 9.12.

FIGURE 9.12

Running the free LeakTest Trojan horse test utility.

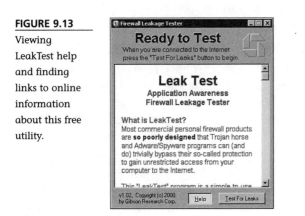

To learn more about the LeakTest utility, click Help, as shown in Figure 9.13. In addition to a brief explanation of the utility, you will find links to information on LeakTest Web pages.

FIGURE 9.13

Viewing LeakTest help and finding links to online information about this free utility.

To run the test, click Test for Leaks. The current version of McAfee Personal Firewall and ZoneAlarm will both block LeakTest's attempt to connect to the Internet.

If you are running BlackICE Defender, LeakTest will succeed in establishing an Internet connection. Remember, BlackICE Defender does not consider LeakTest to be a security threat.

However, running LeakTest this way is not much of a test. The utility is described as a Trojan horse test program. Because Trojan horses usually sneak onto your hard drive and rename themselves so that they appear as a legitimate program, you should rename LeakTest to a name used by one of your Internet applications that is allowed through your personal firewall. For example, try renaming LeakTest with a name such as Internet Explorer and running it again.

Figure 9.14 shows the message displayed by LeakTest when it is blocked from making a connection to the Internet. Hopefully, your personal firewall correctly realized that the copy of LeakTest was really a different program and blocked it. You should also see a pop-up dialog box from your personal firewall informing you of the connection attempt. If it did not, either your personal firewall's security settings are too low or it was unable to detect the security breach.

FIGURE 9.14

LeakTest has been blocked by the personal firewall from connecting to the Internet.

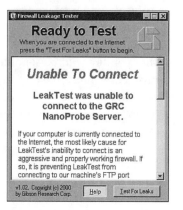

Figure 9.15 shows the message displayed by LeakTest when it is successful in breaching your personal firewall.

The current version of McAfee Personal Firewall and ZoneAlarm are successful in blocking LeakTest. However, versions of the McAfee Personal Firewall prior to version 2.15 have proven vulnerable to the test.

If you are using a version of the McAfee Personal Firewall older than 2.15 you should update your personal firewall immediately!

FIGURE 9.15

LeakTest has breached your defenses and sent information to another computer on the Internet.

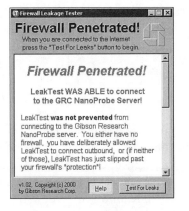

LeakTest also provides a stealth mode, which you can turn on by pressing and holding the Shift key when clicking the Test For Leaks button. When running in stealth mode, the title in the LeakTest title bar changes to indicate this. Unfortunately, no information is available about the differences between these modes.

A Final Analysis

The personal firewall is a relatively new software and hardware product. As such, personal firewall products are constantly being improved and updated. Some products are more mature than others and you should not assume that all firewall products are equal. It is therefore important that you test your personal firewall as soon as you get it up and running. If it performs poorly, it may be that its security settings are set too low and that you can raise them and get better protection. However, it might also be that the personal firewall is not yet ready for prime time. The tests listed in this chapter as well as those listed in Appendix B provide you with the tools for making your own determination.

HABITS OF SECURITY-CONSCIOUS SURFERS

*T*he Internet represents a great leap in human communications. It enables people across the globe to communicate and access information that only a few years ago would have been nearly impossible. Surfing the World Wide Web is an individual experience and it is easy to get lost in the millions of Web sites awaiting you. However, it is very important that you remember that even when you are all alone on your computer surfing the Web, you are never really alone. You are surrounded by millions of other people all sharing and working over the same network.

On the surface, a personal firewall might seem like an unnecessary piece of hardware or software to many users. It does not provide an obvious service such as helping you to do your taxes or kill space aliens. It does not publish Web pages or help you earn money. It just sits there, usually completely unnoticed. It is imperative therefore that people come to understand the inherent dangers of their environment.

This book has endeavored to demonstrate the dangers posed to your computer when it is attached to the Internet, especially when you are connecting via a cable or DSL high-speed connection, and to show you how you can use a personal firewall to protect yourself. The purpose of this chapter is to provide you with additional recommendations that you can use to further strengthen your defenses.

■ Learn how to keep your Microsoft operating system current

■ Learn more about the threats posed by computer viruses and how you can try to vaccinate yourself against them

■ Examine the importance of keeping your firewall's defenses up-to-date

■ Examine other types of Internet threats and how you can combat them

Updating Your Personal Firewall

Most personal firewalls provide a means of keeping themselves updated over time. As they are your primary line of defense against Internet hackers, it is absolutely critical that you keep your personal firewall updated. All three of the personal firewalls covered in this book enable you to apply updates to them. The process of updating each one is outlined in the following sections.

Updating McAfee Personal Firewall

When you purchase the McAfee Personal Firewall you are automatically entitled to one free product upgrade, which must occur within 90 days of purchase. This ensures that you are running the most current version of the firewall. McAfee makes downloads available from its Web site.

Unfortunately, the McAfee Personal Firewall does not have a built-in mechanism for notifying you when an update becomes available. Therefore, you have to visit www.mcafee.com and look for yourself. You can apply the update that you download by double-clicking it and following the instructions that appear. You'll probably have to reboot afterward.

Updating BlackICE Defender

You can set up BlackICE Defender to notify you whenever an update to the personal firewall is available, as described in Chapter 7, "BlackICE Defender." BlackICE Defender notifies you that an update is available by displaying an NI icon in the upper-right corner of its main dialog box. To apply the update, simply click the icon and follow the instructions that are presented.

If you prefer, you can disable the automatic update feature and perform a manual check. To manually initiate an update, click the Download Update option on the BlackICE Defender Tools menu. The firewall then connects to the Network ICE Web site and determines whether a new update is available. If one is available, you are prompted to install it.

Updating ZoneAlarm

You can set up ZoneAlarm to notify you whenever an update to the personal firewall is available, as described in Chapter 8, "ZoneAlarm." To download updates from the ZoneLabs Web site, you must first register your copy of ZoneAlarm, which you are given the opportunity to do during installation. You can also request that ZoneLabs notify you each time a new update is available.

In addition, you can manually check for new firewall updates by clicking the Check for Update option on the ZoneAlarm Configuration panel. ZoneAlarm then connects to the ZoneLabs Web site and determines whether a new update is available. If one is available, the Get Update button on the Configuration panel is enabled. Click it to initiate the update process.

Keeping Your Microsoft Operating System Up-to-Date

With the arrival of high-speed Internet access, people are beginning to realize the importance of personal firewalls. However, even the most security-conscious home users often tend to overlook one of the most basic defenses: keeping their operating systems up-to-date.

Security holes are constantly being found in every software product, including your operating system. Microsoft aggressively addresses these problems as they are discovered. It then publishes free fixes, updates, and services packs on its Web site that you can download and install to plug these holes.

You might be wondering why you need to worry about holes in your operating system now that you have installed your personal firewall. After all, nothing is going to breach your security now, right? Well, let's hope not. However, over time, hackers develop new techniques for penetrating computer systems. After a new hacking technique is identified, your personal firewall developer will probably address it quickly. However, until you download and install the update, you are vulnerable to the new type of attack. Therefore, if someone should break through your personal firewall, you'll want to make sure that you haven't made things easy for the hacker. You can do this by locking down any known holes in your operating system.

Since the arrival of Windows 98, Microsoft has incorporated a new feature in its operating systems called Windows Update that makes it easy to keep your particular operating system updated. You can find the Windows Update on your Windows Start menu. When you click it, Windows opens your Web browser and loads the Windows Update site that applies to your particular Microsoft operating system.

The following procedure outlines the steps involved in using the Windows Update feature using Windows 2000 Professional as an example.

1. Click Start and then Windows Update. Internet Explorer starts and loads the Microsoft Windows Update site appropriate for your operating system as demonstrated in Figure 10.1.

FIGURE 10.1

Each Windows operating system Update Web site provides a single location for finding and downloading fixes for that particular operating system.

2. Click Products Updates. The first time that you use Windows Update, the dialog box shown in Figure 10.2 appears. Click Yes.

FIGURE 10.2

The first time you use Windows Update the Security Warning dialog box appears.

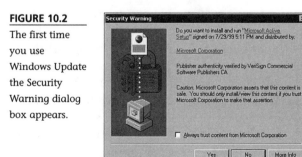

3. Information is collected about your operating system. This information is used by the Windows Update Web site to determine which updates have not been applied to your computer. Within a few moments, a list of software updates that are applicable to your computer are displayed, as shown in Figure 10.3.

FIGURE 10.3

The Windows Update Site analyzes your operating system and presents a listing of updates applicable to your computer.

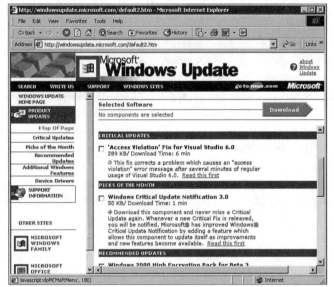

The Windows Update site organizes its list of available updates into different categories. These categories include

- Critical Updates
- Picks of the Month
- Recommended Updates
- Additional Windows Features
- Device Drivers

4. Pay special attention to updates in the Critical Updates and Recommended Updates categories and keep an eye out for any update that relates to fixing a security problem. If you find such an update you should apply it by selecting the update and clicking Download. A Web page will open requesting confirmation of the download.

5. Click Start Download to download and apply the update. You might see a license agreement dialog box appear depending on the update that you selected. If necessary, click Yes to accept the license agreement.

6. The update that you selected is downloaded and installed. Depending on the nature of the update, you might also be required to restart the computer.

Keeping Your Operating System Locked Down Tight

Windows operating systems are not very secure when connected to the Internet. Microsoft obviously recognizes this fact and it's beginning to take steps to address it with its new Windows XP Home operating system. Unless you have a home network you shouldn't need to run many of the networking components that you will find installed on your computer. As Chapter 4, "Locking Down Windows Networking" showed, you do not need the Client for Microsoft Networks and Windows file and printer sharing. Remove them. If you do have a home network, consider using NetBEUI as your home network protocol and removing TCP/IP from all computers except from the one connected to the Internet. If you insist on using TCP/IP as your local area networking protocol, use a firewall, such as ZoneAlarm, that permits you to define security settings for your home and Internet connections separately.

Another option is to consider purchasing a hardware firewall and using it as a barrier between your home network and the Internet. Check out Chapter 11, "Home Networks and Internet Connection Sharing," for more information about home networking.

If your wallet and your computer hardware will both support it, you should also consider upgrading to a more current Microsoft operating system. Windows NT Workstation and Windows 2000 Professional both allow you to require anyone who accesses your computer, either locally or via the Internet, to authenticate themselves. Built-in protection will lock out user accounts when a hacker attempts to run a password-cracking program against them. In addition, these two operating systems allow you to apply security permissions on all files and folders, making them much more secure than files and folders stored on Windows 95, 98, and Me systems.

The only drawback to Windows NT and 2000 is that they might not be 100% backward compatible with all your existing software. Some programs and many games will not work on computers running either of these two operating systems. However, Windows XP, which will be released in the latter part of 2001, will provide you with backwards compatibility to run your old software plus the industrial security and processing power provided by Windows NT and 2000.

You can eliminate another weak spot from your computer by uninstalling any Internet applications that you do not use. For example, if your computer has

Microsoft Personal Web Server installed but you do not use it, go to the Windows Control Panel and use the Add/Remove Programs utility to remove it.

Microsoft Personal Web Server is the "lite beer" of Internet Web servers. It allows you to turn an Internet connected home computer into a little Web server. Its features are limited but many people use it to prototype Web sites that they create before uploading them to a real Web server on the Internet. When active, the Personal Web Server is capable of accepting incoming connection requests and has been known to provide hackers with a back door into home computers.

Other things that you can do to tighten up your computer's security include:

- Password protecting any shared resources.
- Using strong passwords that include a mixture of upper- and lowercase letters as well as numbers and special characters.
- Never use names or words as passwords that any of the freely available password-cracking programs can easily break.
- Never use passwords that are derived from easily obtainable personal information—such as your name or the name of you children.
- Turn off your computer when you are not using it or invoke a personal firewall lock. Alternatively, you can activate a stronger set of personal firewall security policies.
- Take advantage of the encrypted file system (EFS) if you are running Windows 2000 or XP to encode your important files and folders.
- Remember to encrypt the Windows C:\Temp folder when EFS is available because Windows often places copies of files that you open in this folder when you work on them.
- Don't ignore your security just because you have a dial-up connection. You never know when you'll be logged on at the wrong place or the wrong time.

Using Antivirus Software

Computer viruses are software programs that are designed to attack your computer in a number of ways. Before they can strike, they must first sneak onto your system and infect it. They can do so in a number of ways. For example, computer viruses have been known to hide in files and programs downloaded from the Internet, in e-mail attachments, or on floppy disks. In some rare instances, computer viruses have even been known to originate from store-bought software programs.

When it comes to combating computer viruses, there is no substitute for a good virus scanner and a little common sense. The following list presents a number of good rules that you should following to prevent viruses from penetrating your defenses. These include:

- Avoid downloading files and programs from the Internet except from Web sites that you know you can trust.

- Never load a floppy disk received in the mail from someone that you do not know.

- Leave your antivirus scanner running all the time and set it to check everything.

- Download attachments to a temporary file and then run your virus scanner on them before opening them.

- Never open e-mail attachments from a stranger.

- Never open an unexpected e-mail attachment from a friend without first verifying that your friend actually sent it to you.

Some viruses infiltrate a computer's address book and send themselves to everyone listed there—meaning that the virus looks like a legitimate message from someone that the receiver knows!

Fighting Viruses

A *virus* is a program that hides inside another program in order to sneak its way onto your computer where it then hides. Viruses can also sneak onto your computer by hiding in the boot sector of a floppy disk. The boot sector is a small reserved area on a floppy or hard disk where small executable programs can reside. A virus hidden here is executed whenever the floppy disk is loaded. After it has started, the virus then moves to a new hiding place on your local hard drive, maybe even to the boot sector.

Viruses are pesky but smart little programs that usually don't strike right away. After all, striking too quickly might make it easier to track down and discover where they come from. They lie dormant until a specified event occurs such as a particular date or a computer reboot. A virus has two major functions. These are to reproduce and spread copies of themselves to other computer systems and networks and to perform whatever task they were designed to do such as deleting your hard disk or displaying irritating little messages.

Some viruses are so smart that they are able to strike without revealing their presence. For example, a virus might seek out your spreadsheets and randomly change one or two numbers. While the effects of such a change might be tremendous, many people will assume that the change was the result of their own error when they typed the data into the spreadsheet. Because these programs are so clever, the only way to catch them may be your antivirus program.

Viruses can spread in a number of ways, including:

- Hiding inside a file that is passed between multiple users
- Hiding in the boot sector of floppy disks
- Locating your address book and using its entries to e-mail itself to your friends and work associates

A recently popular new form of virus has emerged using Microsoft's VBA (Visual Basic for Applications) language. This language is fairly easy to master and is embedded into many Microsoft applications, including Word and Excel. VBA is intended to provide users with an easy to learn script language that can be used to create macros to automate the process of working with Microsoft Office products.

A *macro* is a small program that automates a particular application procedure. These viruses are typically transmitted as e-mail attachments and can be recognized by their .vbs file extension. Once it's on a user's computer, the virus raids the user's address book and sends copies of itself as attachments to listed addresses. These e-mails usually have a snappy title to help trick people into opening them. As soon as the .vbs attachment is opened, the VBA script runs and the virus is released to spread again.

Watch out for sneaky VBScript virus programs that try to fool you with clever filenames. For example, one might try to trick you into thinking that it is actually a Microsoft Word document by giving itself a filename such as filename.doc.vbs. Microsoft Word documents have a .doc file extension. However, Microsoft operating systems allow filenames to contain periods and only the text after the last period in the filename is considered to be its file extension. At first glance, many people see the .doc portion of the file name and overlook the fact that the file's real file extension is .vbs.

VBA macros are not especially complicated programs and can consist of just a few lines of program code. Microsoft Office programs support the use of macros. For example, you can create a macro for Microsoft Excel 2000 by starting Excel and selecting the macro option on the Tools menu. You then select one of the submenu options that appears, as shown in Figure 10.4.

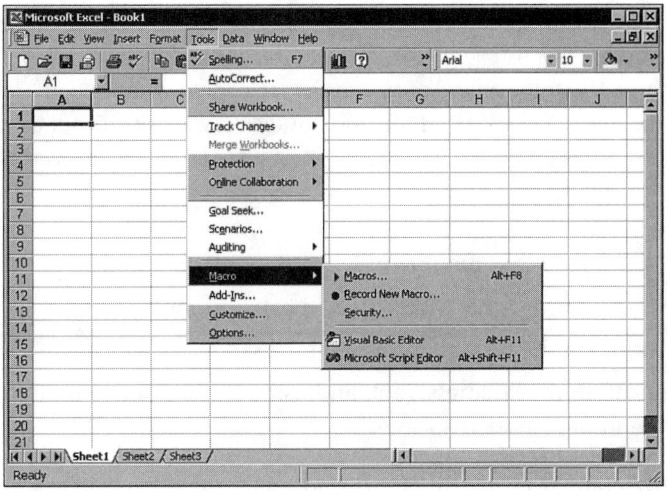

FIGURE 10.4

Creating a macro for use with Microsoft Excel 2000.

VBA code can also be embedded inside documents such as Microsoft Word and Excel files. This means that even .doc and .xls files can contains viruses.

If you do not write scripts or have other programs that depend upon them, you can disable Windows support for VBA by uninstalling the Windows Script Host using the following procedure.

1. Click Start, Settings, and then Control Panel.
2. Double-click Add/Remove programs.
3. Select the Setup property sheet.
4. Double-click Accessories.
5. Clear the entry for Windows Script Host and click OK.

Uninstalling the Windows Script Host is pretty harsh and can prevent other legitimate programs from operating correctly. After all, not all .vbs programs are going to be viruses. In fact very few of them are.

The ZoneAlarm Personal Firewall provides another option called MailSafe. It provides the capability to quarantine all e-mail that contains .vbs attachments and gives you the opportunity to first investigate their origin before deciding whether you want to run them. For more information on MailSafe, refer to Chapter 8.

Defeating Trojan Horses

A Trojan horse is a type of virus that sneaks its way onto your computer and seeks out your personal information, which it then tries to send to its creator. This makes

it very different from a traditional virus because the last thing that it wants to do is attract your attention by disrupting your computer system in any way.

Both the McAfee Personal Firewall and ZoneAlarm provide application filtering that allows you to specify which applications are allowed to traverse the firewall and which ones are not. Anytime an unknown application, such as a Trojan horse, attempts to connect to the Internet, it is temporarily blocked and you are prompted for instructions. This allows you the opportunity to insulate and remove Trojan horse programs. Because BlackICE Defender operates on a different security premise, it does not provide you with the capability to specify trusted and untrusted applications.

Your best bet in defending against Trojan horse programs is to use a personal firewall in combination with an antivirus program. The antivirus program attempts to prevent Trojan horse programs from getting loose on your computer. Should a Trojan horse program get past your antivirus program, your personal firewall will detect and block its attempt to call home to its creator.

Don't Become a Zombie—Help Prevent Distributed Denial-of-Service Attacks

A *zombie* is a computer in which a hacker has planted a Trojan horse-styled program that can be remotely activated and used to make the computer participate in a mass attack on an Internet server. As a zombie, your computer—along with dozens, hundreds, or thousands of other computers—is instructed to flood a particular Web site with service requests, eventually preventing the Internet site from being able to perform any real work. The best way to prevent this hijacking of your computer is to install a personal firewall and keep it regularly updated to defend against the latest types of distributed denial-of-services attacks.

Beware Cookies

Have you ever wondered how Web sites are able to welcome you back by name when you visit them again? This little trick is made possible through cookies. A *cookie* is a little record that Web sites can store on your computer when you visit their sites. A cookie can contain all sorts of information, including any preferences that you set at the Web sites or an ID and password that you specified while visiting the site. A cookie can also store information about what you did while you were at a particular Web site. For example, cookies can track the links that you clicked or the pictures that you viewed. In short, cookies can record a lot of information about your behavior.

Neither Microsoft Explorer nor Netscape Communicator deals with cookies very well. By default, both browsers allow cookies to be stored and retrieved. Both browsers also allow you to turn off cookie support. However, not all cookies are bad. Cookies that remember your user settings or record information that you do not want to have to retype each time you visit a Web site are very nice. However, many people detest the use of cookies that allow Web sites to track their behavior because it is really nobody's business.

Figure 10.5 shows Internet Explorer's Security property sheet. By default, the Internet zone is selected. At the bottom of the property sheet, the Security level for the Internet zone option is shown. By default it is set to Medium. By raising it to High, you can disable all cookies.

FIGURE 10.5

Configure Internet Explorer's support for cookies.

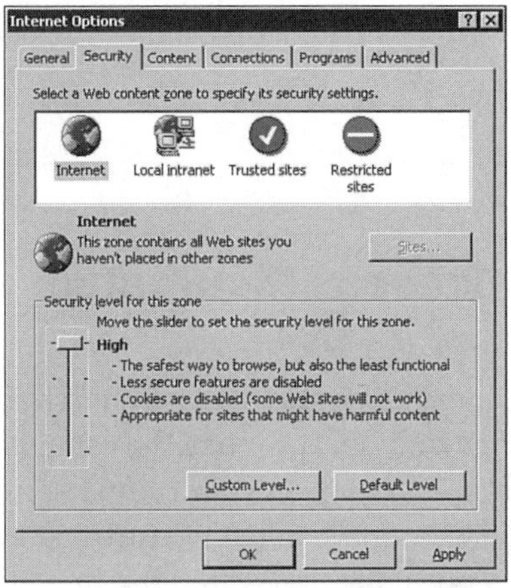

Likewise, Figure 10.6 Shows the Preferences dialog box in Netscape Communicator. Settings for controlling cookies are located under the Advanced category.

FIGURE 10.6

Configure Netscape Communicator's cookie settings.

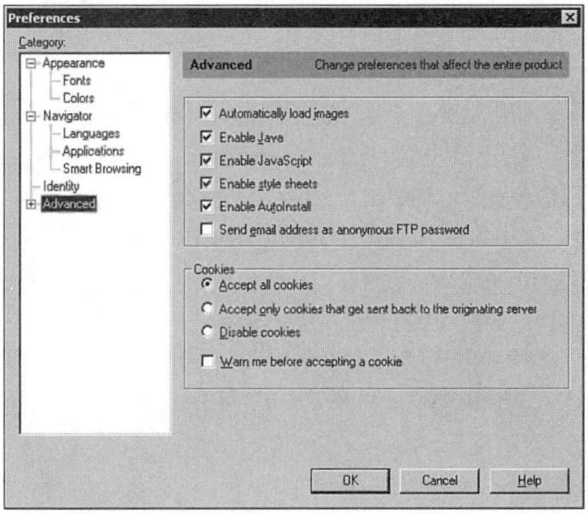

As you can see, Internet Explorer and Netscape Communicator provide limited control over cookies. Fortunately, there are other ways of dealing with cookies. Companies like Norton and McAfee both make software products designed to give you control over which Web sites are allowed to store cookies on your computer and when Web sites are allowed to retrieve cookies. For information on Norton Internet Security 2001, check out www.norton.com. For information on McAfee Watch Dog, refer to www.mcafee.com.

Backing Up Your Data

Although this book strives to help you strengthen your defenses when connected to the Internet, there is always the chance that some clever hacker will find a new way to break into your computer. If your personal data is viewed or even stolen, you should report the crime to your local ISP and perhaps even the authorities.

If the hacker's intent was merely to delete your hard drive or perform some similarly dastardly deed, you can always recover provided you make performing backups a part of your normal routine. With a good set of backups, you should always be able to restore your computer to its previous state.

Windows operating systems provide built-in backup programs. In addition, just about any backup device that you purchase has software of its own. Although you can back up your entire hard disk, all that you really need to copy is your data. After a second copy of your data is safely stored away, all you'll need to do to recover is reinstall your operating system and application using the CDs and floppy disks that contain them. Then install your backup program and use it to restore your data to its original location on your hard disk. Alternatively, if you do not have a tape drive or other backup device—but you do have a read-writeable CD drive— you can use it to store a backup copy of your personal data.

Although backups cannot prevent hackers from taking advantage of stolen data, they can ensure that you never lose access to your own work and give you a much safer feeling when leaving your computer connected to the Internet for long periods of time.

Be Vigilant and Test Often

To test your defenses, you will want to see your computer the same way that a hacker does. As Chapter 9, "How Secure Is Your Computer?" showed, you can do this by running a free Internet security scan against your computer. Appendix B, "Other Web Sites That Will Test Your Security," lists a number of Web sites that provide free scanning services. Many of these scans run in less than a minute. You should

consider running an Internet scan against your computer whenever any of the following conditions occur:

- To test the result of changes to security policies on your personal firewall.
- Anytime you install a new software that does not come from a reputable software developer.
- Anytime you suspect your computer has been compromised in some way or that it may contain a virus, Trojan horse, worm, or similar program.
- Anytime you notice your cable or DSL modem's display lights showing suspicious amounts of Internet activity when you are not actively surfing the Internet or downloading a file.

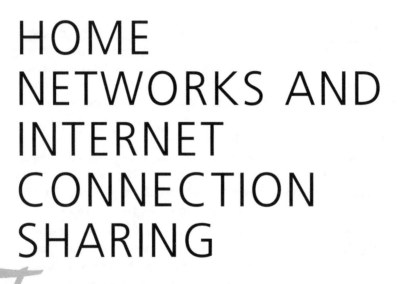

HOME NETWORKS AND INTERNET CONNECTION SHARING

*T*his chapter explains the basics of setting up and securing a home network using a combination of hardware and software personal firewalls. This chapter begins by explaining how the typical home network is configured. You'll learn the basics of creating your own network, including how to share and access network resources such as hard disk drives and printers.

After getting all the basics of home networking down, you'll see how easy it is to modify the network to include a shared high-speed Internet connection. In addition, a number of options and recommendations are presented for securing your network with personal firewalls.

- Review the basic features of home networks
- Learn how to set up your own home network
- Discover how to share disk and printer resources
- Learn how to share a high-speed Internet connection
- Learn different options for securing your home network's Internet connection

What Is a Home Network?

Home networks are just small peer-to-peer local area networks. A peer-to-peer network is one in which all participating computers are equal and control their own security and administrative settings. This is opposed to a client/server network, on which a central server or group of servers administers security for the network. Corporate computer networks are designed on the client/server model and can grow to include many thousands of computers. In contrast, the typical home network consists of 2 to 10 computers. Computers running Microsoft operating systems are designed to work on either type of network.

To set up a client/server-based network, you need at least one computer to be running Microsoft Windows NT 4 Server, Windows 2000 Server, or Windows XP Server. These operating systems cost a lot more, require an advanced level of networking knowledge and experience, and are overkill for home networks.

Each computer on a peer-to-peer network remains responsible for its own security. For Windows NT, 2000, and XP operating systems, this means that you must have a user account set up on each computer that you want to access from the network. For example, if your home network consists of four computers running a combination of these three operating systems, you need an individually configured user account on every machine to log in to the network from the machine. After you're logged in, access is automatically granted to the network.

Windows 95, 98, and Me systems do not require that you authenticate yourself by supplying a username and password. In fact, you can simply click Cancel when prompted to log in and each of these operating systems will happily give you access to every resource on the computer. Obviously, a peer-to-peer network consisting entirely of Windows NT, 2000, and XP systems is going to be more secure than one that includes other Windows operating systems.

Tip

If you have at least one Windows NT, 2000, or XP system, place your most important data there to keep it more secure.

There are two phases to the creation of a home peer-to-peer network: hardware setup and software configuration.

This chapter moves pretty fast through the process of building a home network and assumes a little previous experience on the part of the reader. If you feel that you need additional information beyond what is provided here, check out *Practical Microsoft Windows Peer Networking,* by Jerry Lee Ford, Jr. and published by Que; ISBN: 0-7897-2233-X.

Putting Your Network Together

You are going to need a number of pieces of hardware to connect all your computers into a home network. For each computer on the network, you need to purchase a NIC (network interface card) and a RJ-45 twisted-pair cable. In addition, you will want to purchase a small network hub. The hub is used to connect each computer to the network. This type of network has a star topology. The term topology refers to the physical layout of your network. In the case of a star topology, all computers connect to a central point. Figure 11.1 depicts a typical home network consisting of four computers and a small network hub.

FIGURE 11.1
A depicture of a typical home network consisting of four personal computers and a network hub.

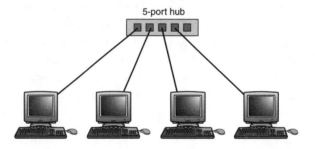

As you can see, the hub ties the network together and ensures that each computer can communicate with every other computer. Assemble your network using the following steps:

1. Centrally locate the network hub and attach its power supply.

2. Power down each computer and install its NIC.

3. Attach each computer to the hub using a RJ-45 twisted-pair cable.

4. Power on each computer and let Windows plug and play take over from here.

Network Software Configuration

As long as plug and play can auto-detect your NIC cards, each computer's Windows operating system should automatically install them. You will be prompted to supply

the CD or disk that accompanied each NIC in order to load the software driver that Windows needs when communicating with the NIC.

As part of the NIC installation process, each Windows operating system will automatically configure itself to join a Microsoft network. Since the introduction of Windows 98, all Microsoft operating systems have been designed to automate their connection to a Microsoft client/server or peer-to-peer TCP/IP based network. In fact, you will find that each computer automatically configures its network connection, leaving you with just a few administrative tasks.

Here is what happens. Your Windows 98, Me, 2000, or XP computer detects the new NIC. It then automatically installs the following software:

- **NIC software driver**—A piece of software provided by the NIC manufacturer that tells Windows how to communicate with the NIC.

- **TCP/IP**—Windows default networking protocol.

- **Client for Microsoft Networks**—Software that enables the computer to communicate with other computers on your home network.

When TCP/IP is installed, it is automatically configured to look for a DHCP server on the local area network and to ask it for an IP address. Because this is a home network you won't have a DHCP server, each Windows computer automatically assigns its own TCP/IP configuration. By default, each computer assigns itself an IP address between 169.254.0.1 and 169.254.0.255. This places each computer on a TCP/IP network of 169.254.0.0. By assigning itself to the same network, each computer ensures that it can communicate with the other computers on the network.

If you are still running Windows 95 on one of your computers you will have to perform a few additional steps. Windows 95 should be able to automatically use plug and play to detect and install its NIC. However, instead of installing TCP/IP, it installs the NetBEUI network protocol. Therefore, you need to manually install and configure TCP/IP, which you can do from the Networking dialog box found in the Windows 95 Control Panel. You also have to manually assign the computer's TCP/IP configuration. Make sure that you assign your Windows 95 computer an IP address in the range of 169.254.0.1 – 169.254.0.255. If you need more help on how to configure TCP/IP on Windows 95, I suggest you refer to *Practical Microsoft Windows Peer Networking*, ISBN: 0-7897-2233-X.

After each Windows computer has configured its new NIC and network connection, your network should be ready to go.

You don't need to concern yourself with the actual IP addresses assigned to your computers. However, if you simply have to know, you can find out a Windows Me, 2000, or XP computer's IP address assignment by typing **IPCONFIG /ALL** at the Windows

command prompt. On Windows 95 and 98 systems, type **WINIPCFG**. More information on how to use the commands is available in Chapter 2, "High-Speed Internet Connections Equal Increased Vulnerability."

 You can test your network's connectivity by sitting at one of its computers and pinging the IP address of the other computers on the network. PING is a TCP/IP command that tests the communications between two computers. For example, after figuring out the IP address assigned to another network computer, open a Windows command prompt by clicking on Start, Programs, Accessories and then Command Prompt and then typing **PING 169.254.0.X** (*X* represents the last part of the other computer's IP address), and press Enter.

Network Administration

At this point, the home network is physically assembled and each computer should be able to talk to every other computer using TCP/IP. However, before you can use your home network, you need to complete a few tasks. These tasks include:

- Naming your computers and setting up a workgroup
- Sharing disks and folders
- Sharing printers

Setting Up Workgroup and Computer Names

Microsoft peer-to-peer networks are based on a workgroup model. A workgroup is simply a logical organization of computers into groups. By placing computers into workgroups, you make it a little easier for members of the same workgroup to find each other's disk drives and printers. For example, when you double-click the Network Neighborhood on a Windows 95 or 98 computer, the first thing you see is a listing of all the computers in your workgroup. To see a list of other workgroups, you must click the Entire Network icon. Things work similarly in other Windows operating systems. For example, with four computers you might want to organize your network into two workgroups—parents and kids—as depicted in Figure 11.2. You can make the two computers used by the children members of the kids workgroup and the other two computers members of the parents workgroup.

However, setting up two workgroups is usually overkill on a home network and a single workgroup will suffice. Figure 11.3 depicts a home network of four personal computers, all of which are part of the same workgroup.

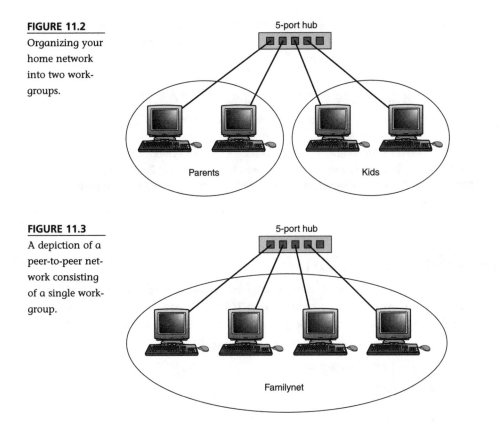

FIGURE 11.2

Organizing your home network into two workgroups.

FIGURE 11.3

A depiction of a peer-to-peer network consisting of a single workgroup.

A workgroup name can be anything you want, as long as it's limited to 15 characters. For example, the workgroup depicted in Figure 11.3 is named FAMILYNET.

In addition to defining a common workgroup for your home network, you must also ensure that each computer has a unique computer name. This name can consist of up to 15 alphanumeric characters. The following procedure outlines how to configure computer and workgroup names on Windows 95, 98, Me, or NT computers on your home network.

1. Click Start, Settings, Control Panel, and then double-click the Network icon. The Network dialog box appears.

2. Select the Identification property sheet, as shown in Figure 11.4.

3. Type the computer name and workgroup name that you want to assign to the computer in the computer name and workgroup fields and click OK.

4. Click Yes when prompted to restart your computer.

FIGURE 11.4

Naming your
computer and
assigning it to a
workgroup.

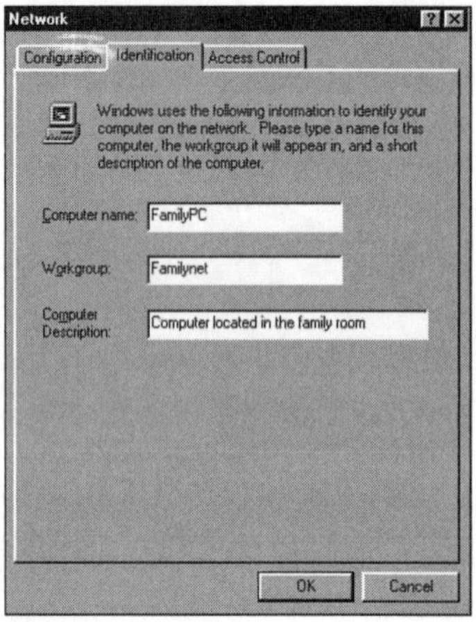

Network

Configuration | Identification | Access Control

Windows uses the following information to identify your computer on the network. Please type a name for this computer, the workgroup it will appear in, and a short description of the computer.

Computer name: FamilyPC

Workgroup: Familynet

Computer Description: Computer located in the family room

OK   Cancel

Note

You can change the name and workgroup on a Windows 2000 computer by opening the Control Panel, double-clicking System, selecting Network Identification, and clicking Properties.

Sharing Network Resources

Now that you have your network running and each computer's name and work-group are set, it's time to configure your shared resources. There are three types of resources that you will probably want to share. These are disk drives, printers, and your Internet connection. Disk and printer sharing is discussed in the next two sections. Internet connection sharing is covered later in the chapter.

Any Windows operating system can share its disk and printer resources. However, before you can share a disk drive or printer on a Windows 95, 98, or ME system, you must turn on file and printer sharing. You can do this using the following procedure:

1. Open the Windows Control Panel and double-click the Network icon. The Network dialog box opens. By default, the Configuration property sheet is displayed, as shown in Figure 11.5.

2. Click File and Print Sharing. The File and Print Sharing dialog box appears, as shown in Figure 11.6.

3. Select I want to be able to give others access to my files to turn on disk and folder sharing. Select I want to be able to allow others to print to my printer(s) to enable printer sharing. Click OK.

4. Click OK to close the Network dialog box.

5. Click Yes when prompted to restart your computer.

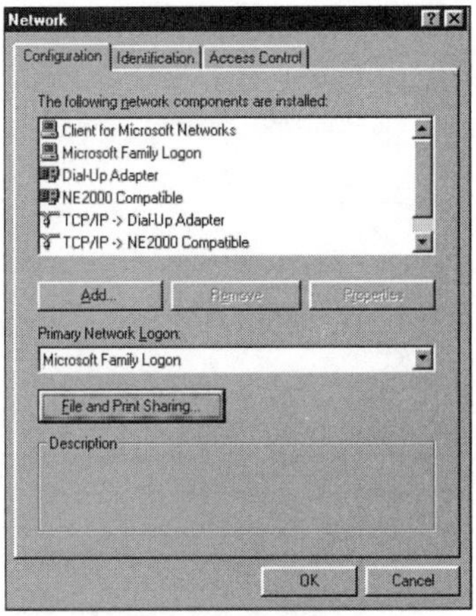

FIGURE 11.5

The Windows network dialog box as shown on Windows 95, 98, and Me computers.

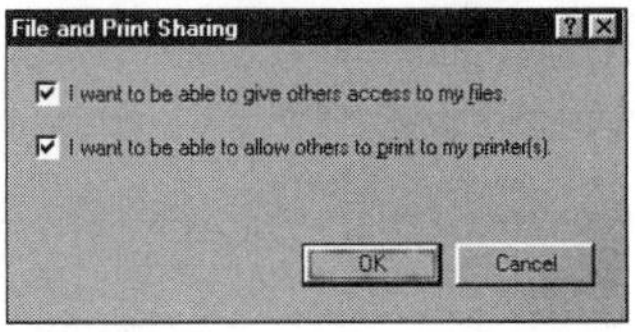

FIGURE 11.6

Enabling file and printer sharing on a network computer.

Note

Now might be a good time to go back to Chapter 4, "Locking Down Windows Networking," and review how to properly secure Windows file and print sharing. This way you'll be ready when you set up Internet connection sharing, as covered later in this chapter.

Sharing Your Disk Drive

You can share any folder or disk drive on your computer with the rest of the computers on your home network. This is a great way to make additional disk space available to network computers that have small hard drives. The same procedure is used to share floppy drives, hard drives, CD-ROM drives, and folders.

The process of sharing a driver or folder is the same on any Windows operating system, except that Windows NT, 2000, and XP also allow you to apply security permissions to each share to limit which network users have access to it.

The following procedure demonstrates how to share a disk drive on a Windows Me system.

1. Double-click the My Computer icon on the Windows desktop. The My Computer window opens, as shown in Figure 11.7.

FIGURE 11.7

The My Computer window shows that there are no shared devices on the local computer.

2. Right-click a local hard drive and select the Sharing option from the context menu that appears. This opens the Properties dialog box for the selected disk drive.

If the Sharing option is not present then Windows file and printer sharing has not been enabled.

3. By default, the Not Shared option is selected. To share the local drive, select the Share As option, as shown in Figure 11.8. This activates several fields on the dialog box.

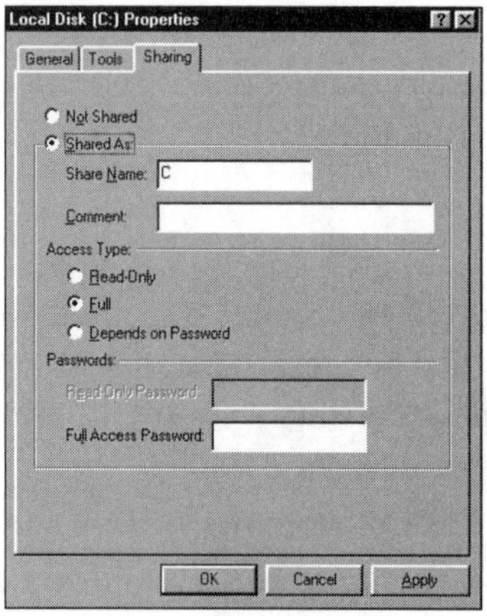

FIGURE 11.8

Sharing a local hard drive on a Windows Me computer.

4. A default name will be provided for the share. You can type a more descriptive name if you want. You can also type additional information in the Comment field. Select the appropriate access level for the shared drive. There are three options:

- **Read-Only**—Lets any network user access the drive and read locally stored files.

- **Full**—Lets any network user access the drive and read, change, or delete its contents.

- **Depends on Password**—Lets any network user who knows the assigned password either have read or full access to the drive and its contents.

5. Click OK—The icon representing the disk drive changes to show a hand underneath it.

Note that after you have established a shared disk drive, it is visible to other network computers and can be seen using any of the following means:

- Windows Explorer

- Internet Explorer

- Network Neighborhood

- Various Windows dialog boxes

For example, you can view the shared drive from the Network Neighborhood of another computer using the following procedure:

1. Double-click the Network Neighborhood icon on the Windows desktop.

2. Double-click the icon representing the computer where the shared drive was created.

3. You will see a list of all the shared resources on the selected computer. To view the contents of a given resource, double-click it.

Networking Your Printer

Sharing a printer is just as easy as setting up a shared disk drive. First, log on to the computer where the printer was installed and make sure that file and printer sharing has been enabled. Use the following procedure to share the printer with other network computers.

1. Open the Printers folder, which is located in the Windows Control Panel.

2. Right-click the printer and select Sharing from the context menu that appears.

3. Select Shared as and type a share name. Optionally you can supply a comment about the printer and apply a password.

4. Click OK. The printer icon will change to show a hand underneath it.

To print to the printer from another computer on your home network, you must first create a network connection for the shared printer. The following procedure demonstrates how to do this using the Windows Me Print wizard.

1. Click Start, Settings, Control Panel, Printers, and then the Add Printer icon to open the Add Printer Wizard.

2. Click Next.

3. Select Network Printer and click Next, as shown in Figure 11.9.

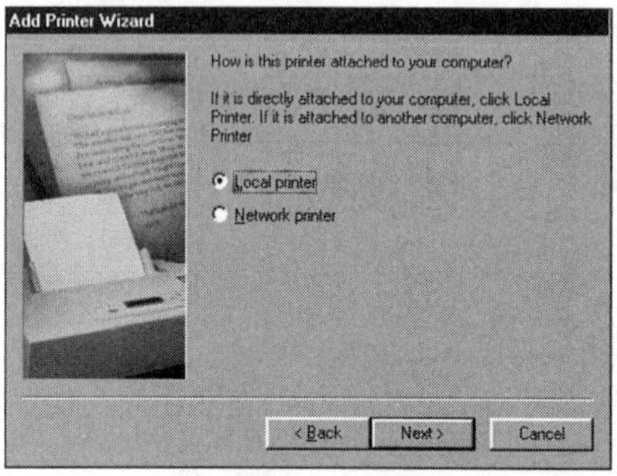

FIGURE 11.9

The Add Printer wizard provides support for installing local and network printers.

4. The Add Printer wizard asks for the location of the network printer. Enter the location using the Universal Naming Convention (UNC) method. If the computer where the printer resides is named FamilyPC and the printer name is ColorPTR, UNC path is \\FamilyPC\ColorPTR. You can also click Browse and browse your home network to find the printer. After specifying the location of the printer, click OK.

5. Next you are prompted to specify the manufacturer and model of the printer. After selecting the manufacturer and printer type, click Next. If the manufacturer or the type of printer is not displayed, click the Have disk button and, when prompted, supply the disk or CD-ROM that contains the printer driver supplied by the printer manufacturer.

6. Finally, type a name that your computer will use to refer to the network printer. If you want this printer to become the default computer, click Yes. Otherwise click No. Then click Finish.

Connecting Your Home Network to the Internet

After you have an operational home network you are ready to share your high-speed Internet connection. Before you do so make sure that you have followed the instructions presented in Chapter 4 to help minimize the security exposure caused

by connecting a home network to the Internet. The easiest way to connect all the computers on your home network to the Internet is to replace your network hub with a multiple port cable/DSL router. In addition to its simplicity, this option also provides the advantage of protecting your home network with the router's built-in hardware firewall feature. This option, depicted in Figure 11.10, involves several steps.

FIGURE 11.10

Sharing your high-speed Internet connection with all the computers on your home network.

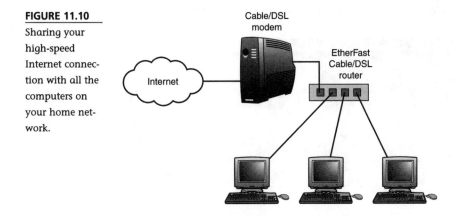

The first step is to purchase and install a cable/DSL router in place of your network hub. You may recall from Chapter 5, "Hardware Firewalls," that one of the built-in features of these devices is the functionality of a network hub.

The second step is to set up the cable/DSL router with your ISP. You can do this in one of two ways. You can either set it up using the MAC address of one of your network computer's NIC cards or you can register the MAC address of your cable/DSL router. If you have already registered the MAC address of one of your home computer's NICs, the easiest thing to do is to clone its MAC address. Otherwise, using the MAC address of the router makes the most sense.

Note

Not all cable/DSL providers require you to register your MAC address, in which case you can skip the processing of configuring your cable/DSL router's MAC address.

Your ISP would like for you to keep you old network hub and register additional network computer's MAC addresses. This fee is usually between $6 and $7 per computer per month. For a home network of four computers, this can significantly impact your monthly fee. To share your Internet connection using this option you must contact your ISP and report the MAC address of NIC cards in each of your network computers. Because Windows computers are automatically set up to accept a dynamic IP

configuration, all that you have to do is wait until your ISP says that the additional computers have been registered. You'll have to install a personal software firewall on every network computer in order to secure your networking using this option.

The easier and less expensive option is to get rid of your old network hub and use your new cable/DSL router and lets its default settings configure your network for you.

Cable/DSL routers come pre-configured to provide home networks with a number of features. As a network hub they can provide all the local area network connectivity for your home network. Cable/DSL routers also provide DHCP services and NAT translation. As you learned in Chapter 5, a multi-port cable/DSL router is automatically configured to create a TCP/IP based home network with an address of 192.168.1.0. The router will automatically assign IP addresses to any computer that asks for it. Because all Windows operating systems since Windows 98 are automatically configured to look for a DHCP server before assigning their own IP addresses, the change of network addresses from a home network of 169.254.0.0 to 192.168.1.0 should be completely transparent to you. The one exception being that if you have any Windows 95 computers with static IP addresses, you'll have to reconfigure them to use DHCP. Because Windows computers seek out DHCP servers by default, everything should work automatically.

The last step in setting your network to share your high-speed Internet connection is to help each network computer set up its own Internet connection. You can do this by running the Internet Connection wizard on each computer. The following procedure outlines the process of setting up an Internet connection using this wizard.

1. Click Start, Programs, Accessories, Communications, and then Internet Connections wizard. The wizard opens as shown in Figure 11.11.

FIGURE 11.11

Set up the Internet connection for each network computer by running the Internet Connection wizard.

2. Select I want to set up my Internet connection manually, or I want to connect through my local area network (LAN) and click Next.

3. You are then prompted to specify how the computer will connect to the Internet. Select I connect through a local area network (LAN) and click Next, as shown in Figure 11.12.

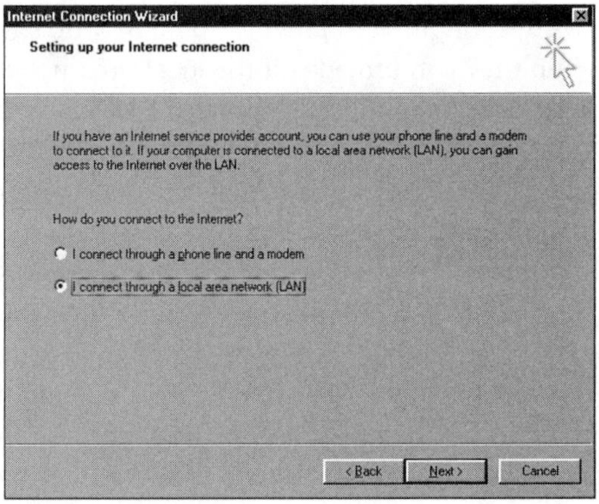

FIGURE 11.12

Selecting your local area network as your means of connecting to the Internet.

4. The next dialog box enables you to tell the wizard how to find the network's proxy server. This is your cable/DSL router. Make sure that Automatic discovery of proxy server is selected and click Next, as shown in Figure 11.13.

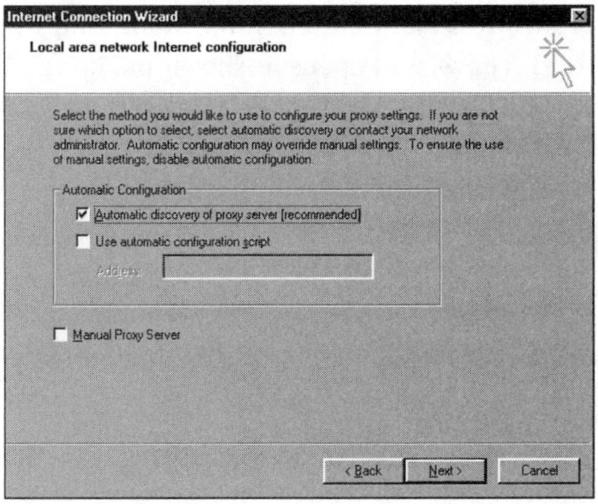

FIGURE 11.13

Let the Wizard automatically detect your cable/DSL router.

5. Click No when prompted to set up an Internet mail account and then click Next.

6. Click Finish. Internet Explorer will automatically start and establish an Internet connection.

One piece of built-in software on the cable/DSL router that helps make everything work is Network Address Translation, or NAT. When a computer on your home network tries to connect to a Web site, its request is intercepted by your router. Using NAT, the router maintains a table of all requests and which home computer they came from. The router then contacts the specified Web site and, when the Web page is downloaded, the router determines which home network computer initiated the request and passes the Web pages on to that computer. This way, each network computer operates as if it is directly connected to the Internet when in fact only the cable/DSL router is connected, as depicted in Figure 11.14. All that your ISP can see is Internet traffic flowing in and out of one IP address. The fact that your router is making connections on behalf of multiple computers is transparent.

FIGURE 11.14

NAT allows your cable/DSL router to translate between connection requests between your home network and the Internet.

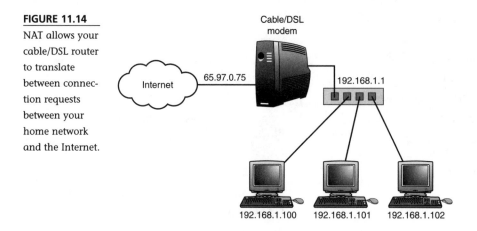

Your cable/DSL router then has two IP addresses associated with it. The first is the external IP address assigned by your ISP. In this example, the IP address is 65.97.0.75. The second IP address is the one that the router uses to communicate on your home network. This IP address is 192.168.1.1. Figure 11.14 also shows the IP addresses of the other home network computers. The addresses are assigned by the DHCP features of the cable/DSL router.

For example, if the computer that your cable/DSL router has assigned a network address of 192.168.0.102 tries to connect to www.microsoft.com, the router intercepts the request, makes a note of who initiated it, then makes the request itself. When the www.microsoft.com main Web page is downloaded, the router determines which network computer initiated the request and passes the Web page to that computer.

Tightening Things Up with a Second Line of Firewalls

At this point your home network should be up and running and all your network computers should be able to access the Internet using shared access to your high-speed Internet connection. In addition, the personal firewall features built into your router protect your entire network. This section discusses how you can further tighten up your security by adding personal firewalls to each of your network computers.

Cable/DSL routers provide a number of hardware firewall features such as port stealth and the capability to block internal computers from gaining access to the Internet. However, as Table 11.1 shows, there are a number of features provided by software firewalls that are not found in these hardware devices.

Table 11.1   Complementary Features of Hardware and Software Firewalls

Hardware Firewall	Software Firewall
Puts ports into stealth mode	Puts ports into stealth mode (All)
Maintains detailed logs	Maintains detailed logs (All)
Blocks unsolicited inbound traffic	Blocks unsolicited inbound traffic (All)
Blocks internal IP addresses	External IP addresses (ZoneAlarm and BlackICE)
Blocks internal MAC addresses	-
Blocks TCP and UDP ports	Blocks TCP and UDP ports (All)
Filters protocols	Filters protocols (ZoneAlarm and McAfee)
-	Filters applications (ZoneAlarm and McAfee)
-	Analyzes packets for threats (BlackICE)
-	Detects Trojan horses (ZoneAlarm and McAfee)
-	Alerts when events occur (All)

As you can see, although there is some duplication of features, hardware- and software-based firewalls provide a complementary set of services. For example, hardware firewalls can block Internet IP addresses, whereas software firewalls often allow you to block external IP addresses. Hardware firewalls allow you to block specific TCP and UDP ports, whereas software firewalls often let you block individual applications and specific protocols.

As Table 11.1 points out, features vary among firewall products. Software firewalls, such as the McAfee Firewall and ZoneAlarm, filter based on application and protocol, whereas BlackICE Defender analyzes data packets for specific threats. In addition, there are some other fundamental differences between the three software firewalls presented in this book:

- **McAfee Firewall**—This firewall allows you to configure separate settings for a dial-up and network connections but does not allow you to establish separate security settings for your Internet and home network. In addition, this firewall does not support Microsoft Internet Connection sharing, which is discussed in the next section.

- **BlackICE Defender**—This firewall does not distinguish between an Internet connection and a home network connection nor does it allow you to specify separate security settings for your Internet and home network connections.

- **ZoneAlarm**—This firewall enables you to set separate security settings for both your Internet connection and your home network, making it a good candidate for the computers on your home network.

McAfee Firewall and BlackICE Defender do not allow you to set up separate security settings for your Internet and home network. ZoneAlarm, on the other hand, provides this capability, as shown in Figure 11.15.

FIGURE 11.15
ZoneAlarm enables you to set different security settings for your home and Internet network connections.

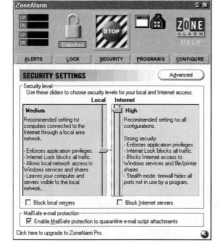

This feature, combined with the fact that ZoneAlarm is free for personal use, makes it an excellent candidate for use on your home network. As you learned in Chapter 8, "ZoneAlarm," you can choose from three security settings for both your home

and Internet network connections. Figure 11.16 depicts how you deploy ZoneAlarm on a home network. This design gives you two layers of Internet security while allowing your home network to operate unaffected at its own security setting.

FIGURE 11.16

Using ZoneAlarm to add maximum security to your Internet and home network connections.

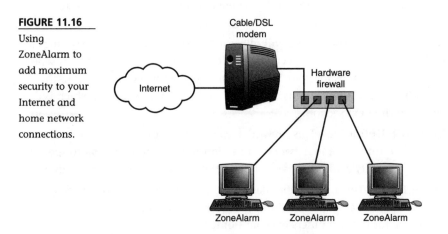

Microsoft's Internet Connection Sharing

Microsoft provides an alternative way to allow computers on a home network to share a broadband high-speed Internet connection. This option requires a regular network hub. If you have ever seen Microsoft Internet Connection Sharing (ICS) used to share a traditional dial-up connection to the Internet, you know that it allows you to configure the dial-up connection. This is so its computer can share it with other home network computers using the computer's NIC, as depicted in Figure 11.17.

FIGURE 11.17

Using Windows built-in ICS to share a dial-up connection.

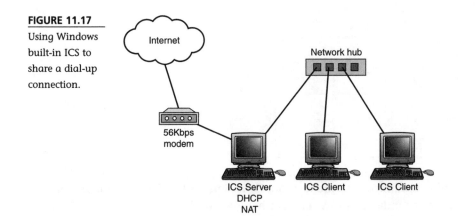

ICS is supported on Windows 98 Second Edition, Windows Me, and Windows 2000. It is installed and configured differently on each operating system. You can consult the Windows help system for specific instructions on setting up ICS for each operating system. In general, you first need to install ICS using the Add/Remove Programs utility. Then you can share the connection. After it's configured, ICS turns a computer into a DHCP server that also provides NAT services. Other network computers can then be configured to use this connection using the Internet Connection wizard.

Only one DHCP server can be active on a home network at any time. If you choose to use Microsoft ICS to share your Internet connection you need to either use a regular network hub or disable the DHCP service on your cable/DSL router.

There are a number of third-party applications, such as WinGate (www.wingate.com), that also allow you to share your Internet connection with your home network.

ICS is more difficult to configure when using it to share a broadband connection. As shown in Figure 11.18, you need to install two NIC cards on the computer where ICS will be installed. Both NICs must be connected to the network hub. One NIC needs to be set up to manage the connection to the Internet and the other NIC provides a regular network connection. You can then configure the computer to share the ICS connection.

FIGURE 11.18
Using Windows built-in ICS to share a dial-up connection via a broadband connection requires two NIC cards.

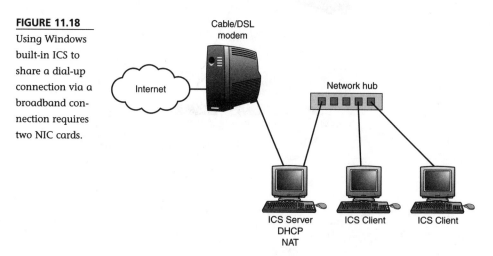

Setting up a dual-NIC connection and running ICS provides shared Internet access with the benefit of personal firewall protection. At a minimum you should install a software personal firewall on the computer sharing the Internet connection. To be

even more secure, you should consider putting personal firewall software on each network computer.

Note	The McAfee Firewall does not support Microsoft ICS.

Securing Home Networks with NetBEUI

Figure 11.19 shows another alterative for configuring a home network. In this example, allowing only TCP/IP on the computer requiring Internet access makes the home network more secure. The NetBEUI protocol, on the other hand, is loaded on every network computer. Because the NetBEUI protocol is non-routable, hackers can't break into any computer on the network other than the one running TCP/IP. The computer with the Internet connection can then be secured by installing any personal firewall. Additional security can be added by replacing the network hub with a cable/DSL router.

FIGURE 11.19
Using the NetBEUI protocol to isolate your network from your Internet connection.

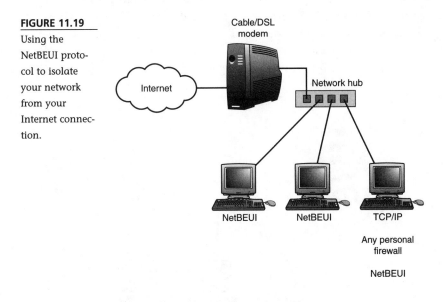

OTHER FIREWALL PRODUCTS

*T*his appendix provides an overview of seven additional software firewalls that you might want to consider when shopping for your own personal firewall. While some of these firewalls may not be as well known as the three software firewalls reviewed previously in this book, most provide an equivalent level of protection and are just as effective. This appendix provides a description of each personal firewall and summarizes its features. In addition, you'll find the Web site for each product where you can go to get additional information.

- Aladdin Knowledge Systems eSafe Desktop 2.2

- Norton Personal Firewall 2000

- PGP Desktop Security 7.0

- Symantec Desktop Firewall 2.0

- Sygate Personal Firewall

- ConSeal PC Firewall

- Tiny Wall Personal Firewall

Aladdin Knowledge Systems eSafe Desktop 3.0

The Aladdin Knowledge Systems eSafe Desktop 3.0 is provided by Aladdin Knowledge Systems and can be found at `www.eAladdin.com/esafe`, shown in Figure A.1.

FIGURE A.1

The Aladdin Knowledge Systems eSafe Desktop 3.0.

It is free for personal use and provides a number of features, including:

- Built-in antivirus application

- Internet content filtering

- Desktop lockdown features

- Personal firewall

The personal firewall feature includes the ability to filter all network traffic. Four security settings are available:

- Off
- Low
- Normal
- Extreme

This personal firewall focuses heavily on restricting ports and might be a little more difficult to work with than some of the other personal firewall products.

Norton Personal Firewall 2001

The Norton Personal Firewall 2001 is provided by Symantec and can be found at www.symantec.com, as shown in Figure A.2.

FIGURE A.2

The Norton Personal Firewall 2001.

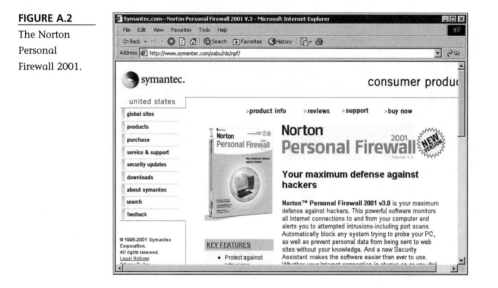

This personal firewall is one of the more expensive personal firewalls. It provides four security settings:

- Minimal
- Medium
- High
- Custom

It includes a Security Assistant wizard that steps you through the process of configuring your personal firewall. Intrusion detection alerts you to attempts to scan your ports and is combined with an AutoBlock feature that is designed to block any computer attempting to launch a scan of your computer.

PGP Desktop Security 7.0

The PGP Desktop Security 7.0 is provided by Network Associates and can be found at www.pgp.com, as shown in Figure A.3.

FIGURE A.3

The PGP Desktop Security 7.0.

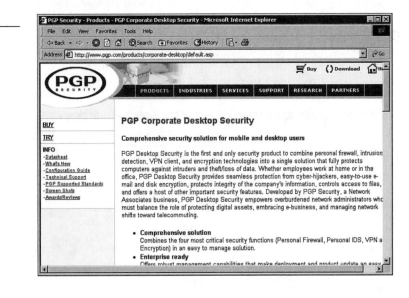

In addition to a personal firewall, this product provides an assortment of features, including

- Virtual Private Networking (VPN) support
- Disk encryption
- E-mail encryption
- Instant message encryption

The personal firewall provides intrusion detection against known types of attacks, can block computers attempting to scan your computer, and will even attempt to reverse-trace the location of intruders. It does a good job of alerting and can even notify you of problems using e-mail.

PGP Desktop Security 7.0 seems to be targeted more at corporate users than home users and is the most expensive of all the personal firewalls reviewed in this book.

Symantec Desktop Firewall 2.0

The Symantec Desktop Firewall 2.0 is provided by Symantec and can be found at www.symantec.com, as shown in Figure A.4.

FIGURE A.4

The Symantec Desktop Firewall 2.0.

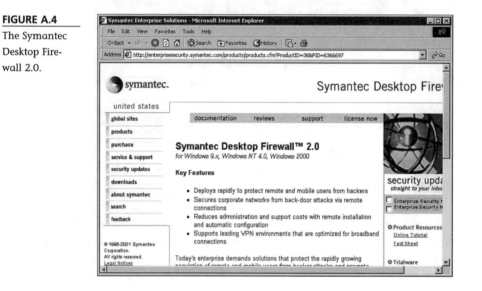

This is one of two personal firewalls provided by Symantec and seems to be over-shadowed by their other personal firewall, the Norton Personal Firewall 2001. A free trial of the personal firewall is permitted so that you can take it for a test drive before deciding if it's right for you.

The Symantec Desktop Firewall 2.0 allows you to block Internet traffic based on application. You can also block specific IP addresses or a range of IP addresses.

Sygate Personal Firewall

The Sygate Personal Firewall is provided by Sygate Technologies and can be found at www.sygate.com, as shown in Figure A.5. It is designed for personal and small business users.

This personal firewall is free for personal use. It features a learning mode where it prompts you about what to do for each application that tries to connect to the Internet, allowing you to block any application. It also allows you to establish a collection of trusted IP addresses and to associate them with specific applications. You can also block the use of specified ports and protocols. Alerts can be delivered to you via e-mail or pop-up messages.

FIGURE A.5

The Sygate
Personal
Firewall.

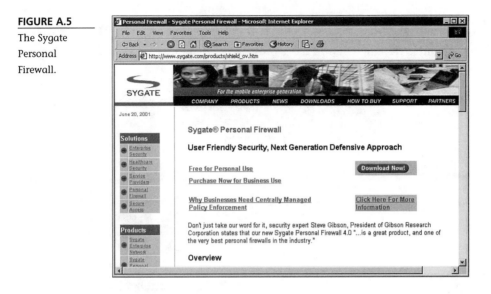

The Sygate Personal Firewall also allows you to set up a schedule by which your security rules can be implemented. This way, you can apply tighter security to your firewall when you are not using it.

ConSeal PC Firewall

The ConSeal PC Firewall is provided by Sygate Technologies and can be found at www.consealfirewall.com, as shown in Figure A.6.

FIGURE A.6

The ConSeal PC
Firewall.

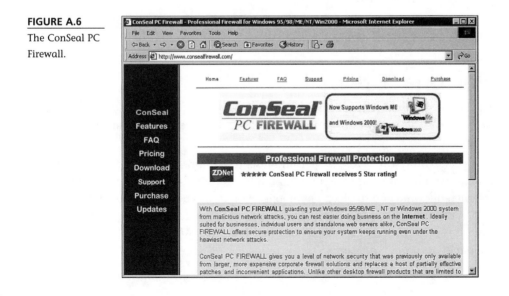

This personal firewall can filter a number of packet types including IP, NetBEUI, and Novell's IPX. It features a learning mode that prompts for instructions and automatically generates security rules. Rule sets can be created for specific applications, network devices, IP addresses, and services. Four security settings are provided:

- Basic
- Cable/ADSL
- Browse
- None

You can password-protect your security settings. The ConSeal PC Firewall is one of the more expensive firewalls. It comes in three versions:

- ConSeal for Server
- ConSeal for Workstation
- ConSeal for Desktop

ConSeal for Desktop is targeted at the home user running Windows 95, 98, or Me. If you are running Windows NT Workstation or Microsoft 2000 Professional, you need to purchase the ConSeal for Workstation version.

Tiny Personal Firewall

The Tiny Personal Firewall is provided by Tiny Software and can be found at www.tinysoftware.com, as shown in Figure A.7.

FIGURE A.7

The Tiny Wall Personal Firewall.

This little personal firewall is small enough to fit on a single floppy disk and is free for personal use. It sports a very nice setup wizard and the automatic detection of applications as they try to access the Internet for the first time. You can define trusted IP addresses, or ranges of IP addresses, that should have greater access through the firewall.

Three security settings are available:

- Minimal Security. Allows all communications to pass through the firewall.
- Medium Security. The default security level which automatically allows common applications such as Internet Explorer through the firewall.
- Maximum Security. Prevents undefined applications from establishing connection through the firewall.

In addition, you can password-protect your configuration settings and schedule the time that your security settings are applied, allowing you to tighten your personal firewall security when you are away from your computer.

OTHER WEB SITES THAT WILL TEST YOUR SECURITY

This appendix provides a list of Web sites on the Internet where you can receive free Internet security scans of your computer. Some sites only provide a quick or basic scan, whereas other sites provide detailed scans that can take up to 30 minutes to complete.

To test the effectiveness of your personal firewall, run a security scan with your personal firewall disabled and then run the same test with your personal firewall enabled and compare the results. Remember that personal firewalls come with different levels of security policies. If you find that you are not comfortable with the results of a security scan when your personal firewall is active, try the scan again after enabling a stronger security policy on your personal firewall.

- HackerWhacker
- Gibson Research Corporation
- Secure Design
- Sygate Online Services
- Symantec
- McAfee
- HackYourself.com

HackerWhacker

You can get a detailed scan of your personal firewall from www.hackerwhacker.com, as shown in Figure B.1.

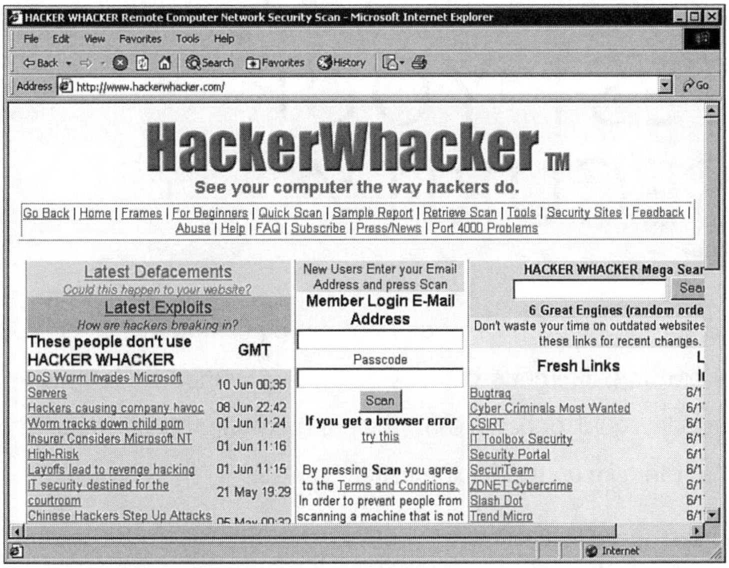

FIGURE B.1

The www.hacker-whacker.com site provides a large collection of links to PC security-related topics as well as a free Internet security scan of your computer.

The HackerWhacker Internet security scan performs a detailed probe of your computer and provides a report of security breaches. To run the HackerWhacker scan, click the Want to test your firewall? link at the bottom of the Web page. You will be prompted for your e-mail address. HackerWhacker uses your e-mail address to send you detailed instructions telling you how to perform the scan.

Gibson Research Corporation

The Gibson Research Corporation's Web site, shown in Figure B.2, also provides a free Internet scan of your computer.

FIGURE B.2

The Gibson Research Corporations Shields UP! Web site provides an abundance of free information and tools in addition to two free Internet security scans.

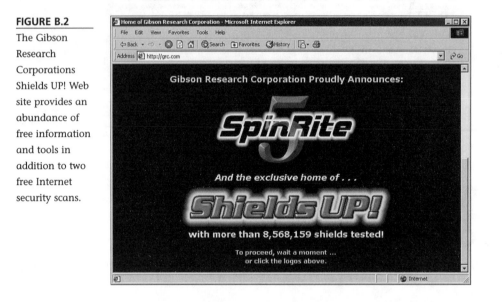

You will find this Web site at `http://grc.com`. To run its free Internet security scans, click the Shields UP! link. You will find an abundance of information found on the Shields UP Web pages. Two free Internet security tests are available.

- **Test My Shields!**—Performs a scan of your computer by attempting to make a connection and gathering information such as your username, your computer's name, and any shared resources.

- **Probe My Ports!**—Performs a port probe using a small subset of well-known TCP/IP ports and displays a list of any discovered vulnerabilities.

Secure Design

Two Internet scan tests can be found at `www.sdesign.com`, shown in Figure B.3.

Click Free Security Test and then Scan me now. You'll see two options:

- **Basic Scan**—Initiates a scan of Windows file sharing and well-known TCP/IP ports.

- **Complete Scan**—Performs a more exhaustive scan of your computer that can take up to 30 minutes. You'll need to supply your IP address before starting this scan.

FIGURE B.3

Two Internet
security scans
are available
from the Secure
Design Web site,
allowing for
both a quick
and a detailed
test of your com-
puter's defenses.

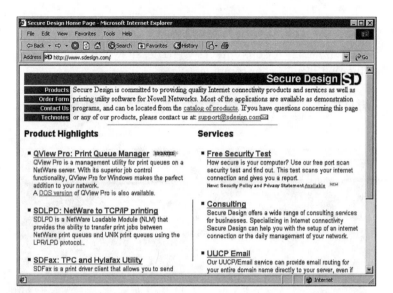

Sygate Online Services

There are a number of free Internet security scans that you can run from the Sygate
Online Services Web site (scan.sygatetech.com), shown in Figure B.4.

FIGURE B.4

The Sygate Web
site provides six
Internet security
scans, allowing
you to probe
your computer's
security in a
variety of ways.

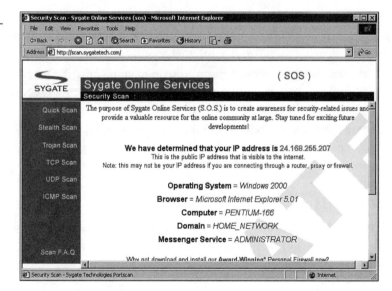

When you first load the Sygate Online Services Web page, you are presented with a
list of information about your computer, as demonstrated in Figure B.4. On the left
side of the screen, you will see the six free scans that you can run. These include:

- **Quick Scan**—Performs a quick port scan of your computer.
- **Stealth Scan**—Performs a test similar to the first one but is supposed to employ techniques for penetrating firewalls.
- **Trojan Scan**—Scans for Trojan horse programs.
- **TCP Scan**—Scans all 1,024 well-known TCP ports.
- **UDP Scan**—Performs a test of how well your UDP ports are protected.
- **ICMP Scan**—Performs a test to determine whether your firewall blocks ping attempts. As of the writing of this book, this test was not available.

Symantec

You can also receive a free Internet security from the Symantec Web site located at www.symantec.com/securitycheck, as shown in Figure B.5.

FIGURE B.5

The Symantec security scan breaks down its analysis of your computer's vulnerability into multiple categories.

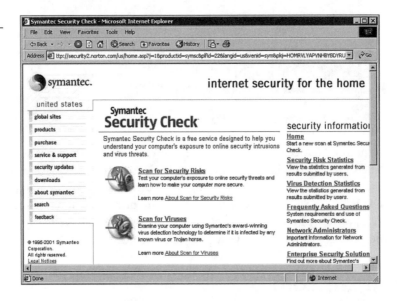

To initiate the scan, click Scan for Security Risks. You will see your IP address displayed while you wait for the results of the scan to appear. A report then summarizes the computer's exposure to the following threats:

- Network vulnerability
- NetBIOS availability
- Active Trojan horses

You can click the Show Details link to the right of any of these categories to get detailed information regarding the results of a particular test.

McAfee

The makers of the McAfee Personal Firewall, reviewed in Chapter 6 of this book, also provide a free Internet Security scan at their Web site, which is located at www.mcafeeasap.com, as shown in Figure B.6.

FIGURE B.6

McAfee provides an Internet security scanning service and allows you to run a free trial test.

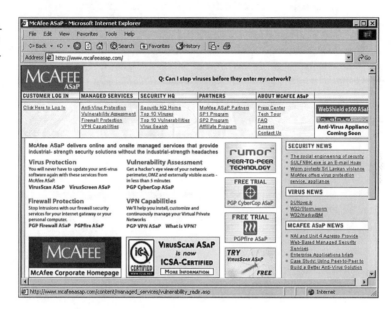

To run the McAfee security scan, click the Vulnerability Assessment link under CyberCop ASaP and then click on Free Trial. You have to provide your e-mail address, name, phone number, company name, and a password to run the scan. Next, click on Submit. The scan will then run and you will receive an e-mail with a link showing you the location of your scan results. You have to supply the password you provided to McAfee to view your scan results.

HackYourself.com

HackYourself.com, located at www.hackyourself.com, provides much of the same information available at www.hackerwhacker.com. In addition, it provides a quick free Internet scan of your computer without requiring your e-mail address. See Figure B.7.

FIGURE B.7

The www.hack-yourself.com site provides a quick scan of your computer's defenses against Internet attacks.

To run the quick scan, click Want to Test Your Firewall?, type your IP address when prompted, and click GO. When the test completes, click Report Details to view the results of the test.

Glossary

@HOME   One of the two largest cable Internet access ISPs in North America.

A

Address   A component of a data packet that identifies either the sending or destination computer.

ADSL (Assymetric Digital Subscriber Line)   A type of DSL connection targeted at home users and small businesses. Provides less bandwidth for uploads than for downloads.

Aladdin Knowledge Systems eSafe Desktop 3.0   A software product that includes personal firewall technology designed to protect your broadband or dial-up Internet connection.

Antivirus program   A software program designed to protect your computer from computer viruses by scanning your disk drives and downloaded files for viruses.

Application gateway firewall (proxy firewalls)   A firewall that filters data packets based on IP addresses and the specific function that an application is trying to execute. This is the model implemented by most personal firewalls.

B

BlackICE Defender   A software-based personal firewall that is designed to protect your broadband or dial-up connected computer when surfing the Internet.

Broadband Internet connection   A high-speed cable or DSL connection to the Internet.

C

Cable modem connection   An always-on, high-speed Internet connection provided by your local cable company using the same cable connection that provides your cable TV.

Cable/DSL router   A built-in feature found in most hardware personal firewalls that provides for the sharing of a single Internet connection.

CableLabs   An organization charged with the responsibility of ensuring compliance with the cable modem DOCSIS standard and labeling certified cable modems as "CableLabs Certified."

Circuit-level firewall   A firewall designed to permit traffic flow with pre-approved IP addresses, networks, and Internet service providers. Packets are filtered only while a connection is being established. Once estab-

lished, packets pass through the firewall unhampered.

Client for Microsoft Networks A software component used on computers running Microsoft's operating systems that allows computers to connect and share resources.

Configuration wizard A software utility provided by most personal firewalls that steps you through the process of installing the personal firewall and establishing its security settings.

Connection A logical session established between two computers communicating over a network.

Cracker An individual who breaks into computer systems and networks with the intent of creating mischief or stealing private information, as opposed to a hacker who has no interest in doing harm but is instead interested in overcoming a technical challenge.

D

Demigod A hacker with decades of experience and a worldwide reputation in the hacker community.

Denial-of-service (DoS) attack An attack on another computer whereby a computer with faster network access attempts to flood the target computer with more network data than it can handle in order to prevent it from being able to accept and process any other network requests or data.

DHCP (Dynamic Host Configuration Protocol) A TCP/IP protocol used by ISPs to dynamically assign IP addresses to subscribers of their Internet services.

Distributed denial-of-service (DDoS) attack An attack on a network computer launched by taking control of a number of other computers and instructing them to flood the target system with data in an effort to overload its processing capabilities.

DOCSIS (Data Over Cable Systems Interface Specification) A cable modem standard introduced in 1998 that has been adopted by the cable industry.

DSL (digital subscriber line) An always-on, high-speed Internet connection provided by your local telephone company over your existing telephone lines using a DSL modem.

Dynamic IP address An IP address that is dynamically assigned or leased to a network computer on a TCP/IP network. In the case of dial-up connections, a new IP address is assigned for each new session whereas cable and DSL connections can usually continue automatically by renewing the same IP address indefinitely.

E

E-mail An electronic means of transmitting messages over networks such as the Internet.

EFS (Encrypted File System) A feature of Windows 2000 and Windows XP that allows you to encrypt the contents of files stored on hard drives in order to prevent unauthorized access to them.

Ephemeral port A TCP or UTP port above the well-known port range that has not been officially assigned to a service or application.

Ethernet A low-level protocol used to connect computers to local area networks and also used to establish a connection between your computer and your high-speed access cable or DSL modem.

F-H

FAT   The original Windows and MSDOS file system. This file system provides for the insecure organization and storage of files using an 8.3 character name format.

FAT32   A 32-bit version of the FAT file system that includes support for long filenames and larger disk drives.

File and printer sharing   A service of Microsoft operating systems that, when enabled, facilitates the sharing of local disk drives, folders, and printers.

File sharing   The process of making the contents of local files, folders, and disk drives available to other computers on a network.

Filtering   The process a firewall uses to examine every packet passing through a network connection in order to determine whether they should be allowed access.

Firewall   A hardware device or software program designed to defend a computer or network against external attack.

FTP   A TCP/IP protocol used by Internet servers to transfer files.

Hacker   A title given to a person having a technical mastery of computing skills who enjoys finding and solving technical challenges, including breaking into computer and network systems, as opposed to a cracker who breaks into computer systems and networks with the intent of creating mischief or stealing private information.

Hardware firewall   An external device connected to your computer and cable or DSL that filters traffic for an Internet connection. These devices are managed using a Web browser.

Hub   A external network device that connects two or more computers to create a local area network.

I-K

IDSL (Integrated Digital Subscriber Line)   A type of DSL connection targeted at telephone customers that are over three miles away from a central office. Provides a slower level of service than other DSL options.

Internet Connection Firewall   A personal firewall provided with the Windows XP Home Edition operating system.

Internet connection sharing   A feature found in Windows 98 Second Edition, Windows Me, and Windows 2000 that allows these operating systems to share an Internet connection with other users on a home network.

Intrusion detection   A capability sometimes found in personal firewalls that enables you to defend against attacks and block access to a computer trying to break into your computer. Intrusion detection involves the examination of data packets and their contents to determine whether they pose any threat.

IP (Internet Protocol)   One of the protocols in the TCP/IP suite of protocols that is responsible for the transport of packets across the Internet.

IP address   A unique 32-bit address made up of a combination of 0s and 1s that identifies computers and network devices on the Internet.

IPX   A protocol that provides similar functionality to TCP on proprietary NetWare networks.

ISA slot   An older type of expansion slot located inside a computer that allows you to expand its capabilities by installing peripheral devices into the slot.

ISP (Internet service provider)   A company that provides leased access to the Internet.

L

Larva   A beginner hacker who has just begun to learn the trade and who idolizes true hackers.

Latency   A measurement of the amount of time required for a packet to traverse the Internet. Latency is typically caused by congestion at your ISP or by slow server response at the Web sites.

Linksys EtherFast cable/DSL router   A hardware-based personal firewall that protects your computer from broadband connection to the Internet.

Log file   A file generated by your personal firewall that contains an assortment of information regarding the operation of the firewall and its activity.

Local area network (LAN)   A small network comprised of two or more computers that share information and resources. In the context of this book, a local area network is equivalent to a home network.

M

MAC address   A 48-bit address encoded on every NIC that provides it with a unique identifier. Ultimately all network communication is based on determining the MAC address of both the sending and receiving computer regardless of the networking protocol being used.

McAfee Personal Firewall   A software-based personal firewall that is designed to protect your broadband or dial-up connected computer when surfing the Internet.

Modem   A device that connects to your computer and allows you to communicate with another computer or network such as the Internet.

Multi-port hub   A hardware device such as a hardware personal firewall that provides more than one Ethernet port so that you can build a home-based local area network.

N

NetBEUI (NetBIOS Extended User Interface)   A local area network protocol designed to support network communication over a small network without requiring any configuration.

NetBIOS   A network communication protocol that is carried over TCP, UDP, and NetBEUI and that facilitates the sharing of Microsoft resources including printers and hard drives.

NIC (Network Interface Card)   A peripheral device that allows your computer to connect to a computer network. NICs are also used to establish network connections between a computer and a cable or DSL modem.

Norton Personal Firewall 2000   A software-based personal firewall that is designed to protect your broadband or dial-up connected computer when surfing the Internet.

NTFS (New Technology File System)   A file system provided by the Windows NT, 2000,

and XP operating systems that enables you to protect files using an advanced set of security permissions.

O-Q

Operating system   Software that is loaded when your computer starts and that manages the computer's hardware and application and provides you with the interface for working with these resources.

Packet   A collection of data sent over a network that contains both the source and destination address of two communicating computers and the data that is being sent between them.

Packet-filtering firewall   A type of firewall designed to monitor packets based on their IP address. Allows only assigned IP addresses to communicate through the firewall.

Password   A secret code associated with a user account or resource that authenticates computer and network users.

Password crackers   Software programs designed to try to crack or decode passwords assigned to user accounts or shared computer resources such as disk and printer shares.

PCI slots   32-bit expansion slots inside a computer that allow you to expand the computer's capabilities by installing peripheral devices into the slots.

Personal firewall   A software product or small hardware device designed to protect a home computer or network from unauthorized access by a range of malicious programs. A personal firewall is also capable of preventing internal applications from communicating with external networks.

PGP Desktop Security 7.0   A software product that includes personal firewall technology designed to protect your broadband or dial-up Internet connection.

Ping   A TCP/IP command that allows you to test for the presence of another computer on a network. You can try to ping any computer on the Internet by typing **PING** followed by its name or IP address.

Port   Any of the 65,534 possible connections to a computer or network device running TCP/IP.

Port scan   An attempt by a individual to locate and ascertain the presence of open TCP/IP ports on a computer and to try to test the ability to establish a connection with these ports.

Printer sharing   The process of making the contents of local printers available to other computers on a network.

Protocol   A collection of rules and standards for establishing network communications.

R-S

Regedit   An advanced software utility that allows you to view and modify the Windows Registry.

RoadRunner   One of the two largest cable-access ISPs in North America.

Samurai   A hacker who hires out his or her skills to corporations to help them improve their network security. Samurai's are often paid by companies to try to break into their networks.

SDSL (Synchronous Digital Subscriber Line)   A type of DSL connection targeted at businesses with heavier Internet access requirements. Features equal bandwidth for uploads and downloads.

Security policy   A built-in policy provided by personal firewalls that implements security rules based upon information that you provided to the firewall's configuration wizard.

Service   A Windows application that performs a specific system-level function.

Software driver   A small software program that is provided with peripheral devices such as NICs that must be installed for the operating system to work with and manage the device.

Software firewall   A software program loaded from your computer's hard drive that is designed to defend against hostile attacks launched from the Internet. Unlike hardware firewalls, software firewalls work with both broadband and dial-up connections.

Stateful inspection firewall   This type of firewall attempts to determine the type of data being transmitted and its possible threat before allowing it to pass through the firewall.

Static IP address   An IP address manually assigned to a computer running TCP/IP; it does not change over time.

Stealth mode   The capability to place a computer's TCP/IP ports into a state whereby they will not be visible over the Internet. This prevents the computer from replying to port scans and revealing its existence to Internet scanners.

Switch   A feature often found in network hubs that creates a temporary dedicated connection between two communicating devices and provides for an uninterrupted communication flow.

Sybergen Networks Secure Desktop 2.1   A software product that includes personal firewall technology designed to protect your broadband or dial-up Internet connection.

Symantec Desktop Firewall 2.0   A software-based personal firewall that is designed to protect your broadband or dial-up connected computer when surfing the Internet.

T

TCP   One of the protocols that comprise the TCP/IP protocol suite that is designed to establish logical connections between networked devices.

TCP/IP   A suite of protocols that provides communications over computer networks such as the Internet (of which TCP and IP are simply two member protocols). TCP/IP is also the default protocol for Windows 98, Me, 2000, and XP.

TCP/IP Receive Window   A feature of TCP/IP in which data packets are stored during communications with other network computers. The size of the TCP/IP Receive Window can significantly impact the efficiency of your computer's communication over the Internet.

Tiny Wall   A software-based personal firewall that you can download from the Internet for free personal use and that provides many of the same features found in other commercially available software-based personal firewalls.

Tracert   A TCP/IP command that allows you to test your level of latency. It identifies

the number of hops that a data packet makes on its way to the destination computer and lists the amount of time that each hop took.

Trojan horse A software program designed to infiltrate your computer and run in stealth mode for the purpose of exposing personal information to the individual who planted it or allowing the complete takeover of your computer. Trojans horses often gain access to computers by masquerading as harmless software or by hiding inside e-mail attachments.

Trusted application An application identified to your personal firewall as one that is allowed to penetrate the personal firewall and communicate over the Internet.

U-Z

UDP (User Datagram Protocol) One of the protocols that comprise the TCP/IP protocol suite that is designed to establish connectionless communication between networked devices.

Virus A software program designed to infect its host computer and cause an assortment of damage ranging from a simple practical joke

to the deletion of the entire contents of your hard drive.

Wannabee An individual who is in the beginning stages of his or her hacking career and who is dangerous mostly because of inexperience.

Whacker A person who engages in hacking activities without possessing the skill set of real hackers. Whackers are less sophisticated in their techniques and capability to penetrate systems.

Winsock A component of Windows operating systems that manages TCP/IP connections with Internet applications.

Worm A software program designed to propagate itself and sneak its way onto your computer where it hides until a predetermined date or event occurs, at which time it activates itself and performs whatever malicious action it was designed to do.

ZoneAlarm A software-based personal firewall that you can download from the Internet for free personal use and that provides many of the same features found in other commercially available software-based personal firewalls.

Index

G - H